KNOWLEDGE-BASED INFORMATION RETRIEVAL AND FILTERING FROM THE WEB

T0137945

The Kluwer International Series
in Engineering and Computer Science

KNOWLEDGE-BASED INFORMATION RETRIEVAL AND FILTERING FROM THE WEB

edited by

Witold Abramowicz
The Poznan University of Economics, Poland

KLUWER ACADEMIC PUBLISHERS
Boston / New York / Dordrecht / London

Distributors for North, Central and South America:
Kluwer Academic Publishers
101 Philip Drive; Assinippi Park
Norwell, Massachusetts 02061 USA
Telephone (781) 871-6600
Fax (781) 681-9045
E-Mail: kluwer@wkap.com

Distributors for all other countries:
Kluwer Academic Publishers Group
Post Office Box 322
3300 AH Dordrecht, THE NETHERLANDS
Telephone 31 78 6576 000
Fax 31 78 6576 254
E-Mail: services@wkap.nl

 Electronic Services <http://www.wkap.nl>

Library of Congress Cataloging-in-Publication Data

Knowledge-based information retrieval and filtering from the Web / edited by Witold Abramowicz.
       p. cm. -- (The Kluwer international series in engineering and computer science ; SECS 746)
    Includes bibliographical references and index.
    ISBN 978-1-4419-5376-6
    1. World Wide Web. 2. Expert systems (Computer science) 3. Artificial intelligence.
    4. Information storage and retrieval systems. 5. Internet searching. 6. Internet--Censorship--Data
    processing. I. Abramowicz, Witold II. Series.

TK5105.888.K58 2003
004.6'78--dc21

                                                                                2003047596

Permission for books published in Europe: permissions@wkap.nl
Permissions for books published in the United States of America: permissions@wkap.com

Printed on acid-free paper.   Printed in the United States of America.

TABLE OF CONTENTS

I FOUNDATIONS OF INFORMATION RETRIEVAL AND INFORMATION FILTERING

CHAPTER 1

Krzysztof Węcel
Department of Management Information Systems
The Poznań University of Economics, Poland

CHAPTER 2

Jakub Piskorski
German Research Center for Artificial Intelligence
Saarbrücken, Germany

CHAPTER 3

David A. Garza-Salazar, Juan C. Lavariega, Martha Sordia-Salinas
ITESM-Campus Monterrey

III CLUSTERING

Willy Picard and Wojciech Cellary
Department of Information Technology
The Poznań University of Economics

Piotr S. Szczepaniak [1, 2], Adam Niewiadomski [1],
[1] Institute of Computer Science, Technical University of Łódź, Poland
[2] Systems Research Institute, Polish Academy of Sciences, Poland

Frank Teuteberg
Business Informatics,
European University Viadrina, Frankfurt (Oder), Germany

IV OTHER ISSUES

Eric Paquet and Herna Viktor
NRC and University of Ottawa

Peter Gerstl, Birgit Kuhn, Hans-Joachim Novak
IBM Germany

Hele-Mai Haav
Institute of Cybernetics at Tallinn Technical University, Estonia

PREFACE
Witold Abramowicz – Editor

INFORMATION RETRIEVAL AND FILTERING – WHAT IS IT AND WHAT IS IT FOR?

The beginning of my professional work was connected with limited access to scientific publications. The **access to the information** was a kind of privilege – not only at that time, for example the sources of Egyptian priests' power aroused from the access to religious, astronomical, economical or political information. In every historical period could be found examples of the key role of information access which was the source of power and other privileges.

The past was characterized not only by limited information access. The **channels of information distribution** were established for relatively long periods of time. In Europe the whole generations of bourgeois' families read the same periodicals. Possessing the channel of information distribution was the source of power. As an example, for Genghis-Khan above source was the net of mounted couriers who delivered information from conquered countries.

This example depicts well the thesis, that in the past acquiring the **information** was tightly bound with **high costs**. Before the print was invented a price of a book was equal to the price of several villages in Poland.

The information lifetime, measured with its usefulness, was initially **long**; then it gradually decreased. At the beginning of my scholar work I remember the good custom of passing the books owned by a professor who died to the university library by the widow. In many well respected libraries there is a lot of information about that kind of donors. By the time, the willingness of librarians to accept such gifts diminished, because the value of professors' personal libraries was outdating even faster.

The information was often **organized** by the media. Not long ago one could go to a record library and notes were kept in a notebook. Today everyone can have such information in the computer, which weights less than 200g and additionally allows watching movies.

The resources of information in particular domains could be embraced by single individuals, taking into consideration our contemporary perception abilities,

Considerable democratization in the information access occurred. In the eighties of the previous century, when I was into hypertext, I believed that the time would come, when information bits scattered worldwide, would be available in the computer network and the mutual connections would make the access easier. By the end of this decade, when I was doing probably the first European tenure about hypertext, I was convinced that the possibility of my vision coming true was quite remote.

Nowadays everyone faces the information overload. Information demanding citizen of Manhattan has five hundred TV channels on his disposal. Annual information production per capita is 250 megabytes. The amount of information in the narrowest domain of human activity exceeds the perception ability of single expert, even if we consider, that the most efficient broadcast means such as movie, animation, graphics which are the most memory-consuming.

In spite of information overload, the information becomes a tradable good, as it never happened in the past. More and more people are willing to pay more for useful information because despite of information overload they lack the most important - the useful information. Such information turns out to be an instrument of competitive advantage. Its holders are willing to give it away only for a decent price. The history shows that it was always worth-knowing, what others did not know, but up to now we have never been information overloaded, so there was no information overburden paradox.

Israel Beer Josephat discovered the meaning of scoop. He built the Reuter's power on it. The scoop in is news published before the competitors. Once publishing was important, because there were little information channels, so that one could assume that after publication the information was used. Today, with the information increase, the number of information channels also increases. The above assumption then can not be held. In my opinion, today scoop should be understood as passing information to the interested ones.

The information becomes a good. Thus, it is reasonable to emphasize this phenomenon; to speak about information consumers instead of information users. The consumers assign increasing amounts of time for information acquisition. On the other side the information suppliers intensify their fight for the valuable good, which is information consumer's attention. This fight will become even more brutal, taking into consideration, that more and more people in economically developed countries confirm that they lack time.

Because the information is still free, it makes numerous users to consume enormous amounts of it. The effect is that we often read with no understanding, watch with no reception and listen but do not hear. Such consumption of information is the manifestation of informational fears. Everybody wants to be informed, while not being aware of the information overburden paradox.

It may be expected, that in a few years time, half of USA citizens will have access to broadband connections of high capacity. The cost of wireless communication will decrease and its capacity will grow bigger. The countries, that do not want to loose their chances, they will follow the example. The devices capable of accessing such channels will replace all what we nowadays call TV, radio, Internet, phone and library. I am convinced that the duration of single séance with the device will shorten, but the accumulated time devoted to media during the day will grow larger.

I am confident that the consequences of such development will be further mergers and takeovers, in order to concentrate possibly largest number of information channels in one company. It probably does not mean unification of information channels. The good examples are CNN or MTV stations, which make domestic versions of their programme on American market. The next step undoubtedly will be the broadcast in local language.

The techniques of dealing with information overload gain special importance – beginning with techniques of speed reading, through personal information systems (e.g. based on Pocket PC technology), to complex information management systems.

Democratization of access to the information and rapidly rising information volume are the reasons for growing number of information distribution channels.

Once recipient paid for all acquired information that the carrier, on which it was written, could hold. Now he has right to choose. He can order a delivery of information that is the subject of his interest and only that much. The sale of information is more often embedded in the system of its distribution. He can decide to use free information. It means that he looks for desired information by himself and bears the personal expenses or increases the internal cost of the organization, which is often not realized. Dissemination of awareness is leading to creation of various payment systems for information, not for media as it was in the past. Growing number of readers will agree to pay more for an article than for the whole journal.

The profit will be derived from savings on superfluous issues and time devoted to reading the pages not being in the area of interest. Similar development will undoubtedly concern TV on demand.

When we buy a newspaper with Stock Exchange information, we buy historical information – yesterdays at best. Using free Internet Stock Exchange services, we get access to outdated information – the quotation is several minutes old. Buying on-line service we have instant picture of the situation, which is useful for day traders. Recently stock exchange information was published by weekly magazines. This example depicts the tendency for diminishing of information at a growing speed.

The boundary between the information access technology used for professional purposes and for leisure fades. The corporations perceive it while speaking of entertainment and media sector.

The above considerations show the importance of information retrieval. I mean by that the tools which are able to focus consumer's attention, because they counteract the paradox of information overburden. Facing the democratization of access to information, they are becoming the subjects of common interest in the information society, which is the society of information consumers.

My adventure with information retrieval began almost 25 years ago in Federal Institute of Technology in Zurich (Switzerland). During the first years even the computer scientists needed explanation what the area of information retrieval systems was. At that time we were involved in text retrieval. Because there were few large textual document databases, many of us thought that database technology was sufficient for:

- text document acquisition,
- their automatic description, pointing at information that is embedded in them,
- organizing the documents,
- representation of information consumer needs,
- searching documents in accordance with information needs,
- and for presentation of obtained results

These are the tasks, which information retrieval systems deal with. These systems are capable of satisfying 'ad hoc' information needs quite good. For those of us who have well crystallized information needs and want to appease them with new information, the information retrieval systems are not particularly useful. They would have to constantly repeat the queries. It would be difficult for them to identify once acquired documents. The concept of information filters arouse, as specialized information retrieval systems, which separate documents, that meet information needs of their users from the stream of information.

I have devoted most of my publications just to information filters. They can be a tool:

- commonly used, they meet the tendency for democratization in access to the information,
- limiting the amount of information that everyone of us has to deal with,
- managing the access to selected information sources,
- lowering the cost of information assessment,
- allowing to control the information acquisition costs,
- for fast access to the information, allowing to use it before it gets outdated
- for retrieving the criteria of information organization,
- managing knowledge derived from information

Hypertext could be acknowledged as the concept which was a model for today's Internet. It is a graph, which vertices are texts and edges are the relations between them. I have to admit self-critically, that having written the book on filtering hypertext documents in 1989 I did not foresee the scale of the revolution in information retrieval and filtering systems applications that the flashing growth of Internet brought.

It was just the dissemination of the Internet that created the awareness of a need to find proper solutions for: the description of the information found on the Internet, the description of the information consumers' needs, the algorithms for retrieving documents and indirectly, the information embedded in them, and the presentation of the information found. That is why the subject of the book: information retrieval systems and information filtering from the Internet seems to be well justified.

Regretfully, most of the deterministic approaches to information retrieval and filtering, that I remember from the lectures of Gerald Salton can not be put into practice, due to their computational complexity in the face of vast number of documents and consumers in the Internet. That is why inviting my colleagues to write the chapters of the book that you hold, I turned to knowledge based issues.

Similar approach can be found among other scientists involved in information retrieval and filtering. There were thirty one chapters submitted for the book from Australia, Austria, Bangladesh, Canada, Czech Republic, Estonia, Finland, Germany, The Netherlands, New Zealand, Poland, Slovenia, Switzerland and the USA. Many of the authors are members of the society participating in BIS conferences (Business Information Systems http://bis.kie.ae.poznan.pl/) regularly. Fifteen chapters appeared in this book after both the authors and the editor had worked for over a year.

Our intention was to prepare the work useful for everyone, who wanted to fight the paradox of information overburden and wanted to create a good scoop. Among them there would be researchers concerned with information retrieval, filtering and managing the information on the Internet. I presume that the book will be helpful for all creators of information retrieval and filtering systems and for the students, who want to build, implement and administer such systems in the future.

The book will be undoubtedly useful for those who are aware of the fact that for decision-making purposes only **the information known** to the decision-makers is used. Therefore they do not need to retrieve it. The tool which is said to try to deliver such information causes the effort not awarded with relevant information. For decision-making purposes the needed but not possessed information is required. Just that realized lack of information is the most common motivation towards using information retrieval and filtering systems. There is also information, the usefulness of which the decision-makers are not aware of. Hence they do not endeavor to acquire it.

We too often realize how important these groups of information are in crisis situations. Donald Rumsfeld, the US Secretary of Defense, during the press conference on June 22nd, 2002 assessing the intelligence activity in the context of the tragedy of September 11th, Washington DC, said: 'There are things we know that we know. There are known unknowns - that is to say, there are things that we now know we don't know but there are also unknown unknowns. There are things we do not know we don't know.'

I wish that The Readers would find the inspirations in this book for building knowledge based information retrieval and filtering systems satisfying not realized information needs.

ACKNOWLEDGEMENTS

Let me express my gratitude for cooperation to all the authors of the chapters, both these who are in this book and those who did not fit in because of limited space. I am really grateful for interesting discussion we led.

The book could not be published without enormous amount of work that my assistants at The Poznan University of Economics, Poland, Tomasz Kaczmarek and Marek Kowalkiewicz put in it. They bore the burden of coordination work involved in creation of this book. Thanks to it they had the opportunity to learn the most interesting aspect of information systems – managing documents' versions. Thank you very much for your cooperation and patience.

This is the second book I prepared with Melissa Fearon's assistance, it was a great pleasure for me and I am grateful for that.

Poznań, Poland, March 2003.

CONTRIBUTING AUTHORS

Witold Abramowicz
Department of Management Information Systems, The Poznań University of Economics, Poland

Roxana Angheluta
Katholieke Universiteit Leuven, Belgium

Rik De Busser
Katholieke Universiteit Leuven, Belgium

Wojciech Cellary
Department of Information Technology, The Poznań University of Economics, Poland

Czesław Daniłowicz
Department of Information Systems, Wrocław University of Technology, Poland

David A. Garza-Salazar
ITESM-Campus Monterrey

Peter Gerstl
IBM Germany

Hele-Mai Haav
Institute of Cybernetics at Tallinn Technical University, Estonia

Harald Häuschen
Department of Information Technology, University of Zurich

Birgit Kuhn
IBM Germany

Juan C. Lavariega
ITESM-Campus Monterrey

Marie-Francine Moens
Katholieke Universiteit Leuven, Belgium

Huy Cuong Nguyen
Department of Information Systems, Wrocław University of Technology, Poland

Ngoc Thanh Nguyen
Department of Information Systems, Wrocław University of Technology, Poland

Adam Niewiadomski
Institute of Computer Science, Technical University of Łódź, Poland

Hans-Joachim Novak
IBM Germany

Eric Paquet
NRC and University of Ottaw, Canada

Willy Picard
Department of Information Technology, The Poznań University of Economics, Poland

Jakub Piskorski
German Research Center for Artificial Intelligence, Saarbrücken, Germany

Hakikur Rahman
SDNP

Martha Sordia-Salinas
ITESM-Campus Monterrey

Piotr S. Szczepaniak
Institute of Computer Science, Technical University of Łódź, Poland
Systems Research Institute, Polish Academy of Sciences, Poland

Edward Szczerbicki
The University of Newcastle, NSW, Australia

Frank Teuteberg
Business Informatics, European University Viadrina, Frankfurt (Oder), Germany

Herna Viktor
NRC and University of Ottawa, Canada

Krzysztof Węcel
Department of Management Information Systems, The Poznań University of Economic, Poland

Feiyu Xu
German Research Center for Artificial Intelligence, Saarbrücken, Germany

Chapter 1

TOWARDS AN ONTOLOGICAL REPRESENTATION OF KNOWLEDGE ON THE WEB

KRZYSZTOF WĘCEL
Department of Management Information Systems
The Poznań University of Economics, Poland

Abstract: This chapter gives a background on recent developments in Web ontologies, which provide basic means to represent semantic knowledge about the Web. We start with Resource Description Framework to show basic syntax, and further develop many examples in OWL Web Ontology Language to show the expressiveness of this language.

Key words: knowledge representation, semantics, Web, ontology, RDF, OWL

1.   INTRODUCTION

Due to the fast growth of information volume, proper description of distributed information is essential for effective information retrieval and filtering. Many proposals have emerged. They have begun with simple metadata, and evolved to more complex and expressive structures. It is inescapable to create more and more classes of information about information. It is advantageous if descriptions of information utilize the same syntax, but it is not sufficient. We also need the same semantics.

The need for expressive syntax and for unambiguous semantics drove to the development of ontologies. Ontologies are introduced as an "explicit specification of a common conceptualization" [Gruber, 1993]. Much of the effort is devoted to creation of Web ontologies, which are expected to greatly improve the search capabilities of the Web. Just these ontologies, which create the foundation for the Semantic Web, are described further in this chapter.

2.   WEB ONTOLOGIES

The history of metadata at the W3C began in 1995 with PICS, the Platform for Internet Content Selection (*http://www.w3.org/PICS*). PICS is a mechanism for communicating ratings of Web pages from a server to clients.

At the Dublin Core meeting in Helsinki in 1997, representatives from the W3C Metadata Project presented the first draft of a new specification for extended Web metadata – the Resource Description Framework (RDF). The development of RDF as a general metadata framework and a simple knowledge representation mechanism for the Web was heavily inspired by the PICS specification. RDF is based on the XML recommendation [XML]. When the term 'ontology' became more popular and the idea of the Semantic Web appeared, RDF and its extensions became Web ontologies.

Ontologies encode knowledge within a domain and also knowledge that spans domains. They include definitions of basic concepts in the domain and the relationships among them. The Semantic Web needs ontologies with a significant degree of structure. These need to specify descriptions for the following kinds of concepts:
– classes in the domains of interest
– relationships that can exist among things
– properties those things may have.

Ontologies are usually expressed in logic-based languages. It is then possible to build tools capable of automatic reasoning based on the facts in the ontology. Such tools found their applications in many areas: semantic search and retrieval, software agents, decision support, speech and natural language understanding, and knowledge management. As we can see, ontologies are critical if we want to search across or merge information from diverse communities.

XML DTDs and XML Schemas are only sufficient for exchanging *data* between parties who have agreed to definitions in advance. However, they lack semantics, and introduction on new XML vocabularies involves next agreements and many changes in software. Moreover, the same term may have different meanings in various contexts, and different terms may have the same meaning. RDF and RDF Schema begin to approach this problem by introducing simple semantics.

3.   RESOURCE DESCRIPTION FRAMEWORK

Resource Description Framework (RDF) is an infrastructure that enables the encoding, exchange and reuse of structured metadata. This infrastructure enables metadata interoperability through the design of mechanisms that support common conventions of semantics, syntax, and structure [RDF].

RDF is an application of XML that imposes needed structural constraints to provide unambiguous methods of expressing semantics [Miller1998]. RDF additionally provides a means for publishing both human-readable and machine-processable vocabularies. Vocabularies are the set of properties, or metadata elements, defined by resource description communities. These vocabularies are designed to encourage the reuse and extension of metadata semantics among disparate information communities.

RDF is designed to support **semantic modularity** by creating an infrastructure that supports the combination of distributed attribute registries. Thus, a central registry is not required. This permits communities to declare own vocabularies that may be reused, extended or refined to address application or domain specific descriptive requirements. Such a solution assures metadata interoperability.

RDF can be used in a variety of application areas, for example [RDFS]:
– resource discovery to provide better search engine capabilities
– cataloging for describing the content and content relationships available at a particular Web site, page, or digital library
– knowledge sharing and exchange by intelligent software agents
– content rating
– describing collections of pages that represent a single logical document
– describing intellectual property rights of Web pages
– expressing the privacy preferences of a user as well as the privacy policies of a Web site.

3.1   Formal Data Model

RDF provides a formal model for describing resources. These descriptions can be modeled as relationships among Web resources.

As specified in [RDF], relations between resources are modeled as named properties with values assigned. RDF properties may be thought of as attributes of resources and in this sense correspond to traditional attribute-value pairs. RDF properties also represent relationships between resources. As such, the RDF data model can therefore resemble an entity-relationship diagram [RDFS].

The basic data model consists of three object types: Resources, Properties, and Statements.

3.1.1   Resource

RDF defines a `Resource` as any object that is uniquely identifiable by a Uniform Resource Identifier as described in [URI]. RDF uses *qualified* URIs, that is, URIs with an optional fragment identifier (a text added to the URI with a "#" between them). RDF considers every qualified URI (with or without fragment identifier) as a full resource by itself.

The RDF model is very simple and uniform. Mostly, the fact that the only vocabulary is URIs allows the use of the same URI as a node and as an arc label. This makes things like self-reference and reification possible, just like in natural languages. This is appreciable in a user-oriented context (like the web), but may pose problems for knowledge-based systems and inference engines.

3.1.2   Property Type

A `PropertyType` is a resource that has a name and can be used as a property (e.g. `Author` or `Title`). It needs to be the resource so that it can have its own properties.

A *property* is a specific aspect, characteristic, attribute, or relation used to describe a resource. Each property has a specific meaning, defines its permitted values, the types of resources it can describe, and its relationships with other properties.

3.1.3   Statement

A `Statement` is the combination of a `Resource`, a `PropertyType`, and a `Value`, for example: "The Author of http://kie.ae.poznan.pl/~kaw is Krzysztof Węcel". The Value can just be a string, for example "Krzysztof Węcel" in the previous example, or it can be another resource, for example "*http://www.kie.ae.poznan.pl* is referenced by *http://www.ae.poznan.pl*".

The statement can also be thought as a triple: subject, predicate, and object, the basic element of the RDF model.

A resource (the *subject*) is linked to another resource (the *object*) through an arc labeled with a third resource (the *predicate*). We will say that <subject> has a *property* <predicate> *valued* by <object>.

All the triples result in a directed labeled graph, whose nodes and arcs are all labeled with qualified URIs.

Figure 1-1. Basic RDF assignment

The triple above could be read as "kaw@kie.ae.poznan.pl is the creator of the page *http://kie.ae.poznan.pl/~kaw*".

In RDF, values may be atomic in nature (also called literal: text strings, numbers, or other primitive data types defined by XML) or other resources, which in turn may have their own properties (see Figure 1-2).

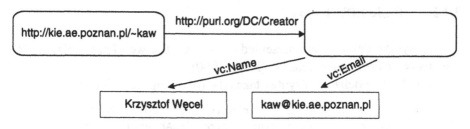

Figure 1-2. Extended RDF assignment

3.2 The RDF Syntax

RDF defines simple, yet powerful model for describing resources. Syntax representing this model is required to store instances of this model into machine-processable files and to communicate these instances among applications.

Creators of RDF decided to use XML syntax which in fact became a standard. RDF and XML are complementary: RDF is a model of metadata, so it defines elements and relationships. Issues such as encoding for transportation and file storage (internationalization, character sets) are only addressed by reference. For these issues, RDF relies on the support of XML.

3.2.1 Namespaces

RDF provides the ability for resource description communities to define their own semantics. Hence, it is important to disambiguate these semantics among communities. Different communities can use the same property type to mean different things. To distinguish these property types, RDF uses the XML *namespace* mechanism [XMLNS].

Namespaces provide a method for unambiguously identifying the semantics and conventions governing the particular use of property types by uniquely identifying the governing *authority* of the vocabulary.

Let us consider the example: the Dublic Core defines "author" as "person or organization responsible for the creation of the intellectual content of the resource" and specifies it in the Dublin Core CREATOR element. An XML namespace is used to unambiguously identify the schema for the Dublin Core vocabulary (abbreviated as DC) by pointing to the Dublin Core resource that defines the corresponding semantics. The full reference is then DC:CREATOR.

3.2.2   Basic RDF Syntax

The syntax descriptions presented below use the well-known Extended Backus-Naur Formalism notation [Naur, 1960].

Basic RDF serialization syntax takes the following form [RDF]:

```
[1] RDF ::= ['<rdf:RDF>'] description* ['</rdf:RDF>']
[2] description ::= '<rdf:Description' idAboutAttr? '>'
    propertyElt* '</rdf:Description>'
[3] idAboutAttr ::= idAttr | aboutAttr
[4] aboutAttr ::= 'about="' URI-reference '"'
[5] idAttr ::= 'ID="' IDsymbol '"'
[6] propertyElt ::= '<' propName '>' value '</' propName '>'
    | '<' propName resourceAttr '/>'
[7] propName ::= Qname
[8] value ::= description | string
[9] resourceAttr ::= 'resource="' URI-reference '"'
[10] Qname ::= [ NSprefix ':' ] name
[11] URI-reference ::= string, interpreted per [URI]
[12] IDsymbol ::= (any legal XML name symbol)
[13] name ::= (any legal XML name symbol)
[14] NSprefix ::= (any legal XML namespace prefix)
[15] string ::= (any XML text, with "<", ">", and "&" escaped)
```

The RDF element is a simple wrapper that marks the boundaries in an XML document between which the content is explicitly intended to be mappable into an RDF data model instance.

3.2.3   Expressing RDF in XML

As mentioned earlier, RDF requires the XML namespace facility to precisely associate each property with the schema that defines this property. Element names are qualified with a namespace prefix to unambiguously connect the property definition with the corresponding RDF schema., or default namespace can be defined as specified in [XMLNS].

Before RDF schema is used, proper namespace should be declared. To associate rdf: with the RDF Schema, RDF description expressed in XML should start with:

```
<rdf:RDF
  xmlns:rdf="http://www.w3.org/1999/02/22-rdf-syntax-ns#">
```

The example statement from Figure 1-1 "Krzysztof Węcel is the creator of the page *http://kie.ae.poznan.pl/~kaw*" in XML syntax is represented as:

```
<rdf:Description rdf:about="http://kie.ae.poznan.pl/~kaw">
  <author>Krzysztof Węcel</author>
</rdf:Description>
```

In the above example the element <rdf:Description> should be interpreted as the element Description in the context of the RDF namespace.

The common practice is to store persons as a separate resource. It is then possible to refer to them many times. We would like to include additional descriptive information regarding the author. It is possible to include elements from other metadata schemas, and we decided to use the Dublin Core CREATOR property type. Unfortunately, in Dublin Core does not define semantics for additional property types, such as "name", "email" and „affiliations". Therefore, an additional resource description standard have to be utilized. Let us assume that there is a schema (similar to the vCard specification) created to automate the exchange of personal information typically found on a traditional business card [Miller1998].

The data model representation for this example with the corresponding business card schema defined as vc would be:

```
<?xml version="1.0"?>
<rdf:RDF
  xmlns:rdf="http://www.w3.org/1999/02/22-rdf-syntax-ns#"
  xmlns:dc="http://purl.org/dc/elements/1.0/"
  xmlns:vc="http://person.org/BusinessCard/">
  <rdf:Description rdf:about="http://kie.ae.poznan.pl/~kaw">
    <dc:creator rdf:href="#Creator_001"/>
  </rdf:Description>
  <rdf:Description ID="Creator_001">
    <vc:Name>Krzysztof Węcel</vc:Name>
    <vc:Email>kaw@kie.ae.poznan.pl</vc:Email>
    <vc:Affiliation>The Poznań University of Economics
    </vc:Affiliation>
  </rdf:Description>
</rdf:RDF>
```

3.3   RDF Schema

The RDF data model provides no mechanisms for declaring new properties, nor does it provide any mechanisms for defining the relationships between the properties and other resources. That is the role of RDF Schema.

[RDFS] defines a *schema specification language*. It defines mechanism to build new schemas and also a core vocabulary to do it. These mechanisms are used to define property types, to define the classes of resources they may be used with, to restrict possible combinations of classes and relationships, and to detect violations of those restrictions. RDF Schema is a collection of RDF resources that can be used to describe properties of other RDF resources (including properties) in order to create application-specific RDF vocabularies.

RDF Schemas might be contrasted with XML Document Type Definitions (DTDs) [XML] and XML Schemas [XMLSCHEMA]. An XML DTD or Schema gives specific constraints on the structure of an XML document. It can be used to verify that an XML document is a well-formed XML by validating the syntax. Unlike an XML Schema, an RDF Schema provides information about the interpretation of the statements given in an RDF data model. A syntactic schema alone (i.e. from DTD) is not sufficient for RDF purposes. RDF Schemas may also specify constraints that should be followed by these data models.

The RDF Schema type system is similar to the type systems of object-oriented programming languages such as C++ and Java. However, RDF significantly differs from such systems. Instead of defining a class in terms of the properties its instances may have, RDF schema defines properties in terms of the classes of resource to which they apply. This is achieved using the `rdfs:domain` constraint (indicates the classes on whose members a property can be used) and `rdfs:range` constraint (indicates the classes that the values of a property must be members of). For example, in a classical OOP system we define a class *Book* with an attribute *author* of type *String*. In RDF we would define the *author* property type to have a domain of *Book* and a range of *Literal*.

In the RDF property-centric approach, it is very easy for anyone to say anything they want about existing resources, which is one of the architectural principles of the Web.

Figure 1-3 presents the concepts of class, subclass, and resource. A class is presented as a rounded rectangle, and a resource is symbolized by a large dot. A subclass is shown by having a rounded rectangle (the subclass) completely enclosed by another (the superclass). Arrows are drawn from a resource to the class it defines.

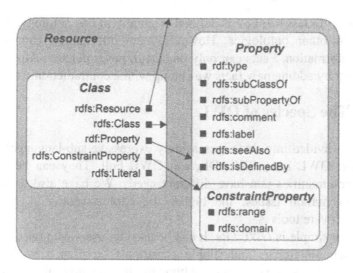

Figure 1-3. Classes and Resources in RDF Schema
Source: [RDFS]

4.   OWL WEB ONTOLOGY LANGUAGE

With RDF Schema, we can define classes that may have multiple subclasses and superclasses, and can define properties, which may have subproperties, domains, and ranges. In this sense, RDF Schema is a simple ontology language. However, the expressive power of RDF is limited. We are unable to assert that Employee and Organization classes are disjoint, or that a soccer team consist of eleven players.

Recent developments in languages for defining and instantiating *Web ontologies* drove to the OWL, Web Ontology Language. It is being designed by the W3C Web Ontology Working Group. OWL is a semantic markup language for publishing and sharing ontologies on the World Wide Web. It can be used to describe the classes and relations between them that are inherent in Web documents and applications.

OWL is developed as a vocabulary extension of RDF (Resource Description Framework) and revises the DAML+OIL web ontology language. It incorporates the lessons learned from the development and applications of DAML+OIL.

OWL development is the next step towards the idea of Semantic Web. Semantic Web from its nature is distributed, and we also require OWL ontologies to be distributed. Therefore, OWL generally makes an *open world* assumption, i.e. descriptions of resources are not limited to one file defining the ontology. It is possible to reference as many external files as required.

For example, if class Worker is defined originally in one ontology, it can be extended in other ontologies. However, new information cannot recall previous information. Facts can only be added, never deleted. After all it is possible that by adding new facts we end up with a contradiction.

4.1   The Species of OWL

OWL is divided into three increasingly expressive sub-languages. These species are: OWL Lite, OWL DL, and OWL Full. They can be used by different communities that have different needs. We have also to consider the implementation issues: the higher the expressiveness is, the more complex software tools is.

The most simple is *OWL Lite*. It can be used by users who need mainly a classification hierarchies and simple constraints on properties. It is best suited to express taxonomies. Although it supports the cardinality constraints, only values of 0 or 1 are valid. The tools for OWL Lite should also be relatively easy to design.

OWL DL supports the maximal expressiveness that is possible without losing computational completeness. OWL DL puts constraints on the mixing with RDF and requires disjointness of classes, properties, individuals and data values (type separation). OWL DL corresponds to description logic. It was designed to support the existing description logic software tools and has desirable computational properties for reasoning systems.

OWL Full supports the maximal expressiveness and also the free syntax of RDF. The ontology can augment the meaning of the pre-defined (RDF or OWL) vocabulary. In OWL Full there is no difference between a class and an instance of this class (an individual). However, there are no computational guarantees. Due to the complexity of OWL Full it is unlikely that it will be fully supported by reasoning software.

4.2   Relation to XML and RDF

There are some important features that distinguish OWL from its predecessors: XML and RDF.

An ontology is a knowledge representation, and XML is only a message format. To be useful, XML documents are accompanied by protocol specifications. They have no meaning in itself. Protocols give them operational semantics, e.g. "After receiving the *travel offer confirmation*, book a *flight* and make a *hotel reservation*". It is not possible to reason outside the transaction context.

The most important advantage of OWL over XML is the possibility to infer new facts based on facts provided. Moreover, this inference is domain-independent. If one introduced such functionality for XML, it would be restricted to specific XML schema. The reasoning systems may be developed separately from ontologies, and ontologies can be developed simultaneously by many communities. Tools has only to base on the formal properties of the OWL language.

OWL, similarly as DAML and OIL, can be viewed as an extension of a restricted view of the RDF language. This implies that every OWL document is an RDF document, but not all RDF documents are OWL documents.

OWL documents use RDF syntax. For example, to define a class we can use the following RDF statement.

```
<rdf:Description rdf:about="#Employee">
<rdf:type rdf:resource="http://www.w3.org/2002/07/owl#Class"/>
</rdf:Description>
```

We can also use the abbreviated syntax:

```
<owl:Class rdf:ID="Employee"/>,
```

where `owl` is the appropriate namespace for OWL (see 5.1 Namespaces).

5.   OWL STRUCTURES

An OWL document consists of an optional *ontology header* and any number of *class axioms*, *property axioms*, and *individual axioms*.

5.1   Namespaces

Similarly to RDF documents, we have to start OWL ontology with XML namespace declarations in an opening `rdf:RDF` tag. A typical declaration look as follows:

```
<rdf:RDF
    xmlns      ="http://www.kie.ae.poznan.pl/business#"
    xmlns:owl ="http://www.w3.org/2002/07/owl#"
    xmlns:rdf ="http://www.w3.org/1999/02/22-rdf-syntax-ns#"
    xmlns:rdfs="http://www.w3.org/2000/01/rdf-schema#"
    xmlns:xsd ="http://www.w3.org/2001/XMLSchema#">
```

The above associations will be used further in this chapter. The most important in this list is `owl` namespace that allows to use OWL vocabulary.

5.2   Ontology Headers

Because ontologies evolve quickly, it is useful to have a track of versions. The metadata about OWL documents can be stored in ontology headers. Such a header has to be marked by owl:Ontology, and can look like this:

```
<owl:Ontology
rdf:about="http://www.kie.ae.poznan.pl/example.owl">
  <owl:versionInfo>
    $Id: example.owl,v 0.99 2002/11/09 kaw $
  </owl:versionInfo>
  <owl:priorVersion rdf:resource=
    "http://www.kie.ae.poznan.pl/example.owl-200107"/>
  <rdfs:comment>An example ontology</rdfs:comment>
  <owl:imports rdf:resource="http://www.w3.org/2002/07/owl"/>
</owl:Ontology>
```

The statement owl:imports implements the distributed nature of the ontology. It allows to include assertions from other ontologies (identified by the rdf:resource attribute) and use them within current ontology for inference purposes. Usually it is accompanied by an appropriate namespace declaration. Importing another ontology, *O2*, will also import all of the ontologies that *O2* imports.

5.3   Class Axioms

5.3.1   Simple Classes

When modeling the domain we usually start with defining basic concepts. These concepts should correspond to classes that are the roots of various taxonomic trees. Much of the power of ontologies comes from class-based reasoning.

Every individual in the OWL is a member of the class owl:Thing. Consequently every class defined by a user is a subclass of owl:Thing. Thing is the superclass of all classes and the class of all individuals. There is also owl:Nothing class, which is empty from definition.

To define classes in OWL we use owl:Class, which is a subclass of rdf:Class. A class definition has two parts: a name introduction or reference and a list of restrictions. Each of the immediate contained expressions in the class definition further restricts the instances of the defined class.

First form, name introduction, allows the creation of new classes. In this case we use the attribute rdf:ID to introduce a name of a class. This attribute is like the ID attribute defined in XML. It is then possible to make references to such defined class using `rdf:resource` attribute.

```
<owl:Class rdf:ID="Activity"/>
```

The above defined class could be referenced as `rdf:resource="#Activity"` or in full form, e.g. `rdf:resource= "http://www.kie.ae.poznan.pl/business#Activity"`.

The fundamental taxonomic constructor for classes is `rdfs:subClassOf`. This property is transitive, i.e. if A is a subclass of B and B is a subclass of C then A is also a subclass of C.

```
<owl:Class rdf:ID="BusinessActivity">
  <rdfs:subClassOf rdf:resource="#Activity" />
  ...
</owl:Class>
```

Second form, name reference, allows the extension of existing classes definitions and is crucial for implementation of distributed ontologies. For this purpose we use `rdf:about` syntax. We can extend the definitions of classes from our ontology or other classes from imported ontologies. Thus we can incrementally construct larger and larger ontologies.

5.3.2 Complex Classes in OWL DL

OWL DL provides additional class constructors that can be used to create so-called *class expressions*. The members of the class are completely specified by the set operation. OWL supports the basic set operations, namely union, intersection, and complement. These are denoted `unionOf`, `intersectionOf`, and `complementOf`, respectively. Additionally, classes can be enumerated. Class extensions can be stated explicitly by means of the `oneOf` constructor. And it is possible to assert that class extensions must be disjoint.

Class expressions can be nested without requiring the creation of names for every intermediate class. This allows the use of set operations to build up complex classes from anonymous classes or classes with value restrictions. For this purpose we have to use `rdf:parseType="Collection"` syntactic element.

```
<owl:Class rdf:ID="NonAmericanCar">
  <owl:intersectionOf rdf:parseType="Collection">
    <owl:Class rdf:about="#Car"/>
    <owl:Class>
      <owl:complementOf>
        <owl:Restriction>
          <owl:onProperty rdf:resource="#producedIn" />
```

```
            <owl:hasValue rdf:resource="#USA" />
        </owl:Restriction>
      </owl:complementOf>
    </owl:Class>
  </owl:intersectionOf>
</owl:Class>
```

This defines the class `NonAmericanCar` to be the intersection of `Car` with the set of all things not produced in USA.

It is also possible to define a class via a direct *enumeration* of its members, using the `oneOf` constructor. No other individuals can be then declared to belong to the class.

```
<owl:Class rdf:ID="Direction">
<owl:oneOf rdf:parseType="Collection">
    <owl:Thing rdf:about="#North"/>
    <owl:Thing rdf:about="#South"/>
    <owl:Thing rdf:about="#East"/>
    <owl:Thing rdf:about="#West"/>
  </owl:oneOf>
</owl:Class>
```

The *disjointness* of a set of classes guarantees that an individual that is a member of one class cannot simultaneously be an instance of a specified other class.

```
<owl:Class rdf:ID="Animalia">
  <rdfs:subClassOf rdf:resource="#Organism"/>
  <owl:disjointWith rdf:resource="#Fungi"/>
  <owl:disjointWith rdf:resource="#Plantae"/>
</owl:Class>
```

5.4   Property Axioms

5.4.1   Properties

Classes allow only definitions of taxonomies. *Properties* let us assert general facts about the members of classes and specific facts about individuals. In OWL, like in RDF, property is a binary relation.

OWL distinguishes two types of properties:
a) *object properties*, have a value range of class individuals, reflect relations between instances of two classes
b) *datatype properties*, have a value range of data values, reflect relations between instances of classes and RDF literals and XML Schema datatypes.

An object property is defined using an `owl:ObjectProperty` class, whereas a datatype property is defined through an `owl:DatatypeProperty` class. Both `owl:ObjectProperty` and `owl:DatatypeProperty` are subclasses of the RDF class `rdf:Property`.

It is also possible to define additional characteristics of properties. The following constructs are supported by OWL:

a) RDF Schema constructs: `rdfs:subPropertyOf`, `rdfs:domain` and `rdfs:range`

b) relations to other properties: `owl:equivalentProperty` and `owl:inverseOf`

c) global cardinality constraints: `owl:FunctionalProperty` and `owl:InverseFunctionalProperty`

d) logical property characteristics: `owl:SymmetricProperty` and `owl:TransitiveProperty`.

Data-valued properties can be specified as functional. Individual-valued properties can be specified as symmetric, functional, inverse functional, or one-to-one.

5.4.2   Superproperties

Properties, like classes, can be arranged in a hierarchy. It also gives some extra information for reasoning systems. The property can be defined to be a specialization of an existing property. In the example below `hasColor` is more specific property than `hasFeature`.

```
<owl:ObjectProperty rdf:ID="hasFeature">
<owl:ObjectProperty rdf:ID="hasColor">
  <rdfs:subPropertyOf rdf:resource="#hasFeature" />
  ...
</owl:ObjectProperty>
```

Object properties cannot be superproperties of data properties, and vice versa.

5.4.3   Property Restrictions

When we define a property there are a number of ways to restrict the relation. The most commonly used are restrictions inherited from RDF: domains and ranges. A *domain* for a property specifies to which individuals the given property can be attributed to. A *range* for a property specifies which individuals or data values can be objects of the property.

```
<owl:ObjectProperty rdf:ID="worksFor">
  <rdfs:domain rdf:resource="#Employee" />
```

```
<rdfs:range  rdf:resource="#Organization" />
</owl:ObjectProperty>
```

In OWL Lite ranges for individual-valued properties are classes, and ranges for data-valued properties are datatypes.

```
<owl:DatatypeProperty rdf:ID="jobSeniority">
  <rdfs:domain rdf:resource="#Employee" />
  <rdfs:range  rdf:resource="&xsd;positiveInteger"/>
</owl:DatatypeProperty>,
```

where &xsd; is defined as http://www.w3.org/2001/XMLSchema#.

The range restriction presented above is global, i.e. it is applied to all instances of the property. There are also similar mechanisms but their scope can be local – only for class where they are contained. In order to define such a restriction we use owl:Restriction. The embedded owl:onProperty element indicates, which property is restricted. We can generally distinguish value restrictions and cardinality restrictions.

Value restrictions are the following:
- allValuesFrom, universal local range restrictions (toClass in DAML+OIL)
- someValuesFrom, existential local range restrictions (hasClass in DAML+OIL).

An example of the restriction is given below.

```
<owl:Class rdf:ID="Manager">
  <rdfs:subClassOf rdfs:resource="#Employee">
  <rdfs:subClassOf>
    <owl:Restriction>
      <owl:onProperty rdf:resource="#manages" />
      <owl:allValuesFrom rdf:resource="#Department" />
    </owl:Restriction>
  </rdfs:subClassOf>
  ...
</owl:Class>
```

Every instance of the class Manager must have an instance of the specified property manages with values that are all instances of the specified restriction class Department. Other classes are unaffected by this restriction, so Coach can still manage a Team.

If we replaced owl:allValuesFrom with owl:someValuesFrom in the example above, it would mean that at least *one* of the manages properties of a Manager must point to an individual that is a Department.

Another important restriction is cardinality restriction, i.e. the number of values the property can have. We can define both minCardinality and `maxCardinality`. In OWL Lite the only valid values for cardinality are 0 and 1. This permits the user to indicate 'at least one', 'no more than one', and 'exactly one'.

```
<owl:Class rdf:about="#Employee">
  <rdfs:subClassOf>
    <owl:Restriction>
      <owl:onProperty rdf:resource="#worksFor"/>
      <owl:cardinality
      rdf:datatype="&xsd;NonNegativeInteger">1</owl:cardinality>
    </owl:Restriction>
  </rdfs:subClassOf>
</owl:Class>
```

This syntax seems rather complicated to assert such a simple thing as cardinality. This is local restriction (i.e. in the context of a given class) and unfortunately, there is no other way to state this. We can also make a global restriction by asserting the property to be functional (then it can have 'at least one value', see 5.4.4).

5.4.4   Property Characteristics

Additional features of the properties provide a powerful mechanism for enhanced reasoning. Thus, properties can be transitive, symmetric, functional, or inverse functional. We have to explicitly use `rdf:type` within `owl:ObjectProperty` to indicate the type, or use appropriate property type instead of `ObjectProperty`.

In the definitions below, the notation (x P y) should be interpreted as individual x having property P, which value is y.

`TransitiveProperty`
If a property P is transitive then for any x, y, and z: (x P y) and (y P z) implies (x P z). The best example of such property is `subClassOf`.

`SymmetricProperty`
If a property P is symmetric then for any x and y: (x P y) implies (y P x). Symmetric properties should have identical domains and ranges to make sense, as in an example below.

```
<owl:SymmetricProperty rdf:ID="worksWith">
  <rdfs:domain rdf:resource="#Employee"/>
  <rdfs:range  rdf:resource="#Employee"/>
</owl:SymmetricProperty>
```

`FunctionalProperty`
If a property P is functional then for all x, y, and z: (x P y) and (x P z) implies y = z. It is equivalent to the statement that property P can have at

most one value. Note that unlike cardinality restriction, this restriction is global.

InverseFunctionalProperty

If a property P is InverseFunctional then for all x, y and z: (y P x) and (z P x) implies y = z. A typical example of an inverse-functional property is Social Security Number:

```
<owl:InverseFunctionalProperty rdf:ID="hasSSN">
  <rdfs:domain rdf:resource="Person"/>
</owl:InverseFunctionalProperty>
```

inverseOf

If a property P1 is the inverseOf P2, then for all x and y: (x P1 y) implies (y P2 x).

```
<owl:ObjectProperty rdf:ID="hasEmployee">
  <owl:inverseOf rdf:resource="#worksFor" />
</owl:ObjectProperty>
```

5.5   Individual Axioms

After definition of classes and properties we can introduce individual axioms, also called *facts*. They are statements about individuals, indicating class membership and statements about relevant properties. An individual is minimally introduced by declaring it to be a member of a class.

```
<Organization rdf:ID="ABComm" />
<Employee rdf:ID="JohnSmith">
  <worksFor rdf:resource="#ABComm" />
</Employee>
```

Here we defined ABComm that is an instance of class Organization. Then we instantiated the Employee, and assigned a property worksFor that references the organization ABComm.

Datatype properties can be added to individuals in a similar fashion. Below we give some more information (note the rdf:about) about the existing instance of Employee.

```
<Employee rdf:about="#JohnSmith">
  <jobSeniority rdf:datatype="&xsd;positiveInteger">1998
  </jobSeniority>
  <dateOfBirth rdf:datatype="&xsd;date">1964-07-14
  </dateOfBirth>
</Employee>
```

In OWL it is possible to treat alike a class and an instance of this class.

6.   ONTOLOGY MAPPING

Ontology mapping is one of the most important issues. On the one hand it is the most difficult and time-consuming task in ontology engineering, and on the other hand it is crucial for reasoning capabilities. In order for ontologies to have the maximum impact, they need to be widely shared.

Instead of developing own ontology from scratches it is suggested to find an existing ontology that is broadly accepted, and adopt it to particular needs. Adoption means extension and refinement. Whatever we do, we have to bind together classes and properties from different ontologies. This is the hardest part of ontology development. And it should be done by single assertions. OWL provides some language structures do achieve this goal.

6.1   Properties and Classes in DAML and OIL

Ontology mapping is also a good place to compare some specific structures of DAML and OIL to OWL. In DAML and OIL there were also specific types of properties, other than in RDF. It was also possible to specify property characteristics.

The previous example with owl:inverseOf property written in DAML would look as follows:

```
<daml:ObjectProperty rdf:ID="hasEmployee">
  <daml:inverseOf rdf:resource="#worksFor"/>
</daml:ObjectProperty>
```

And the same example in OIL:

```
<rdf:Property rdf:ID="hasEmployee">
  <oil:inverseRelationOf rdf:resource="#worksFor"/>
</rdf:Property>
```

There are also some significant differences in property restrictions in class definitions. In DAML we use daml:restrictedBy:

```
<rdfs:Class rdf:ID="Employee">
 <rdfs:subClassOf rdf:resource="#Person"/>
 <daml:restrictedBy>
   <daml:Restriction>
    <daml:onProperty rdf:resource="#hasDepartment"/>
    <daml:toClass rdf:resource="#Department"/>
   </daml:Restriction>
 </daml:restrictedBy>
</rdfs:Class>
```

To introduce restrictions in OIL we use `oil:hasSlotConstraint` instead:

```
<rdfs:Class rdf:ID="Employee">
 <rdfs:subClassOf rdf:resource="#Person"/>
 <oil:hasSlotConstraint>
  <oil:ValueType>
   <oil:hasProperty rdf:resource="#hasDepartment "/>
   <oil:hasClass rdf:resource="#Department"/>
  </oil:ValueType>
 </oil:hasSlotConstraint>
</rdfs:Class>
```

6.2   Equivalent Classes and Properties

Equivalence of classes and properties is the most frequently used mapping when building new ontology based on an existing one. We can use `equivalentClass` to indicate that a particular class in one ontology is equivalent to a class in other ontology. They have precisely the same instances. Similarly `equivalentProperty` can be applied to properties.

```
<owl:ObjectProperty rdf:ID="worksFor">
  <owl:equivalentProperty
   rdf:resource="http://any.org/ontology2#isEmployedBy"/>
</owl:ObjectProperty>
```

All the restrictions of each class apply to every instance.

6.3   Individual Identities

In many languages there is an assumption about "unique names": different names refer to different things in the world. On the web, such an assumption is not possible, and OWL does not make it. Unless an explicit statement is made or the inference can be made that two URI references refer to the same or to different individuals, reasoning systems should in principle assume either situation is possible.

We can declare two individuals to be identical by using `sameIndividualAs`. A typical use is to equate individuals defined in different ontologies, as a part of unifying two ontologies.

```
<owl:Thing rdf:about="&onto1;ChryslerLHS">
  <owl:sameIndividualAs rdf:resource="&onto2;Chr2001" />
</owl:Thing>,
```

where &onto1; and &onto2; define URL's to appropriate ontologies.

Using `sameIndividualAs` to equate two classes is not the same as equating them with `equivalentClass`. It causes that classes are interpreted as individuals, and such ontology is categorized as OWL Full.

We can also explicitly state that two individuals are distinct.

```
<Employment rdf:ID="FullTime" />
<Employment rdf:ID="PartTime">
  <owl:differentFrom rdf:resource="#FullTime"/>
</Employment>
```

If we want to define a greater set of mutually distinct individuals, we can use more convenient mechanism. We can use `owl:AllDifferent` to assert that all members of the set are pairwise distinct.

```
<owl:AllDifferent>
  <owl:distinctMembers rdf:parseType="Collection">
    <Profession rdf:about="#Welder" />
    <Profession rdf:about="#Locksmith" />
    <Profession rdf:about="#Plumber" />
    <Profession rdf:about="#Miner" />
  </owl:distinctMembers>
</owl:AllDifferent>
```

7. SUMMARY

Ontologies play a substantial role in knowledge-based information retrieval and filtering. As a consistent specification of the concepts used within a universe of discourse, they introduce this "knowledge element" that may improve the search for information. Most of the information is available on the Web, and in this context the Web ontologies are in the limelight.

A goal of this chapter was not to teach the exact syntax of RDF and OWL but rather to present the capabilities of newly developed Web ontology language. Numerous examples helped to understand the expressiveness of the presented language. In order to work with real world ontologies we rather use specialized tools, which take care of the syntax, and enable to focus fully on semantics. The most popular tools are: Protégé (Stanford), KAON (Karlsruhe, previously OntoEdit), OilEd (Manchester).

OWL is developing very fast and it is hard to predict future applications of OWL. One can be sure that OWL creates a strong foundation for the Semantic Web. Further development of OWL shall focus first of all on semantic-based search for information. It would allow better matching of information and the needs on a semantic level.

REFERENCES

[Gruber, 1993] Tom Gruber, A translation approach to portable ontology specification.
    Knowledge Acquisition 5(2):199-220, 1993

[Miller, 1998] Eric Miller, An Introduction to the Resource Description Framework, D-Lib
    Magazine, May 1998, http://www.dlib.org/dlib/may98/miller/05miller.html

[Naur, 1960] Peter Naur (ed.), „Revised Report on the Algorithmic Language ALGOL 60",
    Communications of the ACM, Vol. 3 No.5, May 1960, pp. 299-314

[OWL-ABSYN] OWL Web Ontology Language 1.0 Abstract Syntax,
    http://www.w3.org/TR/owl-absyn/

[OWL-FEATURES] Feature Synopsis for OWL Lite and OWL, http://www.w3.org/TR/owl-
    features/

[OWL-GUIDE] Web Ontology Language (OWL) Guide Version 1.0,
    http://www.w3.org/TR/owl-guide/

[OWL-REF] Web Ontology Language (OWL) Reference Version 1.0,
    http://www.w3.org/TR/owl-ref/

[OWL-SEMANTICS] Model-Theoretic Semantics for OWL, Web Ontology Language
    (OWL) Abstract Syntax and Semantics, http://www.w3.org/TR/owl-
    semantics/syntax.html

[RDF] Resource Description Framework (RDF) Model and Syntax Specification, W3C
    Recommendation, 22 February 1999, http://www.w3.org/TR/REC-rdf-syntax/

[RDFS] Resource Description Framework (RDF) Schema Specification 1.0, W3C Candidate
    Recommendation, 27 March 2000, http://www.w3.org/TR/2000/CR-rdf-schema-20000327

[URI] Tim Berners-Lee, R. Fielding, U.C. Irvine, L. Masinter. *Uniform resource identifiers:
    Generic syntax*, RFC 2396, Aug 1998, http://www.ietf.org/rfc/rfc2396.txt

[WEBONT-REQ] Web Ontology Language (OWL) Use Cases and Requirements,
    http://www.w3.org/TR/webont-req/

[XML] The W3C XML Extensible Markup Language Working Group Home Page,
    http://www.w3.org/XML/

[XMLNS] Tim Bray, Dave Hollander, Andrew Layman, *Namespaces in XML*, W3C
    Recommendation, 14 January 1999, http://www.w3.org/TR/1999/REC-xml-names-
    19990114.

[XMLSCHEMA] *XML Schema Part 1: Structures*, W3C Recommendation 2 May 2001,
    http://www.w3.org/TR/xmlschema-1/

Chapter 2

ADVANCES IN INFORMATION EXTRACTION

Jakub Piskorski
German Research Center for Artificial Intelligence
Saarbrücken
Germany

Abstract: Nowadays, knowledge relevant to business of any kind is mainly transmitted through free-text documents. Latest trends in information technology such as Information Extraction (IE) provide dramatic improvements in conversion of the overflow of raw textual information into valuable and structured data. This chapter gives a comprehensive introduction to information extraction technology including design, processing natural language, and evaluation issues of IE systems. Further, we present a retrospective overview of IE systems which have been successfully applied in real-world business applications which deal with processing vast amount of textual data, and we discuss current trends. Finally, we demonstrate an enormous indexing potential of lightweight linguistic text processing techniques in other areas of information technology closely related to IE.

Keywords: information extraction, free text processing, natural language processing

1.   INTRODUCTION

For years possessing sound information at the right time has been an essential factor in the strategic planning and facilitating decision making in the area of business of any kind. Today's companies, governments, banks, and financial organizations are faced with monitoring a vast amount of information in digital form in a myriad of data repositories on Intranets and Internet. Unfortunately, the major part of electronically available information like newswire feeds, corporate reports, government documents or litigation records is transmitted through free-text documents und thus hard to search in. One of the most difficult issues concerning applying search technology for retrieving information from textual data collections is the process of converting such data into a shape for searching. Hence, an ever-growing need for effective, efficient and intelligent techniques for analyzing free-text documents and discovering valuable and relevant knowledge from them in form of structured data can be observed.

Conventional Information Retrieval (IR) techniques used in WWW search engines (e.g., boolean queries, ranked-output systems) applied even to homogenous collections of textual documents fall far from obtaining optimal recall and precision simultaneously. For this reason, more sophisticated tools are needed that go beyond simple keywords search and are capable of automatically analyzing unstructured text documents in order to build expressive representations of their conceptual content and determine their relevance more precisely. Recent trends in information technology such as Information Extraction (IE) provide dramatic improvements in conversion of the overflow of raw textual information into structured data which could be further used as input for data mining engines for discovering more complex patterns in textual data collections.

The task of IE is to identify predefined set of concepts in a specific domain and ignoring other irrelevant information, where domain consists of a corpus of texts together with a clearly specified information need. Even in a specific domain it is a non-trivial task due to the phenomena and complexity of natural language. For instance, there are obviously many ways of expressing the same fact, which on the other side could be distributed across several sentences. Furthermore, implicit information is not easy to discern and an enormous amount of knowledge is needed to infer the meaning of unrestricted natural language. The process of understanding language comes quite naturally to most humans, but it is very difficult to model this process in a computer, which has been frustrating the design of intelligent language understanding software.

The potential value of automatically structuring natural language data has been already recognized in the 1950's and 1960's. Currently, Natural Language Processing[1] (NLP) techniques are applied in both IR and IE in order to build rich representations of the analyzed texts. However, it has been shown that from technical point of view realizing high accurate general full text understanding system is at least today impossible. Recent advances

---

[1] "NLP is a branch of computer science that studies computer systems for processing natural languages. It includes the development of algorithms for parsing, generation and acquisition of linguistic knowledge; the investigation of time and space complexity of such algorithms; the design of computationally useful formal languages (such as grammar and lexicon formalisms) for encoding linguistic knowledge; the investigation of appropriate software architectures for various NLP tasks; and consideration of the types of non-linguistic knowledge that impinge on NLP" [Gazdar, 1996].

in NLP concerning new robust, efficient and high-coverage shallow text processing techniques instead of fully-fledged linguistic analysis contributed to the size in the deployment of IE techniques in real-world business information systems dealing with huge amount of textual data. The use of light-weight linguistic analysis tools instead of full text understanding systems may be advantageous since it might be sufficient for the extraction and assembly of the relevant information and it requires less knowledge engineering, which means a faster development cycle and fewer development expenses.

The rest of this chapter is organized as follows. Section 2 introduces the IE task, issues concerning design and evaluation of IE systems, and utilization of shallow text processing. The IE systems successfully applied in the financial, insurance and legal domain are presented in section 3. Section 4 focuses on presenting some fields in information technology closely related to IE, such as Text Mining which benefit from applying similar light-weight linguistic analysis techniques. Finally, we end with a summary in section 5.

2. INFORMATION EXTRACTION

2.1 Information Extraction Task

The task of *Information Extraction* (IE) is to identify instances of a particular pre-specified class of entities, events and relationships in natural language texts, and the extraction of the relevant arguments of the identified events or relationships [SAIC, 1998]. The information to be extracted is pre-specified in user-defined structures called templates (e.g., product or company information, management succession event), each consisting of a number of slots, which must be instantiated by an IE system as it processes the text. The slots are usually filled with: some strings from the text, one of a number of pre-defined values or a reference to other already generated template. One way of thinking about an IE system is in terms of database construction since an IE system creates a structured representation (e.g., database entries) of selected information drawn from the analyzed text. From the viewpoint of NLP information extraction is very attractive since its task is well defined, it uses real-world texts and possesses difficult and interesting NLP problems.

In the last decade IE technology has progressed quite rapidly, from small-scale systems applicable within very limited domains to useful systems which can perform information extraction from a very broad range of texts.

IE technology is now coming to the market and is of great significance to publishers, banks, financial companies, and governments. For instance, a financial organization want to know facts about company take-overs, executive successions and foundations of international joint-ventures happening in a given time span. In figure 2-1 an example of an instantiated template for joint-venture foundation event is presented.

"Munich, February 18, 1997, Siemens AG and The General Electric Company (GEC), London, have merged their UK private communication systems and networks activities to form a new company, Siemens GEC Communication Systems Limited."

$$\begin{bmatrix} \text{VENTURE} : \textit{Siemens GEC Communication Systems Limited} \\ \text{PARTNERS} : \textit{Siemens AG, The General Electric} \\ \text{TIME} : \textit{February } 18, 1997 \\ \text{PRODUCT} : \textit{communication systems, network activities} \end{bmatrix}$$

Figure 2-1. An instantiated template for joint-venture foundation event

The process of extracting such information involves locating names of companies and finding linguistic relations between them and other relevant entities (e.g., locations, temporal expressions). However, in this scenario an IE system requires some specific domain knowledge (understanding the fact that ventures generally involve at least two partners and result in the formation of a new company) in order to merge partial information into an adequate template structure. Generally, IE systems rely always to some degree on domain knowledge. Further information such as appointment of key personnel, announcement of new investment plans, or other market related data could also be reduced to instantiated templates.

The templates generated by an IE system may be incomplete (partially instantiated templates), but incomplete information is still better than no information at all since it could be used to focus users attention on the passage of text containing targeted information.

2.2   Designing IE Systems

There are two basic approaches to designing IE systems: Knowledge Engineering Approach and Learning Approach [Appelt and Israel, 1999]. In the knowledge engineering approach the development of rules for marking and extracting sought-after information is done by a human expert through inspection of the test corpus and his or her own intuition. Therefore, the skill of the knowledge expert is a major factor which impacts the level of performance of an IE system built in this way. Constructing a set of high-coverage extraction rules is usually done iteratively. Initially, a set of rules is written and tested against a test corpus in order to check whether they undergenerate or overgenerate. Subsequently, the rule set is appropriately modified and the process iterates till no significant improvement can be achieved.

In the learning approach the rules are learned from an annotated corpus and interaction with the user. This involves utilization of machine learning techniques based on Hidden Markov Models, Maximum Entropy Modeling, and Decision Trees [Manning and Schütze, 1999]. In this approach, large quantities of training data are a major prerequisite for achieving high accuracy. Obviously, the annotation of texts for the information being extracted requires less skill than manual construction of extraction patterns, but it is still a laborious task. Once a suitable training corpus is provided, the system can be ported to a new domain in a relatively straightforward manner. A debate on advantages and disadvantages of both approaches is given in [Appelt and Israel, 1999]. Generally, higher performance can be achieved by handcrafted systems, particularly when training data is sparse. However, in a particular scenario automatically trained components of an IE system might outperform their handcrafted counterparts. Approaches to building hybrid systems based on both approaches are currently being investigated.

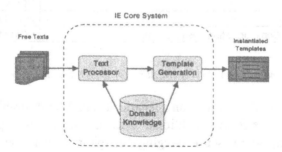

Figure 2-2. A coarse-grained architecture of an IE system

IE systems built for different tasks often differ from each other in many ways. Nevertheless, there are core components shared by nearly every IE system, disregarding the underlying design approach. The coarse-grained architecture of a typical IE system is presented in figure 2-2. It consists of two main components: text processor and template generation module. The task of the text processor is performing general linguistic analysis in order to extract as much linguistic structure as possible [Piskorski and Skut, 2000].

The scope of information computed by the text processor may vary depending on the requirements of a particular application. Usually, following steps are performed:

– Segmentation of text into a sequence of sentences, each of which is a
  sequence of lexical items representing words together with their
  lexical attributes,

– Recognition of small scale-structures (e.g., abbreviations, core
  nominal phrases, verb clusters and named entities),

– Parsing, which takes as input a sequence of lexical items and small-
  scale structures and computes a dependency structure of the sentence,
  the so called parse tree.

FRAGMENT	TYPE
Munich,	LOCATION
February 18, 1997	DATE
Siemens AG	COMPANY NAME
and	CONJUNCTION
The General Electric Company (GEC), London	COMPANY NAME
have merged	VERB GROUP
their UK private communication systems and networks activities	NOUN PHRASE
to form	VERB GROUP
a new company	NOUN PHRASE
Siemens GEC Communication Systems Limited	COMPANY NAME

Figure 2-3. Recognition of small-scale structures for the sentence presented in the figure 2-1

Depending on the application scenario it might be desirable for the text
processor to perform additional tasks, such as: part-of-speech
disambiguation, word sense tagging, anaphora resolution or semantic
interpretation, i.e., translating parse tree or parse fragments into a semantic
structure or logical form. A benefit of the IE task orientation is that it helps
to focus on linguistic phenomena that are most prevalent in a particular
domain or a particular extraction task. An example of a result of recognition
of small-scale structures for the sentence in figure 2-1 is given in the table in
figure 2-3. Recently, a general tendency towards applying partial text
analysis instead of computing all possible interpretations could be observed.
We explore this issue in the next subsection.

The task of the template generation module is to merge the linguistic
structures computed by the text processor and to derive scenario-specific
relations in form of instantiated templates using domain knowledge (e.g., via
domain-specific extraction patterns and inference rules). Since linguistic
analysis, except anaphora resolution operates within a scope of individual
sentences, and due to the fact that filling certain templates requires merging
structures extracted from different sentences, the process of template

generation is usually divided into: (a) creation of templates representing event and entity description, and (b) template merging. In the first step, domain-specific pattern/action rules map linguistic structures into corresponding templates, whereas in the second step, similarity between templates triggers appropriate template merging procedures in order to assemble scattered information pieces. Similarity measures usually rely on the distance and the degree of the overlap between the templates considered [Kehler, 1998]. In figure 2-4, we give an example of template merging.

"<u>Mr. Diagne</u> would leave his job as a <u>vice-president</u> of <u>Yves Saint Laurent</u>, Inc. to become operations director of <u>Paco Raban</u>. <u>John Smith</u> **replaced** <u>Diagne</u>."

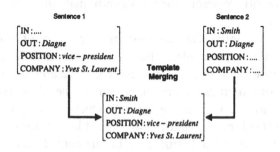

Figure 2-4. Template Merging

In practice, the boundary between text processor and template generation component may be blurred.

2.3   Shallow vs. Deep Text Processing

The main problem one has to cope with when processing free texts is the fact that natural languages are massively ambiguous. The problem of ambiguity pervades all levels of natural language processing. Individual words may have often number of meanings and are used to refer to different things on different occasions of utterance. Further, words or phrases contained in a sentence may be related to one another in more than one way. To illustrate this, consider the following sentence "Simpson saw the terrorist with the telescope" which is structurally ambiguous since it can be interpreted as providing information about which terrorist Simpson saw (the one with a telescope) or about what instrument Simpson used to see the terrorist. The problem we are dealing here with, is the so called PP-Attachment (prepositional phrase attachment). Ambiguities regarding sentence boundaries, clause boundaries and structure, part-of-speech labels and word meanings all complicate sentence analysis. Many sources of ambiguity become simplified when the domain is restricted. For instance, the word "joint" appearing in news articles focusing on business tie-ups is mostly used as an adjective and denotes some sort of joint business activity, whereas in the medical articles one might expect that the word "joint" would be used more frequently as a noun.

The task of *deep text processing* (DTP) is the process of computing all possible interpretations and grammatical relations in natural language text. Because of the high complexity of such full linguistic analysis [Cole et al., 1996] and due to fact that correctly determining such information is not always necessary and may be a waste of time, there is an increased tendency towards applying only partial analysis, so called *shallow text processing* (STP) which is generally considerably less time-consuming and could also be seen as trade-off between simple pattern matching and fully-fledged linguistic analysis.

STP could be briefly characterized as a process of computing text analysis which are less complete than the output of DTP systems. It is usually restricted to identifying non-recursive structures or structures with limited amount of structural recursion, which can be identified with a high degree of certainty. Language regularities which cause problems are not handled and instead of computing all possible readings a STP-engine computes only underspecified structures. Let us consider as an example the recognition of compounds which are massively used in business texts (e.g., in the German "Wirtschaftswoche" corpus consisting of business news, circa 7,2% of the words are compounds). The syntactic structure of a compound may be complex and ambiguous. For example, the structure of the German compound "Biergartenfest" (*beer garden party*) could be [beer [garden party]] (*garden party with beer*) or [[beer garden] party] (*party in the beer-pub*). Furthermore, a compound may have more than just one valid syntactic segmentation (e.g., the German compound "Weinsorten" could be decomposed into "Weins + orten" (*wine places*) or "Wein + sorten" (*wine brands*). Since semantically correct segmentation of compounds as well as computation of their internal structure requires a great deal of knowledge, a STP engine would usually compute a single syntactically valid segmentation and determine the head while leaving internal bracketing underspecified [Neumann and Piskorski, 2002]. On the other side, computing information about all possible segmentations and internal bracketings might be even unnecessary for successfully performing most of the real-world IE tasks.

The term shallow text analysis usually refers to identifying named entities and some phrasal constituents (e.g., base noun phrases, verb clusters) without indicating their internal structure and function in the sentence, but does not have to be restricted to recognizing only this kind of information. Currently developed STP systems are usually based on finite-state technology. The tendency towards applying finite-state technology can be briefly motivated in two ways. Firstly, finite-state devices are time and space efficient due to their closure properties and the existence of efficient optimization algorithms. Secondly, the local natural language phenomena can be easily and intuitively expressed as finite-state devices. Moreover, the linguistic description of a given phenomena can be usually broken into a number of autonomous finite-state sub-descriptions. In this way, a finite-state cascade allows for a strong decomposition of the linguistic analysis into many subtasks, ordered by increasing complexity. The strongly incremental character of this approach entails simplicity of the grammars w.r.t. both size and facility of modification. Obviously, there exist much more powerful formalisms like context-free or unification based grammars [Cole et al., 1996] which allow to describe phenomena beyond the descriptive capacity of finite-state devices, but since industry prefers more pragmatic solutions finite-state based approaches are recently in the center of attention. It is not only due to the higher time complexity, but also due to somewhat more recursive character of these formalisms, which causes debugging and modifying higher-level grammar a more elusive task (e.g., changes to a rule in a context-free grammar may in principle influence the application of any rule in the grammar). Furthermore, finite-state approximation grammars [Mohri and Nederhof, 2001] have been shown to provide a surprisingly effective engine for partial parsing system design. STP-engines based on the finite-state cascades proved to be almost as accurate as those based on more complex formalisms.

One of the major bottlenecks of DTP systems is the lack of robustness, i.e., they either return large number of concurrent analyses or none at all. STP tackles this problem via underspecification and ranking (weighted grammars), which limits the number of analyses and guarantees higher probability of producing at least one analysis [Aït-Mokhtar et al., 2002].

2.4   IE-oriented NLP Platforms

Since the beginning of 90's, the development of shallow and robust parsing systems has emerged [Chanod, 2000]. On the one pole various efficient monolingual shallow text processors have been introduced. [Piskorski and Neumann, 2000] presents SPPC, an efficient, robust and high-performance STP-engine which make exhaustive use of finite-state technology. It consists of several linguistic components ranging from tokenization to subclause and sentence structure recognition. SPPC provides IE-oriented tools, such as frequency-based term extraction and automatic generation of lexico-syntactic patterns based on a bag of seed words [Finkelstein-Landau and Morin, 1999]. For instance, patterns like: [ORG] "and" [ORG] "merge" [NP] "and" [NP], which covers partially the joint-venture foundation event from the sentence in figure 2-1 can be automatically acquired. The current version of SPPC has been in particular fine-tuned for analyzing German business documents up to several megabytes with an average of processing 30 000 words per second, which together with its high linguistic coverage reflects the state-of-the-art performance and functionality of STP systems, and demonstrates their real-world application maturity.

An Achilles heel of early STP systems was the fact that they were dedicated to processing texts in a single language (mainly English and couple of other major languages) and tailored to a specific domain, and had somewhat black-box character. Therefore, the emphasis on multilinguality and reusability has grown, which is crucial for increasing the suitability of end-user IE applications in the process of customization. [Cunningham, 2002] presented GATE, a framework for development of language processing components and systems. It provides a set of prefabricated ready-made and reusable software blocks for basic operations such as tokenization, morphological analysis, or finite-state transduction on annotated documents. They can be coupled in order to form a system instance in a straightforward manner. GATE allows for integrating of new and external processing resources at run-time. Further, it provides a visual system development environment and resources management tools. Several multilingual text extraction tools were built on top of it, including mainly named-entity recognition systems [Maynard et al., 2002]. Ellogon, a text-engineering platform presented in [Petasis et al., 2002] resembles to large extent the GATE framework. Its key added values as the authors claim are full Unicode support, an extensive multilingual GUI, reduced hardware requirements (implemented in C++, whereas GATE is mainly implemented in JAVA), and supporting a wide range of operating systems. Mainly the user-friendly graphical environment for development and integration of linguistic components makes this platform particularly attractive w.r.t. constructing IE systems.

An important aspect in the context of development of IE systems is the specification language for grammar writing. The possibly most widely spread system GATE (over 2500 users worldwide) uses JAPE (Java Annotation Pattern Engine). A JAPE grammar contains pattern/action rules, where the left-hand side (LHS) of a rule is a regular expression over atomic feature-value constraints, while the right-hand side (RHS) of a rule is a so called annotation manipulation statement for output production, which calls native code (C++, Java), making rule writing difficult for non-programmers. An attempt to find a compromise between processing efficiency and expressiveness was done in SProUT [Becker et al., 2002], another platform for development of STP engines. The grammar formalism of SProUT can be seen as an amalgamation of finite-state and unification-based techniques, where a grammar is a set of pattern/action rules, where the LHS of a rule is a regular expression over typed feature structures with functional operators and coreferences, representing the recognition pattern, and the RHS of a rule is a seqeuence of typed feature structures, specifying the output structure. Coreferences provide a stronger expressiveness since they create dynamic value assignments and serve as means of information transport into the output descriptions. The typed feature structures are used as a uniform I/O data structure which ensures a smooth communication between components, and supports cascaded architectures.

2.5 Evaluation of IE Systems

The input and output of an IE system can be defined precisely, which facilitates the evaluation of different systems and approaches. For the evaluation of IE systems the *precision* and *recall* measures were adopted from the IR research community. These metrics may be viewed as estimating systems effectiveness from the user's perspective, since they measure the extent to which the system produces all the appropriate output (recall) and only the appropriate output (precision). We define these measures formally. Let N_{key} be the total number of slots expected to be filled according to a reference comprising of an annotated corpus representing ground truth, and let $N_{correct}$ be the number of correctly filled slots in the system response. Further, let $N_{incorrect}$ denote the number of incorrectly filled slots, where a slot is said to be filled incorrectly, either if it does not allign with a slot in the reference (spurious slot) or if it is scored as incorrect (i.e., has invalid value). Then, precision and recall are defined as follows:

$$precision = \frac{N_{correct}}{N_{correct} + N_{incorrect}} \qquad recall = \frac{N_{correct}}{N_{key}}$$

Intuitively, it is impossible for an IE system to achieve 100% recall except on the trivial tasks, since textual documents offer differing amounts of relevant information to be extracted and the proper answers ocassionally do not come from a closed set of predetermined solutions. Sometimes the *F-measure* is used as a weighted harmonic mean of precision and recall, where β value is used to adjust their relative weighting (β gives equal weighting to recall and precision, and lower values of β give increasing weight to precision). Formally we define the F-measure as follows:

$$F = \frac{(\beta^2 + 1) \times precision \times recall}{\beta^2 \times precision + recall}$$

On top of these measures a further, less known measure, the so called *slot error rate*, *SER* [Makhoul et al., 1999] is defined as follows:

$$SER = \frac{N_{incorrect} + N_{missed}}{N_{key}}$$

,where N_{missed} denotes the number of slots in the reference that do not allign with any slots in the system response. It is simply the ratio between the total number of slot errors and the total number of slots in the reference. For particular need, certain error types may be weighted in order to deem them more or less important than others.

2.6   IE vs. IR

An IR system finds relevant texts and presents them to the user, whereas typical IE system analyzes texts and presents only specific user-relevant information extracted from them. IE systems are obviously more difficult and knowledge intensive to build and they are in particular more computationally intensive than IR systems. Generally, IE systems achieve higher precision than IR systems. However, IE and IR techniques can be seen as complementary and can potentially be combined in various ways. For instance, IR could be embedded within IE for pre-processing a huge document collection to a manageable subset to which IE techniques could be applied [Gaizauskas and Robertson, 1997]. On the other side, IE can be used as a subcomponent of an IR system to identify terms for intelligent document indexing (e.g., conceptual indicies). Such combinations clearly represent significant improvement in retrieval of accurate and prompt information (cf. figure 2-5). For instance, [Mihalcea and Moldovan, 2001] introduced an approach for document indexing using named entities, which proved to reduce the number of retrieved documents by a factor of 2, while still retrieving relevant documents.

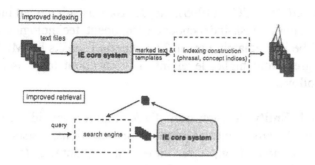

Figure 2-5. The advanced IE technologies improve intelligent indexing and retrieval

The main gain obtained by enriching the texts with named-entity tags, is that this enables the formation of queries that include answer types in addition to the keywords specified in the input question.

2.7   Message Understanding Conferences

The rapid development of the field of IE has been essentially influenced by the Message Understanding Conferences (MUC). These conferences were conducted under the auspices of several United States government agencies with the intention to coordinate multiple research groups and government agencies seeking to improve IE and IR technologies [Grishman and Sundheim, 1996]. The proceedings of MUC provide an important reference to the current state-of-the-art results and techniques used in the field of information extraction. The MUC conferences defined several generic types of IE tasks. These were intended to be prototypes of IE tasks that arise in real-world applications and they illustrate the main functional capabilities of current IE systems. The tasks defined in these conferences are of central importance to the field, since they constitute the most rigorously defined set of information specifications, information representation formats, and a set of corpora that are widely available to the research community. Hence, they provide a framework within which current approaches and systems may be evaluated.

The MUC-1 (1987) and MUC-2 (1989) focused on automated analysis of military messages containing textual information about naval sightings and engagements, where the template to be extracted had 10 slots. Since MUC-3 (1991) the task shifted to information extraction from newswire articles (e.g., concerning terrorist events, international joint-venture foundations, management succession, microelectronics, and space vehicle and missile launches) and templates became somewhat more complex. In MUC-5 the joint-venture task required 11 templates with a total of 47 slots for the output. Further, in MUC-5, the nested template structure and multilingual IE were introduced. In MUC-6 (1995), the IE task was subdivided into subtasks in order to identify task-independent component technologies of IE task which could be immediately useful. The generic IE tasks for MUC-7 (1998) provide progressively higher-level information about texts and they were defined as follows:

(NE) Named Entity Recognition Task requires the identification and classification of named entities such as organizations, persons, locations, temporal expressions (e.g., date, time), and quantities (e.g., monetary values), which has been singled out for this task.

(TE) Template Element Task requires the filling of small-scale templates for specified classes of entities in the texts, such as organizations, persons, certain artifacts with slots such as name, name variants, title, nationality, description as supplied in the text, and subtype. Generally, attributes of entities are used as slot fillings (see template for organization and person in figure 2-6). In other words, TE associates descriptive information with the entities.

(TR) Template Relation Task requires filling a two-slot template representing a binary relation with pointers to template elements standing in the relation, which were previously identified in the TE task. This might be, for instance, an employee relation between a person and a company (cf. figure 2-6), a 'product-of' relation (cf. figure 2-7), or a subsidiary relationship between two companies. The possibilities in real-world applications are endless.

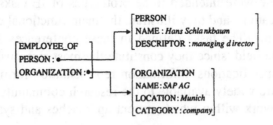

Figure 2-6. An instantiated template representing the "employee-of" relation

(CO) Co-reference Resolution requires the identification of expressions in the text that refer to the same object, set or activity. These include variant forms of name expressions, definite noun phrases and their antecedents, and pronouns and their antecedents (e.g., in the sentence in figure 2-1 the possessive pronoun "their" has to be associated with "Siemens AG" and "The General Electric Company". The CO task can be seen as a bridge between NE task and TE task. It differs from other MUC tasks since it constitutes a component technology.

(ST) Scenario Template Task requires filling a template structure with extracted information involving several relations or events of interest, for instance, identification of partners, products, profits and capitalization of joint ventures (see figure 2-6). Scenario templates tie together TE entities and TR relations into event descriptions. ST task is intended to be the MUC approximation to a real-world IE problem.

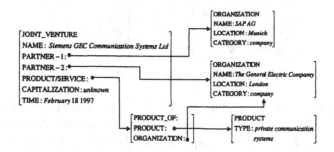

Figure 2-7. An instantiated scenario template for joint-venture

The table in figure 2-8 gives an overview of the tasks evaluated in MUC-3 through MUC-7.

Con\Task	NE	CO	RE	TR	ST
MUC-3					YES
MUC-4					YES
MUC-5					YES
MUC-6	YES	YES	YES		YES
MUC-7	YES	YES	YES	YES	YES

Figure 2-8. Tasks evaluated in MUC-3 through MUC-7

In a MUC evaluation, participants were initially given a detailed description of the scenario along with the annotated training data (*training corpus*) in order to adapt their systems to the new scenario (1 to 6 months). After this, each participant received a new set of documents (*test corpus*), applied their systems to extract information from these documents, and returned the extracted templates to the conference organizer. These results were then compared to the manually filled set of templates (*answer key*). State-of-the-art results for IE tasks for English reported in MUC-7 are presented in figure 2-9. Some experiments were conducted in order to compare the best system results and results obtained by human annotators.

For instance, in the NE task for MUC-7 two human annotators achieved an F-measure of 96.9% and 98.6%. Hence, NE recognition can now be said to function at human performance level. However, for all other tasks IE systems are less accurate than human annotators. The human score for TE and ST task can be around 93% and 80% respectively, where the latter result illustrates the complexity involved. [Appelt and Israel, 1999] argued that 60% can be considered as an upper bound on the proportion of relevant information which is expressed in an explicit and straightforward way, and can be extracted without involving sophisticated linguistic analysis.

MEASURE\TASK	NE	CO	RE	TR	ST
RECALL	92	56	86	67	42
PRECISION	95	69	87	86	65

Figure 2-9. Maximum results reported in MUC-7

In MUC-7, for the first time, the evaluation of some tasks (e.g., NE task) was run using training and test corpus from comparable domains for all languages considered (Chinese, Spanish and Japanese). The results were on an average slightly worse than the results for English (e.g., F-measure of ca. 91% and 87% for Chinese and Japanese respectively) [Chinchor, 1998]. [Sang, 2002] reported on the evaluation of systems participating in a shared language-independent NE task conducted within the Conference on Natural Language Learning (CoNLL-2002). Twelve different systems have been applied to Spanish and Dutch corpora, where the best systems achieved an F-measure of 81.4% and 77.1% respectively.

3. IE SYSTEMS IN THE BUSINESS DOMAIN

3.1 Early IE Systems

The earliest IE systems were deployed as commercial product already in the late eighties. One of the first attempts to apply IE in the financial field using templates was the ATRANS system [Lytinen and Gershman, 1993], based on simple language processing techniques and script-frames approach for extracting information from telex messages regarding money transfers between banks. JASPER [Andersen et al., 1992] is a IE system that extracts information from reports on corporate earnings from small sentences fragments using robust NLP methods. SCISOR [Jacobs et al., 1990] is an integrated system incorporating IE for extraction of facts related to the company and financial information (corporate mergers and acquisitions).

These early IE systems had a major shortcoming, namely they were not easily adaptable to new scenarios. On the other side, they demonstrated that relatively simple NLP techniques are sufficient for solving IE tasks narrow in scope and utility.

3.2   LOLITA

The LOLITA System [Costantino et al., 1997], developed at the University of Durham, was the first general purpose IE system with fine-grained classification of predefined templates relevant to the financial domain. Further, it provides a user-friendly interface for defining new templates. LOLITA is based on deep natural language understanding and uses semantic networks. Different applications were built around its core. Among others, LOLITA was used for extracting information from financial news articles which represent an extremely wide domain, including different kind of news (e.g., financial, economical, political, etc.). The templates have been defined according to the "financial activities" approach and can be used by the financial operators to support their decision making process and to analyze the effect of news on price behavior. A financial activity is one potentially able to influence the decisions of the players in the market (e.g., brokers, investors, analysts etc.).

The system uses three main groups of templates for financial activities: company related activities – related to the life of the company, company restructuring activities - related to changes in the productive structure of companies and general macroeconomics activities, including general macro-economics news that can affect the prices of the shares quoted in the stock exchange. The table in figure 2-10 gives some examples of templates extracted by the LOLITA system.

Company related activities	ownership, shares, takeovers, mergers, new issue of shares, privatization, market movements, dividend announcement, sales forecasts, investigations, profits/sales results, legal action
Company restructuring activities	new product, joint venture, staff change, new factory
General macroeconomi cs activities	interest rate movements, currency movements, inflation, unemployment, trade deficit

Figure 2-10. Templates extracted by the LOLITA IE system

In the "takeover template" task, as defined in MUC-6, the system achieved precision of 63% and recall of 43%. However, since the system is based on DTP techniques, the performance in terms of speed can be, in particular situations, penalized in comparison to STP-based systems. The output of LOLITA was fed to the financial expert system [Constantino, 1999] to process an incoming stream of news from on-line news providers, companies and other structured numerical market data to produce investment suggestions.

3.3   MITA

IE technology has been recently successfully used in the insurance domain. MITA (Metalife's Intelligent Text Analyser) was developed in order to improve the insurance underwriting process [Glasgow et al., 1998]. The Metalife's life insurance applications contain free-form textual fields (an average of 2.3 textual fields per application) such as: physician reason field - describing a reason a proposed insured last visited a personal physician, family history field – describing insured's family medical history and major treatments and exams field which describes any major medical event within the last five years.

In order to identify any concepts from such textual fields that might have underwriting significance, the system applies STP techniques and returns a categorization of these concepts for risk assessment by subsequent domain-specific analyzers. For instance, MITA extracts a 3-slot template from the family history field. The concept slot in the output structure describes a particular type of information that can be found in a specific field, the value slot is the actual word associated with particular instance of the concept and the class slot denotes the semantic class that the value denotes (cf. figure 2-11).

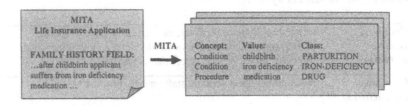

Figure 2-11. An example of output generated by MITA

The MITA system has been tested in a production environment and 89% of the information in textual field was successfully analyzed. Further, a blind testing was undertaken to determine whether the output of MITA is sufficient to make underwriting decisions equivalent to those produced by an underwriter with access to the full text. Evaluation of the results showed that only up to 7% of the extractions resulted in different underwriting conclusions.

3.4   History Assistant

[Jackson et al., 1998] presents History Assistant - an information extraction and retrieval system for the juridical domain. It extracts rulings from electronically imported court opinions and retrieves relevant prior cases and cases affected from a citator database, and links them to the current case. The role of a citator database enriched with such linking information is to track historical relations among cases. On-line citators are of great interest to the legal profession because they provide a way of testing whether a case is still good law.

History Assistant is based on DTP. In particular, it uses context-free grammars for computing all possible parses of the sentence. The problem of identifying the prior case is a non-trivial task since citations for prior case are usually not explicitly visible. History Assistant applies IE for producing structured information blocks, which are used for automatically generating SQL queries to search prior and affected cases in the citator database. Since information obtained by the IE module might be incomplete, additional domain specific knowledge (e.g., court hierarchy) is used in cases when extracted information does not contain enough data to form a good query. The automatically generated SQL query returns a list of cases which are then scored using additional criteria. The system achieved a recall of 93.3% in the prior case retrieval task (i.e., in 631 out of the 673 cases the system found the prior case as a result of an automatically generated query).

3.5   Trends

The most recent approaches to IE concentrated on constructing general purpose, highly modular, robust, efficient and domain adaptive IE systems.

FASTUS [Hobbs et al., 1997] is a very fast and robust general purpose IE system for English and Japanese, built in the Artificial Intelligence Center of SRI International. It is conceptually very simple, since it works essentially as a set of cascaded nondeterministic finite-state transducers. The main design goal of this system was to take full advantage of finite-state technology and represent each stage of processing as finite-state device. The composite output structures of successive stages of processing provide the input for the next stage. FASTUS was one of the best scoring systems in the MUC competitions and was utilized by a commercial client for discovering an ontology underlying complex Congressional bills, for ensuring the consistency of laws with the regulations that implement them. Further, parts of FASTUS were converted into a commercial product for purposes of named entity recognition.

[Humphreys et al., 1998] describe LaSIE-II, a highly flexible and modular IE system, which was an attempt to find a pragmatic middle way in the shallow vs. deep analysis debate which characterized the last several MUCs. The result is an eclectic mixture of techniques ranging from finite-state recognition of domain-specific lexical patterns to using restricted context-free grammars for partial parsing. Its highly modularized architecture (9 submodules) enabled one to take deeper insight into strengths and weaknesses of the particular subcomponents of the system and their interaction. Furthermore, this system provides graphical tools for selecting the control flow through different module combinations. Lasie-II was the only system which took part in all of the MUC-7 tasks and achieved fairly good results (e.g., in ST task recall of 47 % and 42% precision).

Similarly to LaSIE-II, the two top design requirements of the IE2 system [Aone et al., 1999], developed at SRA International Inc. were modularity and flexibility. SGML was used to spell out system interface requirements between the sub-modules of the system, which allow an easy replacement of any sub-module in the workflow. Hence, each module can be developed, tested and improved independently of the other. Further, IE2 provides annotation tool for creating training corpora and visual diagnostic tools for evaluating and debugging the IE submodules which obviously speeds up the development process significantly. The IE2 system achieved the highest score in TE task (recall: 86%, precision 87%), TR task (recall: 67%, precision: 86%) and ST task (recall: 42%, precision: 65%) in the MUC-7 competition.

REES (Relation and Event Extraction System) – a close cousin of IE2, presented in [Aone and Santacruz, 2000], was the first attempt to constructing large-scale event and relation extraction system based on STP methods. It can extract more than 100 types of relations and events related to the area of business, finance and politics, which represent much wider coverage than is typical of IE systems. For 26 types of events related to finance it achieved an *F*-measure of 70%.

[Maynard et al., 2002] presented MUSE, a cross-genre entity recognition system, which borrows some ideas of LaSIE-II, but is mainly based on the finite-state transduction grammar formalism provided in the GATE framework. It was designed to robustly process multiple types of text, with minimal adaptation requirements, through the use of a set of resource switches, which operate according to certain linguistic or other features of the text (e.g., text format triggers different grammar rules). The evaluation of the system demonstrated that the robustness of NE extraction in the context of multiple genres is comparable to robustness achieved by single-genre systems.

Pinocchio, is another environment for developing and running IE applications, which is based on a finite-state approximation of full parsing is presented in [Ciravegna et al., 2000].

3.6   Commercial Systems

The rapid progress in the field of IE fueled an ever-growing interest in the development of commercial IE software for the use in an industrial, governmental and educational context.

Teragram, (http://www.teragram.com) presented Concepts Extractor, a customizable system which automatically detects and extracts concepts from text and documents (based on simple linguistic analysis), such as people's names, company names, publicly traded companies, people's titles and positions, and geographical locations. Additionally, it can also output information associated with the extracted concepts. For example, the extracted publicly traded companies are associated with their ticker symbol and the stock market where they are listed.

The Insight Discoverer Extractor developed by Temis (http://www.temis-group.com), based in France, uses finite-state based shallow processing techniques (morpho-syntactic and semantic tagging and named entity recognition) to extract concepts and relations between concepts. In particular, the extraction patterns are regular expressions over lemmata (cannonical word forms), and syntactic or semantic labels. Furthermore, the patterns allow for defining roles to the extracted entities. For instance, the pattern: [PERSON: IN] "replaced" [PERSON:OUT], would help to fill the template for the second sentence in the example of template merging given in figure 2-4. This product has been deployed in various contexts, including customer email analysis, automatic internet watch for relevant information, and news-wires summarization.

One of the best known commercial ventures that has been spun out of the research work in the field of IE at university, is Cymfony, based in Buffalo, USA (http://www.cymfony.com). Cymfony's InfoXtract is a system which utilizes a leveraged combination of state-of-the-art statistical and grammar-based approaches for extracting entities, relationships between entities, and events of interest. In particular, this tool is capable of identification of numerous key relationships involving industries, companies, people and brands. In order to achieve high speed and robustness, the technique of cascaded shallow grammars has been exploited, where each level of the cascade contributes to increasingly deeper levels of IE. InfoXtract engine, provides the core technology for other advanced text processing tools developed by Cymfony such as text summarization and question answering which will be addressed in the next chapter.

The commercial systems outlined here reveal an enormous application potential of IE technology, and encourage utilization of more advanced NLP techniques in the future. Other US-based companies with similar technology in development include GTE Labs (http://www.gte.com), AT&T Labs (http://www.research.att.com), and MITRE (http://www.mitre.org).

4.   BEYOND INFORMATION EXTRACTION

The last decade has witnessed great advances and interest in the area of information extraction based on STP. In the very recent period, new trends in information processing from texts based on lightweight linguistic analysis closely related to IE have emerged.

4.1   Textual Question Answering

Textual Question Answering (Q/A) aims at identifying the answer of a question in large collections of on-line documents, where the questions are formulated in natural language and the answers are presented in form of highlighted piece of text containing the desired information. The current Q/A approaches integrate existing IE and IR technologies [Gaizauskas and Humphreys, 2000]. An IR system treats a question as a query and returns a set of top ranked documents. Knowledge extracted by an IE system from documents may be modeled as a set of entities extracted from text and relations between them and further used for concept-oriented indexing, which facilitates localization of the answer to the stated question. [Srihari and Li, 1999] presented Textract - a Q/A system, based on relatively simple IE techniques using NLP. This system extracts open-ended domain independent general event templates expressing the information like WHO did WHAT (WHOM) WHEN and WHERE (in predicate-argument structures). Such information may refer to argument structures centering around the verb notions and associated information of location and time. The results are stored in a database and used as a basis for question answering, summarization and intelligent browsing. Figure 2-12 shows a simplified general event template corresponding to the joint-venture foundation event template presented in figure 2-1.

$$\begin{bmatrix} \text{PREDICATE}: merge \\ \text{ARGUMENT1}: Siemens\ AG \\ \text{ARGUMENT2}: The\ General\ Electric \\ \text{TIME}: February\ 18, 1997 \\ \text{LOCATION}: Munich \end{bmatrix}$$

Figure 2-12. General event template corresponding to joint-venture foundation event

Textract, and other similar systems based on lightweight NLP techniques [Attardi and Burrini, 2000], [Harabagiu et al., 2000] achieved surprising good results in the competition of answering fact-based questions in TREC (Text Retrieval Conference) [Voorhess, 1999].

4.2   Text Classification

The task of *Text Classification* (TC) is assigning one or more pre-defined categories from a closed set of such categories to each document in a collection. Traditional approaches in the area of TC use word-based techniques for fulfilling this task. Intuitively, a word like "joint" would either occur in medical or financial texts, but the typical phrases for these two domains, which contain this word, would have probably a slightly different structure. This observation led to a growing exploration of text categorization methods based on NLP which goes beyond simple stemming. [Riloff and Lorenzen, 1998] presented AutoSlog-TS, an unsupervised system that generates domain specific extraction patterns, which was used for automatic construction of high-precision text categorization system. Autoslog-TS retrieves extraction patterns (with a single slot) representing local linguistic expressions that are slightly more sophisticated than keywords. For instance, for extracting information from sentence in figure 2-1 Autoslog-TS would use following patterns: "[SUBJECT] have merged" and "have merged [DIRECT OBJECT]", where such patterns are not simply extracting adjacent words since extracting information depends on identifying local syntactic constructs (verb and its arguments). AutoSlog-TS takes as input only a collection of pre-classified texts associated with a given domain and combines simple STP and statistical methods for automatic generation of a bag of extraction patterns for TC. This new approach to integrating STP techniques in text classification proved to outperform classification using word-based approaches.

Further, similar unsupervised approaches [Yangarber et al., 2000], using light linguistic analysis were presented for acquisition of lexico-syntactic patterns (syntactic normalization: transformation of clauses into common predicate-argument structure), and extracting scenario-specific terms and relations between them [Finkelstein-Landau and Morin, 1999], which shows an enormous potential of shallow processing techniques in the field of text mining.

4.3   Text Mining

Text mining (TM) combines the disciplines of data mining, information extraction, information retrieval, text categorization, probabilistic modeling, linear algebra, machine learning, and computational linguistics to discover valid, implicit, previously unknown, and comprehensible knowledge from unstructured textual data [Gotthard et al., 1997]. Obviously, there is an overlap between TM and IE, but in text mining the knowledge to be extracted is not necessarily known in advance. [Rajman, 1997] presents two examples of information that can be automatically extracted from text collections using simple STP methods: probabilistic associations of keywords and prototypical document instances. Association extraction from the keyword sets (e.g., named entities and nominal phrases) allows to satisfy information needs expressed by queries like "find all associations between a set of companies including Siemens and Microsoft and any person". Prototypical document instances may be used as representative of classes of repetitive document structures in the collection of texts and constitute good candidates for a partial synthesis of the information content hidden in a textual base. They can be computed by extracting frequent term sets, which in turn can be extracted from a training corpus by utilizing STP methods. All document parts (e.g., sentences, paragraphs) which instantiate any of the top-scoring frequent term sets flow into the prototypical document. Prototypical documents can be used in the process of generating text summaries discussed in the next section.

Text mining contributes to the discovery of information for business and also to the future of information services by mining large collections of text [Abramowicz and Zurada, 2001]. It will become a central technology to many businesses branches, since companies and enterprises "don't know what they don't know" [Tkach, 1999].

4.4   Text Summarization

The goal of *Text Summarization* (TS) is a compression of a textual document or a text collection into a short text, usually limited to a few hundreds of words, which compactly represents information content of the document or collection. The standard summarization techniques are based on sentence extraction, where clues like sentence location, word frequency or linguistic clues are used for estimating sentence significance. [Sekine and

Nobata, 2002] proposed an approach which integrates IE techniques into summarization. The used five independent scores for estimating the sentence significance, including sentence position, sentence length, tf/idf-based measure (average of the tf/idf scores of all words in the sentence), similarity measure between headline and the sentence, and a measure based on the weights of lexico-syntactic IE patterns which match the sentence, with the assumption that patterns appearing more often in a domain are more important. These scores were then combined by interpolation in order to calculate the total score of a sentence. The integration of the IE-pattern-based measure paid off since the performance of this summarization system was better than that of all other systems participating in the Single Document Summarization Task in Document Understanding Conference (DUC) in 2001.

[Harabagiu and Lăcătuşu, 2002] have presented GISTEXTER, which shows that high-quality multi-document summarization can be achieved by integrating IE techniques. An IE system is used in order to extract the information base needed for creating a summary. Lexico-semantic patterns (e.g., [CASUALTY-EXPRESSION] to [NUMBER] from [DISASTER-WORD]) are matched against the document collection in order to identify topic relevant information. Additionally, a mapping from template slots to the text fragments containing the information that fills the slots is generated. Further, all the entities from the text collection that corefer with the information filling any slot are stored in coreference chains since they claim that in order to be comprehensible, summaries should include sentences or text fragments that contain the antecedents of all anaphoric expressions from relevant text fragments. A multi-document summary is generated incrementally by inspecting the most representative templates, in order to select sentences containing the text fragments mapped from these templates. The importance of the templates is measured as a sum of all frequency counts of all it slots. An additional factor integrated in the importance measure is a preference for templates that have larger number of mapped text fragments traversed by coreference chains. The set of highly ranked sentences for creating the summary is extended by sentences which contain antecedents of the anaphoric expressions appearing in the highly ranked sentences. Since the final summary length is a parameter of GISTEXTER, various additional procedures are deployed for enhancing/compacting the summary. GISTEXTER was one of the best scoring systems in the DUC 2002 evaluation.

5.   SUMMARY

Prompt, sound and timely information is an essential factor in competition in business today. We have learned that IE technology can provide dramatic improvements in conversion of the overflow of raw textual information into valuable and structured data which is easier to search in. In particular, IE technology has been successfully used in financial, insurance and legal domain in various real-world applications dealing with processing vast amount of textual data. Interestingly, very good results can be achieved by applying relatively simple and efficient shallow text processing techniques that do not require much linguistic sophistication.

The recent trend towards applying partial linguistic analysis in IE systems does not mean that such partial parsing is adequate for solving all problems dealing with processing huge collections of textual data. For instance, for some extraction tasks it is worthwhile to spend hours rather than minutes of CPU time if this produces better results. Hence, further important research direction will be the integration of shallow and deep text processing such that a DTP might be called for those structures recognized as being of great importance. Further, deep processing could be applied to text fragments which might have some relevance, but could not have been successfully processed by the STP engine. An initial work in this area has been presented in [Crysmann et al., 2002] and [Feiyu and Krieger, 2003].

In this chapter we demonstrated also that STP – core IE technology has been successfully applied in other fields of information technology which are closely related to IE. The diagram in figure 2-13 reflects an enormous application potential of STP in various fields of information technology. STP can be considered as an automated generalized indexing procedure. The degree and amount of structured data a STP component is able to extract plays crucial role for subsequent high-level processing of extracted data. In this way, STP offers distinct possibilities for boosting productivity in workflow management, e-commerce and data warehousing [Abramowicz et al., 2002]. Potentially, solving a wide range of business tasks can be substantially improved by using IE. Therefore, an increased commercial exploitation of IE technology could be observed.

The question of developing text processing technology base that applies to many problems is still being major challenge of current research. In particular, future research in this area will focus on multilinguality, cross-document event tracking, automated learning methods to acquire background knowledge, portability, greater ease of use and stronger integration of semantics.

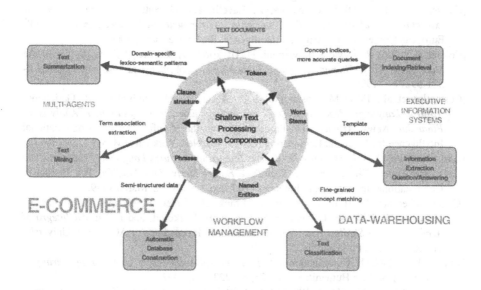

Figure 2-13. Application potential of shallow text processing

REFERENCES

[Abramowicz at. al. 2002] W. Abramowicz, P. Kalczyński, K. Węcel. *Filtering the Web to Feed Data Warehouses*. Springer, ISBN 1852335793, London, 2002.

[Aït-Mokhtar et al., 2002] S. Aït-Mokhtar, J. Chanod, C. Roux. *Robustness beyond shallowness: incremental deep parsing*. In the Journal of Natural Language Engineering, Volume 8 (2/3), pages 121-144, Cambridge University Press, United Kingdom, 2002.

[Andersen et al., 1992] P.M. Andersen, P.J. Hayes, A.K. Heuttner, L.M. Schmandt, I.B. Nirenburg, S.P. Weinstein. *Automatic extraction of facts from press releases to generate news stories*. In Proceedings of ANLP 1992, Trento, Italy, pages 170-177, 1992.

[Aone et al., 1999] C. Aone, L. Halverson, T. Hampton, M. Ramos-Santacruz, T. Hampton. *SRA: Description of the IE2 System used for MUC-7*. Morgan Kaufmann, 1999.

[Aone and Ramos-Santacruz, 2000] C. Aone, M. Ramos-Santacruz. *RESS: A Large-Scale Relation and Event Extraction System*. In the Proceedings of ANLP 2000, Seattle, USA, 2000.

[Appelt and Israel, 1999] D. Appelt and D. Israel. *An Introduction to Information Extraction Technology*. A Tutorial prepared for IJCAI Conference, 1999.

[Becker et al., 2002] M. Becker, W. Drożdżyński, H.U. Krieger, J. Piskorski, U. Schäfer, F. Xu. *SProUT - Shallow Processing with Typed Feature Structures and Unification*. In Proceedings of ICON 2002, Mumbai, India, December, 2002.

[Chanod, 2000] Jean-Pierre Chanod. *Robust Parsing and Beyond.* In: Robustness in Language Technology, G. Van Noord and JC Junqua eds., Kluwer, 2000.

[Chinchor, 1998] – N. A. Chinchor. *Overview of MUC7 /MET-2.* In Proceedings of the Seventh Message Understanding Conference (MUC7), 1998.

[Ciravegna et al., 2000] F. Ciravegna, A. Lavelli, and G. Satta. *Bringing information extraction out of the labs: The Pinocchio environment.* In Proceedings of the 14th European Conference on Artificial Intelligence, Berlin, Germany, 2000.

[Cole et al., 1996] R. A. Cole, J. Mariani, H. Uszkoreit, A. Zaenen, V. Zue. *Survey of the State of the Art in Human Language Technology.* Cambridge University Press ISBN 0-521-59277-1, 1996.

[Costantino et al., 1997] M. Costantino, R.G. Morgan, R. J. Collingham, R. Garigliano. *Natural Language Processing and Information Extraction: Qualitative Analysis of Financial News Articles.* In Proceedings of the Conference on Computational Intelligence for Financial Engineering (CIFEr '97), New York City, March 23-25, 1997.

[Costantino, 1999] M. Costantino. *IE-Expert: Integrating Natural Language Processing and Expert System Techniques For Real-Time Equity Derivatives Trading.* The Journal of Computational Intelligence in Finance, Vol.7, No.2, pp.34-52, March 1999.

[Crysmann et al., 2002] B. Crysmann, A. Frank, B. Kiefer, H. Krieger, S. Müller, G. Neumann, J. Piskorski, U. Schäfer, M. Siegel, H. Uszkoreit, and F. Xu. *An Integrated Architecture for Shallow and Deep Processing.* In Proceedings of ACL-2002, University of Pennsylvania, Philadelphia, July 2002.

[Cunningham, 2002] H. Cunningham. *GATE, a General Architecture for Text Engineering.* In Computing and the Humanities, Vol. 36, pp. 223-254, 2002.

[Finkelstein-Landau and Morin, 1999] M. Finkelstein-Landau, E. Morin. *Extracting Semantic Relationships between Terms: Supervised vs. Unsupervised Methods.* In proceedings of International Workshop on Ontological Engineering on the Global Information Infrastructure, Dagstuhl Castle, Germany, pages 71-80, 1999.

[Gaizauskas and Robertson, 1997] R. Gaizauskas R, A. Robertson. *Coupling Information Retrieval and Information Extraction: A New Text Technology for Gathering Information from the Web.* In Proceedings of RIAO'97, Canada, pages 356-370, 1997.

[Gaizauskas and Humphreys, 2000] R. Gaizauskas and K. Humphreys. *A Combined IR/NLP Approach to Question Answering Against Large Text Collections.* In Proceedings of RIAO 2000, Paris, 2000, pages. 1288-1304.

[Glasgow et al., 1998] B. Glasgow, A. Mandell, D. Binney, L. Ghemri, D. Fisher. *MITA : An Information-Extraction Approach to the Analysis of Free-Form Text in Life Insurance Applications.* AI magazine, 19(1) :59--71. 1998.

[Grishman and Sundheim, 1996] R. Grishman and B. Sundheim. *Message Understanding Conference -- 6: A Brief History.* Proceedings of the 16th International Conference on Computational Linguistics (COLING), pages 466--471, Kopenhagen, Denmark, 1996.

[Harabagiu et al., 2000] S. Harabagiu, M. Pasca, S. Maiorano. *Experiments with open-domain textual question answering.* In Proceedings of the COLING-2000. Association for Computational Linguistics, Morgan Kaufmann, 2000.

[Harabagiu and Lăcătuşu, 2002] S. Harabagiu and F. Lăcătuşu. *Generating Single and Multi-Documat Summaries with GISTextrer.* Workshop on Text Summarization in conjunction with the ACL 2002, Philadelphia, USA, 2002.

[Hobbs et al., 1997] J. Hobbs, D. Appelt, J. Bear, D. Israel, M. Kameyama, M. Stickel, M. Tyson. *FASTUS - A cascaded Finite-State Transducer for Extracting Information from Natural Language Text.* Chapter 13 in [Roche and Schabes, 97], 1997.

[Humphreys et al., 1998] K. Humphreys, R. Gaizauskas, S. Azzam, C. Huyck, B. Mitchell, H. Cunningham, Y. Wilks. University of Sheffield: *Description of the LaSIE-II System as used for MUC-7.* In the MUC-7 Proceedings, 1998.

[Jackson et al., 1998] P. Jackson, K. Al-Kofahi, C. Kreilick and B. Grom. *Information extraction from case law and retrieval of prior cases by partial parsing and query generation.* In Proceedings of the ACM 7th International Conference on Information and Knowledge Management, pages 60-67, Washington United States, 1998.

[Jacobs et al., 1990] P. Jacobs and L. Rau. *SCISOR: extracting information from online news.* Communications of the ACM, 33, 11, pages 88-97, 1990.

[Kehler, 1998] A Kehler. *Learning Embedded Discourse Mechanisms for Information Extraction.* In Proceedings of the AAAI Spring Symposium on Applying Machine Learning to Discourse Processing, Stanford, CA, March 1998.

[Lytinen and Gershman, 1986] S. Llytinen and A. Gershman. *ATRANS: Automatic Processing of Money Transfer Messages.* In Proceedings of the 5th National Conference of the American Association for Artificial Intelligence, IEEE Computer Society Press, 1993.

[Makhoul et al., 1999] J. Makhoul, F. Kubala, R. Schwartz, and R. Weischedel. *Performance measures for information extraction.* In Proceedings of DARPA Broadcast News Workshop, Herndon, VA, Feb. 1999.

[Manning and Schütze, 1999] C. Manning, H. Schütze. *Foundations of Statistical Natural Language Processing.* The MIT Press, Cambridge, Massachuusetts, London, England, 1999.

[Maynard et al., 2002] D. Maynard, V. Tablan, H. Cunningham, C. Ursu, H. Saggion, K. Bontcheva, and Y. Wilks. *Architectural elements of language engineering robustness.* In the Journal of Natural Language Engineering, Volume 8 (2/3), pages 257-274, Cambridge University Press, United Kingdom, 2002.

[Mihalcea and Moldovan, 2001] R. Mihalcea and D. Moldovan. *Document Indexing Using Named Entities.* In Studies in Informatics and Control Journal, Vol. 10, Number 1, March 2001.

[Mohri and Nederhof, 2001] M. Mohri and M. Nederhof. *Regular Approximation of Context-Free Grammars through Transformations.* In J.C. Junqua and Gertjan van Noord, editors, *Robustness in Language and Speech Technology*, pages 153-163. Kluwer Academic Publishers, The Netherlands, 2001.

[Neumann and Piskorski, 2002] G. Neumann and J. Piskorski. *A Shallow Text Processing Core Engine.* In the Journal of Computational Intelligence, August, 2002, vol. 18, no. 3, pp. 451-476(26) Blackwell Publishers Inc, Boston, USA and Oxford, UK, 2002.

[Petasis et al., 2002] G. Petasis, V. Karkaletsis, G. Paliouras, I. Androutsopoulus, and C. Spyropoulus. *Ellogon: A New Text Engineering Platform.* In the Proceedings of LREC 2002, Las Palmas, Gran Canaria, Spain, 2002.

[Piskorski and Skut, 2000], J. Piskorski, W. Skut. *Intelligent Information Extraction.* In the Proceedings of Business Information Systems 2000, Poznan, Poland, 2000.

[Piskorski and Neumann, 2000] J. Piskorski, G. Neumann. *An Intelligent Text Extraction and Navigation System.* In the Proceedings of RIAO 2000, Paris, France, 2000.

[Rajman, 1997] M. Rajman. *Text Mining, knowledge extraction from unstructured textual data.* In Proceeding of EUROSTAT Conference, Frankfurt, Germany, 1997.

[Riloff and Lorenzen, 1998] E. Riloff, J. Lorenzen. *Extraction-based text categorization: Generating domain-specific role relationships automatically.* In Strzalkowski, T., ed., Natural Language Information Retrieval, Kluwer Academic Publishers, 1998.

[SAIC, 1998] SAIC, editor. *Seventh Message Understanding Conference (MUC-7).* http://www.muc.saic.com, 1998.

[Sang, 2002] Tjong Kim Sang Erik F. *Introduction to the CoNLL-2002 shared task: language-independent named entity recognition.* In Proceedings of CoNLL-2002, Roth Dan (editor), Taipei, p. 155-158, 2002.

[Sekine and Nobata, 2002] S. Sekine, CH. Nobata. *Sentence Extraction with Information Extraction technique.* Workshop on Text Summarization in conjunction with the ACL 2002, Philadelphia, USA, 2002.

[Srihari and Li, 1999] R. Srihari and W. Li. *Information extraction supported question answering.* In Proceedings of the Eighth Text Retrieval Conference (TREC-8)., 1999.

[Tkach, 1999] D. Tkach. *The pillars of knowledge management.* In Knowledge Management 2(3), page 47, 1999.

[Voorhess and Tice, 1999] E. Voorhess and D. Tice. *The TREC-8 Question Answering Track Evaluation.* National Institute of Standards and Technology, Gaithersbugh, 1999.

[Yangarber et al., 2000] R. Yangarber, R. Grishman, P. Tapanainen and S. Huttunen. *Unsupervised Discovery of Scenario-Level Patterns for Information Extraction.* In Proceedings of ANLP-NAACL 2000, Seattle, USA, 2000.

[Xu and Krieger, 2003] F. Xu and H.-U. Krieger, Extraction of Domain Specific Events and Relations via a Combination of Shallow and Deep NLP. Research Report, DFKI, Saarbrücken, Germany, to appear in 2003.

Chapter 3

INFORMATION RETRIEVAL AND ADMINISTRATION OF DISTRIBUTED DOCUMENTS IN INTERNET.
The Phronesis [1,2] Digital Library Project

David A. Garza-Salazar, Juan C. Lavariega, Martha Sordia-Salinas
ITESM-Campus Monterrey

Abstract: This chapter presents an approach for information retrieval and administration of distributed documents in Internet. The work is presented in the context of the Phronesis Project. The main result for the project is free open-source software intended for the creation of digital libraries over the Internet. The software, known as Phronesis Server or Phronesis for short, allows the creation, administration, and maintenance of distributed digital libraries. Phronesis can be accessed and managed from a WWW browser and provides services for submission of digital documents, indexing and compression of documents, searching of documents written either in Spanish or English, accessing of the entire document, and services for access control. Documents on Phronesis can be images, audio, video, text, and any type of digital document. Phronesis is also built from open-source freeware software, and in the chapter we illustrate the successful use of this type of tools in the development of Internet-based applications such as Phronesis.

Key words: Digital Libraries, Information Retrieval, Web-Based Applications.

1.   INTRODUCTION

Today there's a great amount of knowledge and information widely available in multiple formats: printed books and journals, video and audiocassettes, and electronic documents through the Internet. The great challenge is to access that knowledge in a fast and efficient way, and then obtain relevant information that could be applied to the solution of problems.

Libraries have been traditionally the repositories of the accumulated wisdom of humanity, from the ancient times of the famous Library of Alexandria (48 B.C.) that contained more than 500,000 volumes to the present time where we have large libraries such as the Library of Congress in the U.S.A with a collection of 23 million volumes.

Nowadays, most of the libraries have computer systems to ease the searching for information. Some libraries have tried to go further on, and include a considerable amount of material in digital format. Therefore is more often to hear that traditional libraries have become *Digital Libraries*. Digital libraries play an important role for dissemination of information, and there exist efforts in several countries for research, development and application of digital libraries [1,2,7,8,11,12,14]. Usually, digital library projects fall into one of two categories: 1) projects oriented toward the implementation of digital libraries, and 2) projects oriented toward the research and development of technologies and tools for the efficient implementation of digital libraries. Phronesis falls into the second category.

After four years of work in Phronesis, we came with the following results: a single system that integrates the functionality required for the efficient creation use and administration of distributed digital library collections (where a collection may include Spanish and English documents). The resulting system is not restricted to a specific domain. Phronesis is freely available and open source, this as a consequence of using freely available software components and open standards during the development of Phronesis. The present chapter describes the technical aspects of Phronesis, including its architecture, components, functionality, and relevance to the information retrieval and digital library research community.

The rest of the chapter is organized as follows. Section 2 presents the fundamentals in digital libraries and addresses the impact that Internet has had in the dissemination of information. Section 2 concludes with a general overview of the Phronesis project and its relationship with Internet distributed digital libraries. Section 3 presents the components and services provided by Phronesis, it also illustrates the use of open-source software in the development of our project. Section 4 addresses issues of Phronesis' interoperability with other digital libraries and some of the purpose-specific applications that have been developed with Phronesis as a basis for document management. Section 5 presents the New Phronesis Architect that our group is working on. Finally, Section 6 concludes the chapter and presents opportunity areas of research on digital libraries, and future work on Phronesis.

2.   DIGITAL LIBRARIES AND THE INTERNET

In this section we present an introduction to fundamental concepts in digital libraries, including basic definitions, services that a digital library must provide; and problems related to the construction and administration of digital collections. We also discuss of the relevance of Internet as a global information resource. By the end of the section we present and overview of Phronesis and how the project is related to information retrieval, digital libraries and the Internet.

2.1   Fundamentals of Digital Libraries

A *Digital Library* (DL) can be defined as an organized collection of documents stored in digital format. A *digital document* can be text, image, video or any combination of these formats.

A digital library should offer services for submission, classification, searching, retrieval, and administration of the digital documents within its *collection* or *collections*. A *collection* is defined as a set of documents that belong to a specific area. Therefore a library may be of general purpose with multiple collections or focused on a specific knowledge area with just one collection.

There are several services that a digital library must offer [4, 9, 22] including, digital document creation, efficient storage, classification and indexing, capabilities to search, filter and summarize big volumes of data, images and information, use of interfaces suitable for the presentation of results, distribution of the library content to the end user, administration and access control. Notice that the services provided by digital libraries go beyond the services offered by traditional library-catalog systems that are only focused on searching library records based on title, author, description or keywords.

Due to the increase in the scope of digital library's services, there are many technological challenges [4] that must be overcome to obtain a full DL implementation

– **Digital document creation**. The first challenge for building a digital library consists of having the documents in the collection in the proper digital format. Materials in digital format already exist and can be placed in a DL. However, there are materials that we would like to preserve and share in a DL, that are not in digital format and must be transformed into an appropriate digital representation.

- **Classification and indexing**. The documents that are part of a collection must be classified and indexed in order to improve the effectiveness of the retrieval process. Ideally, the indexing should be intuitive to the user and based in the semantic content of the documents in the DL. However classifications schemes depend on the format of the documents (text, video, audio), presenting additional challenges to the DL implementation.
- **Search and retrieval**. The information stored in the DL must be accessible to users in an efficient manner. This implies that the library must include an efficient implementation of advanced searching and retrieval techniques. This feature should be also based on the semantic content of the documents within the collection in order to give meaningful answers to user's queries.
- **Distribution**. Full documents that are stored in the digital library must be accessible to end-users in a reliable and fast way.
- **Administration and access control**. In order to avoid the unauthorized access of documents the DL must incorporate mechanisms to restrict access to unauthorized users. The digital library must also provide mechanisms for the easy administration of digital collections.

One of the social objectives for digital libraries is to serve as public available repository of valuable information. The intention for such a repository is to be used by professionals working on specific knowledge areas, around the globe. If we want to accomplish this objective, then we have to consider the following issues in addition to the technical challenges expressed above [15].

- **Non-restrictive documents**. Documents in the collection can be placed in the public domain. Documents within copyright laws may bring restrictions on the free sharing of information among colleges working in similar areas.
- **Quality of the documents**. It is important that the documents in the collection have some level of quality that is acceptable for the community making use of them. Quality of a huge amount of text available to the public has a quality not suitable to be included in a library.
- **Variety of formats**. Documents in the collections may be coming from different sources.
- **Catalogs**. A library should offer a catalog or a set of catalogs to ease the finding of appropriate bibliographic material.
- **User Interfaces**. Uniform easy-to-use, publicly accessible interface is necessary for information retrieval.

In Phronesis, we have followed the approach for having publicly available digital libraries grouped in collections. Where a collection group documents relevant to a knowledge area, or relevant to a group of people. By doing so, Phronesis is not restricted to a specific domain. The quality of the documents is controlled by different levels of authorization for accessing the collection for document search and retrieval, or accessing the collection for placing documents. Phronesis support documents in different formats such as Postscript, PDF, and RTF in addition to plain text. Even though our main approach for cataloging documents is through the concept of collections, we attach metadata (i.e., title, subject, author, description, language, publisher, publishing date, type and format) to the documents to support advanced search within a collection. Phronesis interface with users is through friendly web pages as we will see in the following sections.

2.2   The Impact of Internet

It is estimated that there are over 4,000 Gigabytes of data on the Web. This number continues to grow at an exponential rate and duplicates every 6 months. Some authors refer to the WWW as the largest library in the world. Making available for almost anyone a great amount of knowledge within the selection of just few mouse clicks. Including the database research community has stated the following goal [21].

"The Information Utility: Make it easy for everyone to store, organize, access, and analyze the majority of human information online."

However, there are some problems associated with this vision. The first one is the unstructured nature of the information available in the web, therefore making the retrieval of information from a search in most of the cases with a large amount of entries that are not relevant to our query statement. Other major problem is the quality of the documents and the fact the most of the web content is not peer-reviewed.

Documents of interest such as research reports, committee reports, conference papers government reports theses and dissertations produced by universities and other organizations are available through the web but without a proper cataloging and without attached metadata that can help us to find the appropriate documents for a specific search. Digital libraries can help to cope with this type of "gray literature" [15], because such documents are publicly available, not produced for profit, often released in an electronic format, and freely distributed in the web. What a digital library can offer for retrieving and administrating such documents have been our objectives for building Phronesis.

2.3   Phronesis Objectives and Architecture

We defined the following objectives in Phronesis

1. The system should be a single-system that integrates the functionality that is required for the efficient creation, use, and administration of distributed digital library collections.
2. The system should not be restricted to a specific domain. It should be possible to use the system to create collections in very different subject areas.
3. The system must be built using freely available software components and open standards. The resulting software should also be freely available and open source.
4. The functionality of the system should meet the following technical requirements:

    a) The searching, submission, and retrieval of digital documents as well as the administration of the library must be done via WWW over the Internet.
    b) It should be possible to store and retrieve any digital document (audio, video, software, text, etc.) and the system should provide efficient storage, searching and retrieval services for text-based documents.
    c) It must include support for indexing, searching and retrieving documents written in English or Spanish. The user interface must also be available in both languages.
    d) It should include some form of access control in order to restrict the users that can contribute and access documents in the digital collection.

We built a system that meets all of our design goals stated above. The key component of the system is the Phronesis server that is used for the creation of digital library collections. Several Phronesis servers can be installed on the Internet yielding to a distributed digital library as illustrated in Figure 3-1. Where each server is autonomous and it is locally managed. More than one Phronesis server can reside in a single computer. With respect to our objective for building a system that is open source, Phronesis is built from freely available software in Unix platforms including MG[15], HTML, PERL scripts, and format conversion tools such as *pstotext*.

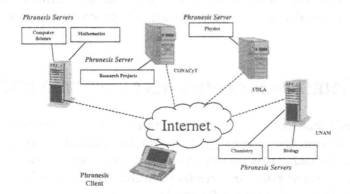

Figure 3-1 A Distributed Digital Library Based on six Phronesis Servers

The architecture of the Phronesis system is based on the client-server model. The client is a WWW browser where users can search, retrieve and submit documents. Users with the proper access rights can perform collection administration tasks via WWW. Figure 3-2 shows a conceptual diagram of the Phronesis architecture. As it can be seen from the diagram, the server is the key component of the system and it performs several tasks such as user control access, document submission and documents retrieval.

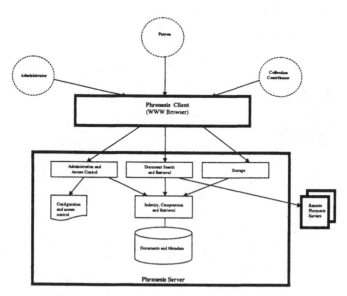

Figure 3-2. Architecture of the Phronesis System

In the following section, we will discuss on the Phronesis System components and the services they provide for the construction of digital libraries.

3.   PHRONESIS COMPONENTS AND SERVICES

Phronesis follows a client server architecture, with the server being the main component and consisting it of several internal subcomponents: *Administration and access control, document search and retrieval, storage, and indexing, compression and retrieval.* In this section we will cover the features of clients and servers in Phronesis

3.1   Phronesis Client

Phronesis clients are users accessing the system for performing actions such as document search and retrieval as well as document submission. Clients are World Wide Web interfaces using HTTP, HTML and PERL Common Gateway Interfaces (CGI's) technology. Figure 3-3, shows one of the users' interfaces that Phronesis provides, in particular, Figure 3-3 shows the interface used for document submission.

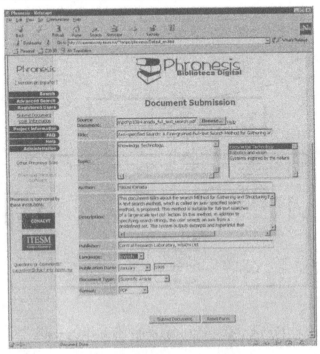

Figure 3-3. Document Submission

3.2   Phronesis Server.

The server is the key component of the system and it performs the following tasks:

- administration and access control,
- physical storage of documents,
- indexing
- local and distributed searching and retrieval

3.2.1   Access Control and Administration.

The Phronesis system defines three classes of users: *administrators*, *collection contributors* (authors or editors), and *patrons* (end users accessing the library). These classes of users are completely independent from the users of the host computer (the computer where the Phronesis server is running).

Administrators are users that maintain a Phronesis server. The system allows administrators to configure the server, to manage the document collection, and to grant access to users that would submit documents to the collection. It is also possible to restrict access to the users that can search the collection or even grant access to users to allow them to perform administrative tasks. The administrator can, at any time, configure the server allowing users to do a distributed search over a set of remote Phronesis collections. An administrator can easily enable this feature on the server by just providing the URL and name of remote Phronesis servers available on the Internet.

Collection contributors are users that have the proper permissions to submit documents to the collection. The quality of any digital collection depends on its contents. Therefore, it is the collection contributor's responsibility to decide what documents to include in the collection.

Finally, *Patrons* are users that access the server to search and retrieve full documents. Most of the time, patrons are not required to have a password to access a Phronesis server. However, the server can be configured to require passwords from patrons

3.2.2   Document Storage and Classification

Documents' authors or editors contribute documents to the Phronesis Server. Authors send their materials through a web interface running on any computer connected to Internet. Authors fill out a form (Figure 3-3) with information about the document being submitted. The information about the document (metadata) includes the following: *Title*, *Topic*, Author, Description, Publisher, Language (English or Spanish), Publication Date, Document Type, and Format (PostScript, PDF, RTF, JPEG, GIFF, MPEG, etc.). Our specification of document's metadata is based on the Dublin Core Standard [5].

Once a document is submitted, the original document and its metadata are stored on the server for inclusion on the collection. With this mechanism for document submission it is possible to increase a library collection in just a few minutes.

With respect to the physical storage of documents, Phronesis is based on the functionality provided by MG [15,16,17], a public available software for the compression, indexing and retrieval of textual documents. MG uses their own format for storage of documents that it processes. In Phronesis, we have extended MG for processing of both the document and the document's metadata. We can also mention that the size of a digital collection stored in a Phronesis server is always smaller than the original size of the documents that are part of the collection as we will discuss in the following section.

3.2.3   Indexing, Compression, and Text Retrieval

A building process performs the integration of newly submitted documents into existing collections. The building process consists of three main tasks. Firstly, the text is extracted from the original document (*text extraction phase*). Secondly the metadata and text are indexed (*indexing phase*). And finally, the original document and the extracted text are compressed and stored in the server (*compression phase*).

The ***text extraction phase*** is performed for the different formats for digital documents supported in Phronesis in addition to the text representation that MG provides. Phronesis supports text extraction from postscript (PS), Rich Text Format (RTF), Portable Data Format (PDF) and Hypertext Markup Language (HTML) documents. Due to the high relationship with MG and the requirement by this software for extracting text from only textual files, it is needed to convert the PS, RFT and PDF documents into text. Using freely available utilities such as *pstotext*, *rtftotext*, *xpdf* and *html2ps* does conversion to text files from PS, PDF and RTF documents. Phronesis includes and additional own analysis tool for PDF documents that under some circumstances are not converted properly by the open utilities.

During the text extraction phase some text analysis is performed for Spanish documents in order to identify special characters (such as *ñ, á, é,* and so on) and substitute them by characters accepted by the indexing phase (*n, a, e,* etc). Additionally, roots of word are extracted from the document in order to create indices on family of words rather than individual entries. This process is done for documents written in Spanish and in English.

The *indexing phase* uses the text and metadata information and builds a very efficient and compact index. This phase is also based on the MG system. We have extended MG to accommodate the use of metadata information and to associate this information with documents. For documents where text cannot be extracted such as MPEG, QuickTime, GIFF, or JPEG files, just metadata information is indexed.

The *compression phase* compresses the original document, its metadata and the extracted text using the *zip* utility. These files are kept in the server. Extracted text is kept in the server for speeding up further builds of the library, since the build time is dominated by the text extraction phase.

We said that size of a digital collection stored in a Phronesis server is always smaller than the original size of the documents in the collection. Table 3-1 shows the amount of space required by the original document collection and the total space used by the same documents once that they have been submitted to the server. Table 3-1 shows the space used in the server by the compressed documents, and the space used by the index files for the metadata and the text. The collection size is the sum of these two amounts. The information is shown for collections consisting of PostScript, PDF and RTF documents and a collection consisting of a combination of these three document formats. It can be seen that the size of the collection is always smaller than the size of the original document collection. For PostScript based collections there is a 51% reduction in disk space, for RTF based collections there is an estimated 15% and for PDF based collections there is a 9 % of savings. The small savings observed for PDF files is due to the fact that PDF files are already very compact and the compression yields very small savings. It is important to notice that the space used by the collection reported in Table 3-1, includes the original document as well as its metadata information and index files. Other systems have very high disk space requirements per collection. It is not uncommon to find systems that store collections using from 120% up to 200% of extra disk space when compared to the original document collection, some of these systems require to keep the original document adding an extra 100% to the disk space requirements.

Table 3-1. Disk Space Requirements for Four Phronesis Collections

Doc. Collection Format	Number of Docs	Original Collection Size (MB)	Extracted Text Size (MB	Compressed Files Size (MB)	Index Size (MB)	Phronesis Collection Size (MB)	Savings (%)
PostScript	32	20.08	1.59	7.85	1.95	9.80	51.21
PDF	21	20.10	0.14	17.78	0.38	18.16	9.61
RTF	125	20.12	10.00	8.98	8.07	17.06	15.21
Combined	46	19.55	3.77	9.83	3.83	13.67	30.08

The building process consists of extracting text from text-based documents (PostScript, PDF and RTF) and building the index for the textual documents and all documents' metadata. Every time that a new document is added to the collection the collection must be built to be up-to-date. In practice, the building of a collection is programmed to be performed either once a day or twice a day. Table 3-2 shows the time required to build a new collection on a Sun UltraSparc 5 workstation (270 MHZ, 128 MB RAM). Table 3-2 shows the time spent in text extraction as well as in text indexing and compression for each of the different collections formats. It can be seen that the time required to build a 20 MB collection is very good. The PostScript based collection takes more time to build than the rest of the collections, because the process of text extraction from PostScript documents is slower compared to the other text extraction filters. Text extraction and file compression is performed just for the newly added documents. The indexing is performed for all the documents that belong to the collection every time that the build process is executed. In this experiment, all documents are considered as newly added documents.

Table 3-2. Times for Text Extraction, Indexing and Compression for Four Phronesis Collections

Document Collection Format	Number of Documents	Original Collection Size (MB)	Text Extraction Time (sec.)	Indexing and Compression Time (sec.)	Total Building Time (sec.)
PostScript	32	20.08	1078.62	27.00	1105.62
PDF	21	20.10	444.05	9.24	453.29
RTF	125	20.12	145.12	123.37	268.49
Combined	46	19.55	664.36	49.09	713.45

3.2.4   Document Search and Retrieval

Patrons can search and retrieve documents from Phronesis via WWW (Figure 3-4). The search facilities include five different types of full-text document and/or metadata search. The search query can include diacritic characters common in the Spanish language. When searching for words that include diacritic characters the server tolerates simple mistakes, common in Spanish language, such as the omission of an accent. For example, a search for the word computing in Spanish will be performed using the search query "computación", however, the search query "computacion" (accent omitted) will find the same documents as the previous one

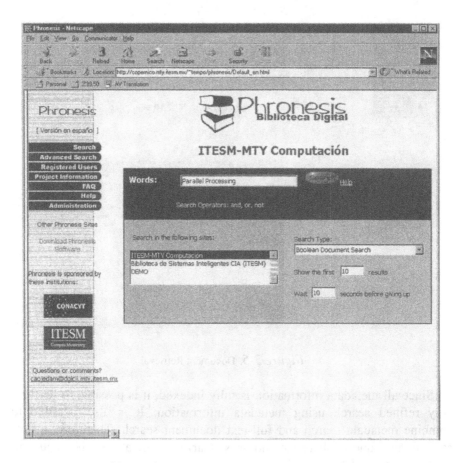

Figure 3-4. User Interface for Searching Documents

The result of a search is always a list of documents that match the search query. For each document a subset of the metadata information is presented and the user is provided with options to view the full document's metadata, view the document's text or retrieve the full document. For retrieving the full

document the user can obtain the document in compressed or in its original
format (Figure 3-5).

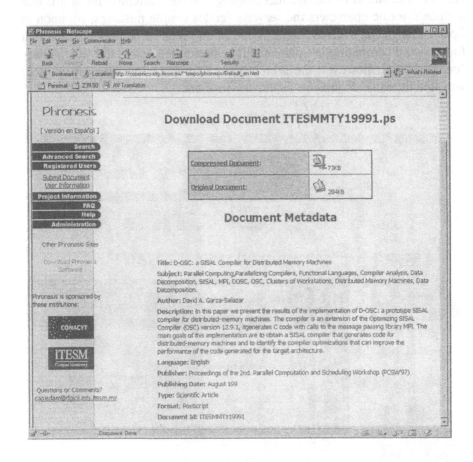

Figure 3-5. Document Retrieval

Since all metadata information is fully indexed, it is possible to perform
very refined search using metadata information. It is also possible to
combine metadata search and full-text document search. Therefore, a user
can submit a query where the author is "Garza o García" and the document
contains the word "compiler".

The Phronesis system allows the following five types of search
- *Document Boolean search.* This is a full-text document search allowing
  the use of Boolean expressions in the search query.
- *Metadata Boolean search.* This type of search is similar to the above
  search, however, they differ in that this one performs the search just on
  the metadata information.

- *Metadata and document Boolean search*. This search combines the document Boolean search and the metadata Boolean search.
- *Ranked search*. This type of search uses an algorithm to rank the documents that match the search query and returns the documents found sorted according to its relevance
- *Advanced Search*. This search allows the specification of Boolean search queries for each of the metadata fields as well as for the documents full-text.

When a Phronesis server has been configured to allow distributed search over remote Phronesis servers, patrons can issue a single search query on different Phronesis collections in a very transparent manner as illustrated by Figure 3-7. The user just selects the type of search she or he wants to perform and the collections where she/he wants to direct the search to (*Form* send to *local support*, indicted with arrow 1 on Figure 3-6). The search queries are forwarded to each of the Phronesis servers both local (arrows 2, 3, 4, 5 on Figure 3-6) and remote (arrows 7, 8, 9, 10 and 11, on Figure 3-6) or a combination of local and remote servers. Results from each of the sites(arrows 13 and 14 on Figure 3-6) are presented to the user (arrow 6 on Figure 3-6), however the user is unaware of the actual location of the collections she/he is querying.. The user can restrict the amount of documents to retrieve from each collection as well as the timeout that he wants to consider before a connection with a specific collection gives up. This feature is accomplished via the HTTP protocol, C programs and PERL scripts that issue a search query in parallel to each of the remote collections.

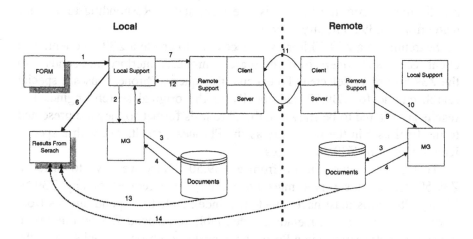

Figure 3-6. Local Site and Remote Site Search

4.   INTEROPERABILITY, APPLICATIONS AND IMPROVEMENTS

In this section, we present ongoing advances on the Phronesis project and their use on practical applications. Phronesis originally was though as a tool for creation of digital libraries or repositories that could interact with other Phronesis repositories, however there is an increase need for sharing documents among digital libraries disperse around the world that are not Phronesis repositories. In the first part of this section we cover our efforts for achieving interoperability with other digital libraries projects.

In the second part of this section, we present some of the applicability that different users have found for Phronesis. Our presentation appears in chronological order and includes the major improvements that Phronesis has suffered over the years since its initial conception.

4.1   Phronesis Interoperability

There are two major efforts in the Phronesis group with respect to provide a wider range of distributed search of documents. One is on the direction of providing interoperability with other digital libraries through the open archives initiative [20]. This is still an ongoing effort in Phronesis. The other approach for interoperability is with digital libraries that use the Z39.50 protocol that we discuss next.

Z39.50 is a standard protocol developed by the USA Congress Library with the objective of allowing the communication among different world library catalogs. This protocol is the most used in the library world.

The Phronesis interoperability is divided in two parts: 1. Searching in a Z39.50 library from the Phronesis interface; and 2) Responding to a query made from a Z39.50 library interface

Searching in a Z39.50 library is necessary to create a Z39.50 client. The client receives the query form the search Phronesis interface and sends it to the Z39.50 library selected. To execute this query, Phronesis uses a special search engine for Z39.50 additionally to the original search engine. The results are filtered to be shown in the Phronesis format so they are presented to the final user in the same way as the Phronesis results but with a special icon representing Z39.50 libraries.

To respond a query made from a Z39.50 library we have to install a Z39.50 server; this server must be waiting for a request of any Z39.50 library. Phronesis must have a metadata index table to respond queries from Phronesis queries and a metadata index table to respond Z39.50 queries so when a Z39.50 searches in a Phronesis repository, Phronesis looks for in the

Z39.50 index table of the repository. These indexes are create in the
Phronesis sending process

4.2   Phronesis Applications and Improvements

Phronesis project started in 1998, when CONACyT approved it as a
Research Projects for Information Technologies. By the summer of 1999 a
fully functional version was released and Phronesis began to be widely used
in universities, research centers and business organizations.

The first user of Phronesis outside our own Institution was the Center for
Information and Computation of the National Polytechnic Institute in
Mexico. They applied Phronesis for constructing a digital library for the
documents generated within the CIC. The actual collection for the CIC
Digital Library consists of 3000 documents [23]. We decided to apply
Phronesis for keeping a Digital Library of Computer Science formed by
documents generated around the globe by well-know institutions. The
collection consists of 10,000 documents and can be consulted through our
web page.

Phronesis 1.2 was completed in 2000. It includes stemmer functionality
and interoperability with Z39 protocol. During 2000, the interest in
Phronesis moved from Universities to business organizations. A major retail
store chain organization [24] initiated a project focused on Knowledge
Management and used Phronesis for the administration of their ISO9000
documents. An ad-hoc interface for such an application was developed in the
form of a web portal. Also a more restrictive access control to the one
defined in Section 2 was developed specifically for the application.

During 2001 the Phronesis Team started exploring the use of new
technologies such as JAVA, and XML in the redoing of some Phronesis
components in order to achieve more interoperability with other digital
library projects. Additionally, some sidelines utilities were developed and
released in version 1.3. Those utilities are not essential for Phronesis to work
correctly, but facilitate the work of the system administrator in charge of
creating Phronesis Repositories and granting access rights to users.

By 2002, the major improvement in the project is the complete
reengineering of the Phronesis architecture. The current version of Phronesis
as we write this chapter is based on the description given in Section 3. But,
due to the initial basic tools that we used (PERL and CGI technology,
HTML, and MG) updates to Phronesis have been painful to grasp for new
members in the development team. A major change was needed also to add
functionality and modularity to Phronesis. Also our initial goal of allowing

the community to contribute to the improvement of Phronesis through the use of open source software will benefit by a more modular architecture [25]

5.   PHRONESIS NEW ARCHITECTURE

The current internal architecture of a Phronesis repository is a set of programs working together to satisfy the services of a digital library, however all of this services are tightly-coupled, therefore making improvements is a painful process. The new architecture is based in distributed services, which will give Phronesis more flexibility to create new digital library services. Each one of these services exports methods that can be called remotely from other services to search and store documents, to record users, etc. Services can be in different computers and communicate via XML-RPC to achieve more flexibility in the management of a digital library.

Services for the new Phronesis architecture include the following:

- **Search engine and indexation:** It takes a Boolean expression as a query and responds with a list of documents that satisfies the request.
- **Storage:** It stores the documents and their metadata.
- **Distribution:** It searches documents in different digital libraries.
- **Configuration:** It manages the information related to the services of a digital library.
- **Interoperability:** It gives the necessary tools to handle a bi-directional communication with other digital libraries.
- **User interface:** It manages the interaction between the final user and the digital library services.
- **Authentication:** It manages the access to a digital library and gives and validates the authentication of a user.
- **User record:** It manages all the data and information related to simple users and a group of users.
- **Names:** It searches a resource like a digital document, a user, or a group of users.

Figure 3-7 shows the interaction among all the services of the new Phronesis architecture. Each Phronesis repository has an interface server to allow final users see the digital library as a unit from a web browser. A user can make a query to different repositories through the distribution service. This service sends this query to the search engine service of each repository where creates a data structure with the document's id sending this information to the user interface service. The user interface service generates a HTML report and creates links with the names service help to get the documents form the storage service. A digital library can have associated one or more search engine services; each search engine service has associated one or more storage services, each repository has associated a name service, user interface service, setting service, interoperability service and a user record service

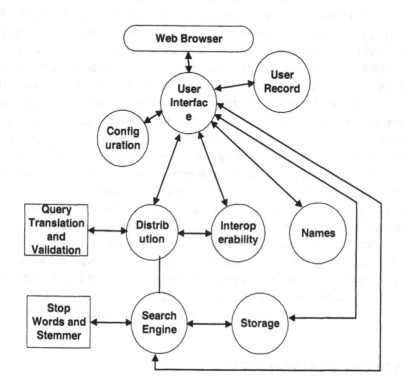

Figure 3-7. Phronesis New Architecture Services

6.   CONCLUSIONS AND FUTURE RESEARCH

Through this chapter we have presented the Phronesis project as a tool for the creation and administration of digital libraries in the Internet. We included in our presentation the fundamental concepts with respect of digital libraries, the impact that Internet has had in the dissemination of information and the need for administering large volumes of documents in this means. We focused our description on the Architecture, components and services of Phronesis.

There are several projects that are related to Phronesis. We can cite NCSTRL [10], MeDOC [6], InQuery [3] and NZDL [11, 16]. Some of these projects have inspired many of the ideas found in Phronesis. However, the design of our system is different from existing projects and none of these systems include all the features previously shown. Phronesis' design approach has been to find a balance between simplicity, functionality and efficiency, we have integrated existing software tools into a single-system that can be easily used to build distributed digital libraries

As open research areas in Phronesis we can mention the need for supporting configurable metadata [18, 19], the full compliance with the Open Archives Initiative and as a consequence to have a major interoperability with other digital libraries project. Also the use of web technologies such as XML is being applied to Phronesis for achieving interoperability with other collections. Other opportunities of research and improvement to include in Phronesis are: natural and spoken language user interface, user profiles, smart indexing and retrieval of non-textual documents, concept based searching for Spanish documents, and automatic classification. Currently, we are re-engineering our current architecture. The overall idea is to develop a component based architecture, which can be enhanced by anyone interested in doing some enhancement to Phronesis. We just started a project for providing an architectural framework for digital libraries services on mobile environments, where is possible to have a natural language interface. In the short run, we continue to work into achieving compliance with the open archives initiative, and into using new and freely available technology such as XML. There is also wok to do on providing configurable metadata suited for users with more specific needs.

ACKNOWLEDGEMENTS

The Phronesis project and its success is the result of the work and effort of many wonderful students from ITESM-Campus Monterrey. To all of them our most sincere gratitude

NOTES

1. The name of Phronesis is taken from the Greek word for "practical wisdom" Phronesis can be found at http://copernico.mty.itesm.mx/~tempo/Projects/
2 Project developed with funding from CONACyT (Mexican National Council for Science and Technology) and ITESM-Campus Monterrey.

REFERENCES

1 Alexandria Project Home Page. http://alexandria.sdc.ucsb.edu, 1997.

2 Bibliotheca Universalis Digital Library Project Home Page. http://www.culture.fr/index.html, 1997

3 Broglio John, Callan James, and Croft W.B., "INQUERY System Overview", *In Proceedings of the TIPSTER Text Program (Phase 1)*, San Francisco, CA: Morgan Kaufmann, pp. 47-67.

4 Adam, N.I., Holowczak., Halem, M., Lal, N., and Yesha, Y., "Digital Library Task Force," *IEEE Computer*, Vol. 29, No. 8, August 1996, pp. 89-91

5 Dublin Core Element Set: Reference Description. http://www.purl.org/DC/about/element_set.htm. OCLC, 1997.

6 Endres, A., Fuhr, Norbert. "Students Access Books and Journals through MeDoc," *Communications of the ACM*, Vol. 41, No. 4, 76-77 April 1998.

7 Infobus Project Home Page. http://walrus.stanford.edu/diglib, 1997.

8 InforMedia Project Home Page. http://www.informedia.cs.cmu.edu, 1997.

9 Lesk, M., *Practical Digital Libraries: Books, Bytes & Bucks*, Morgan Kaufmann Publishers, San Francisco CA, 1997.

10 NCSTRL Overview. http://www.ncstrl.org/Dienst/htdocs/Info/architecutre.html

11 New Zeland Digital Library Home Page. http://www.cs.waikato.ac.nz/cgi-bin/nzdlbeta/gw

12 Open Book Project home Page. http://www.library.yale.edu/preservation/pobweb.htm

13 University of Illinois Digital Library Project Home Page. http://dli.grainger.uiuc.edu, 1997.

14 University of California Berkley Digital Library Project Home Page. http://elib.cs.berkeley.edu , 1997.

15 Witten, I., Moffat, A., Bell, T. *Managing Gigabytes: Compressing and Indexing Documents and Images Second Edition*, Morgan Kaufmann Publishers 1999.

16 Witten, I., Nevill-Manning, Craig, Cunningham, S.J., "Building a Digital Library for Computer Science Research: Technical Issues," *Proceedings of the 19th Australasian Computer Science Conference*, Melbourne, Australia, January 1996.

17 Witten, I., Nevill-Manning, C., McNab, R., and Cunningham, S.J., "A Public Library Based on Full Text Retrieval," *Communications of the ACM*, Vol. 41, No. 4, April 1998, pp. 71-75.

18 Soto-Cervantes, Omar. Parallelization of a vector space technique for finding related documents in a digital library. Master Thesis, ITESM-Campus Monterrey, March 1999. (Available in Spanish).

19 Piña-González, Orlando. Automatic metadata extraction from thesis documents. Master Thesis Proposal, ITESM-Campus Monterrey, March 1999. (Available in Spanish).

20 Paepcke, A., Chan, C-Ch K., García-Molina, H., and Winograd, T., "Interoperability for Digital Libraries Worldwide," *Communications of the ACM*, Vol 41,No 4, April 1998, pp. 33-43.

21 Berstein, P., et al "The Asilomar Report on Database Research," ACM SIGMOD RECORD, Vol. 27. No. 4, December 1998

22 Special Issue on Digital Libraries, *Communications of the ACM*, Vol. 44, No. 4, May 2001

23 http://copernico.mty.itesm.mx/~tempo/REDII/cic/

24 FEMSA http://www.femsa.com/retail.html

25 Jones, P., "Open Sourcing the Doors", *Communications of the ACM*, Vol. 44, No. 4, May 2001, pp. 45-46.

Chapter 4

HARD AND SOFT MODELLING BASED KNOWLEDGE CAPTURE FOR INFORMATION FLOW MANAGEMENT

Edward Szczerbicki
The University of Newcastle, NSW, Australia

Abstract: This Chapter addresses the problem of formal (quantitative) and soft (qualitative) modelling of an information flow in autonomous systems that in real life context are formed by agents consisting of people, machines, robots, etc. Models in management science are designed and applied to describe, understand, and finally support processes and activities that are primarily intellectual. The problems attacked by these models may arise so frequently that the benefits of routinization are sought or they may be one-of-a-kind situations of such importance that steps are taken to improve the quality for the decision outcome. In other words, models are developed mainly to create knowledge. This is also the main purpose of the modelling platform proposed in this Chapter.

Key words: information, information value, information management, soft modelling

1.   BACKGROUND AND INTRODUCTION

Imagine that you are to make an important decision that is based on a number of pieces of relevant information. Each piece of information describes the state of changing environment. You have two options in such situations:
-   you make your decision after gathering all relevant information - you have full (or complete) information but some of it is not current (it is delayed) as gathering takes time and your environment changes during this time;
-   you make your decision after gathering only some information - you have incomplete information but more current (less delayed) as you spent

less time gathering it and changes in the environment may be smaller (less significant for your decision making).

In other words we have to be able to address frequent situations in which the following should be answered: *"What is better, complete information but heavily delayed, or incomplete information less delayed?"*

The above is the essence of informational balance. It can be further explained as follows:

The value of information that flows within a given subsystem is different for different information structures and different environments [1,2,3,4]. It can be considerably affected by two major attributes of information: incompleteness and delay. Intuitively, we understand that the highest value will be possessed by full information. On the other hand, gathering information in dynamic environment takes time, so information becomes outdated (delayed). Both delay and incompleteness can be represented by losses in the value of information in the decisionmaking process.

In informational balance mechanism delay and incompleteness represent two contrary information attributes. This simple idea is depicted in a general form in Fig. 1.

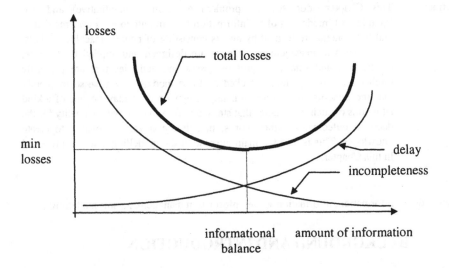

Figure 4--1. Fundamentals of the adverse character of losses caused by incompleteness and delay of information

Currently, there are no modelling tools and there is no modelling perspective to provide decision making support in situations where we try to achieve informational balance. At the same time, as information becomes a dominant and decisive resource in all kinds of business, industrial, and service operations, informational balance problem becomes increasingly important and is often mentioned as the major challenge of the new millennium in the area of intelligent decision support systems development [1,4,5,6,7,8,9].

To meet this challenge, the more general issue of the role of information management in systems operation should be addressed. Understanding and knowledge about the above role is an extremely important requirement in managing complex industrial systems (manufacturing, processing, distribution, servicing, mining, etc) that function in changing and uncertain information-rich environments. To gain this understanding, a modelling platform is needed that could be used to model and evaluate information flow in different real life situations. Such a platform, that lies at the interstices of engineering, information technology, cybernetics and management, is presented in this Chapter.

Systems become increasingly complex. Their decomposition into smaller units is the usual way to overcome the problem of complexity. This has historically led to the development of atomised structures consisting of a limited number of autonomous subsystems (agents) that decide about their own information input and output requirements, i.e. can be characterised by what is called an information closure. These ideas are recently gaining very strong interest in both academia and industry, and the atomised approach to systems modelling, design and development is an idea whose time has certainly come [7,10,11]. In a real-world context autonomous subsystems consist of groups of people and/or machines tied by the flow of information both within a given subsystem and between this subsystem and its external environment [2,12]. This Chapter is focusing on information flow for autonomous subsystems.

2.   THE PROBLEM AND THE MODELLING APPROACH

An autonomous subsystem/agent is usually functioning in the external environment which determines the decision-making process. Its knowledge could be described by the following:

(i) characteristic of the external environment (relationship between variables describing the environment and its dynamics),

(ii) characteristic of the internal environment, i.e. the relationship between the actions of the members of an agent,

(iii) the range of information about variables describing external environment.

The formal representation of the above knowledge is presented in this Section. For the knowledge extraction purposes, a general approach is needed that captures the whole of the behaviour of an agent. Such an approach, based on correlation between information and energy, is outlined next. Certain features implemented in previous research presented in [13,14,15] are included for the sake of completeness.

Let A represent the set of possible actions which can be undertaken by the members of an agent, Z the set of corresponding consequences, and X random variables describing the actual state of the external environment. It can be assumed that

$$z=f(a,x) \tag{1}$$

as the particular consequence (z) depends usually on an action (a) undertaken in the particular state of the environment (x). On the other hand, the decision about particular action depends on information that is available about the state of the environment. If ß stands for the decision function, we have

$$a=\text{ß}(d) \tag{2}$$

where d represents information.

For general description of the function f(a,x) let us consider certain correlation between information, action, and energy. Its theory is relatively young, but is has already been pointed out that in certain situations energy can be replaced by information and vice versa [16,17]. This replacement is of statistical character and can be expressed graphically as in Figure 2.

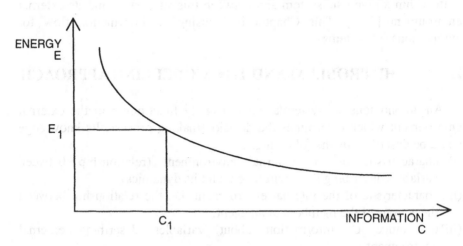

Figure 4-2. The general character of energy/information replacement

According to the curve in Figure 2 the more information one has the less energy he/she needs to perform a given task. This is true for a limited amount of information only (the problem of complexity for large volumes of information) so the curve in Figure 2 approaches asymptotically certain energy level and never goes below it. For the amount of information described in Figure 2 as C_1 certain task can be done using E_1 energy, and let us assume that

$$E_1 = E_{min} \tag{3}$$

Then, for a given C_1 there exists the best way (action A_{opt}) to fulfill the job, i.e. the action which uses E_1 energy. Actions different than A_{opt} result in more energy consumption. The above concept is shown in Figure 3.

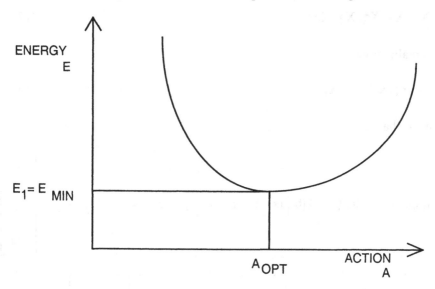

Figure 4-3. Action/energy dependence for given amount of information

For the preference evaluation we have

$$z = e = f(a,x) \tag{4}$$

where e stands for energy, and

$$a_{opt} = minf(a,x), \tag{5}$$

where a_{opt} represents optimal action which uses minimum of energy given by the function $f(a,x)$. Generally, $f(a,x)$ is a certain function specified in n-dimensional space and its min can be found using the second order of Taylor series representation [18,19]. This is the basis for f(a,x) approximation by quadratic form:

$$f(a,x) = B_0 - 2B^T A + A^T Q A, \tag{6}$$

where $B_0 = b_0(x)$, $A = [a_i]$, $B = [b_i(x)]$, symmetric matrix $Q = [q_{ij}]$ $(i,j=1, 2, ...,$ n) and n represents the number of members of an agent. Minimum of (6) exists if $A^T Q A$ is positively defined.

To arrive at the best decision functions β_i $(i=1, 2, ..., n)$ let $n=4$. The external environment of an agent is described by random variables

$$X = \{X_1, X_2, X_3, X_4\} \tag{7}$$

with realizations

$$x = \{x_1, x_2, x_3, x_4\}. \tag{8}$$

Thus we have:

$$f(a,x) = b_0(x) - 2[b_1(x_1) \quad b_2(x_2) \quad b_3(x_3) \quad b_4(x_4)] \begin{bmatrix} a_1 \\ a_2 \\ a_3 \\ a_4 \end{bmatrix} +$$

$$[a_1 \quad a_2 \quad a_3 \quad a_4] \begin{bmatrix} q_{11} & q_{12} & q_{13} & q_{14} \\ q_{21} & q_{22} & q_{23} & q_{24} \\ q_{31} & q_{32} & q_{33} & q_{34} \\ q_{41} & q_{42} & q_{43} & q_{44} \end{bmatrix} \begin{bmatrix} a_1 \\ a_2 \\ a_3 \\ a_4 \end{bmatrix} \tag{9}$$

Matrix Q is a symmetric one and thus:

$$f(a,x)=b_0(x)-2b_1(x_1)a_1-2b_2(x_2)-2b_3(x_3)-2b_4(x_4)+q_{11}a_1{}^2+q_{22}a_2{}^2+q_{33}a_3{}^2+$$
$$q_{44}a_4{}^2+2q_{12}a_1a_2+2q_{13}a_1a_3+2q_{23}a_2a_3+2q_{14}a_1a_4+2q_{24}a_2a_4+2q_{34}a_3a_4 \qquad (10)$$

Second derivative $\delta^2 f/(\delta a_i \delta a_j)$ describes the relation between actions a_i and a_j because, for certain x, it characterizes the way in which the change in a_j affects $f(a,x)$ dependence on a_i. Thus, q_{ij} can formalize an internal environment of an agent, i.e. the interaction between the members of an agent. For the sake of simplicity, let the interaction q_{ij} be constant:

$$q_{ij}=1 \text{ for } i=j, \text{ q for } i \neq j \quad (i,j = 1,2,3,4) \qquad (11)$$

and q is called the coefficient of interaction. If q=0 the agent members actions are independent. They are dependent for $q \neq 0$. For given information d={d_1, d_2, d_3, d_4}, where d_i stands for ith member information (i=1, 2, 3, 4), action a_{opt}={a_1, a_2, a_3, a_4} is chosen as the one for which we have minE[f(a,x)|d]. Because f(a, x) is a convex function the best decisions $a_1=\beta_1(d_1)$, $a_2=\beta_2(d_2)$, $a_3=\beta_3(d_3)$, $a_4=\beta_4(d_4)$ will be obtained from:

$$E(f_i|d_i) = 0, \ i=1, 2, 3, 4, \qquad (12)$$

where $f_i=\partial f/\partial a_i$ (i=1, 2, 3, 4).

We have:
$$f_1=\partial f/\partial a_1=-2b_1+2a_1+2a_2q+2a_3q+2a_4q$$
$$f_2=\partial f/\partial a_2=-2b_2+2a_2+2a_1q+2a_3q+2a_4q$$
$$f_3=\partial f/\partial a_3=-2b_3+2a_3+2a_1q+2a_2q+2a_4q \qquad (13)$$
$$f_4=\partial f/\partial a_4=-2b_4+2a_4+2a_1q+2a_2q+2a_3q$$
and

$$f_1|d_1=-2b_1|d_1+2a_1|d_1+2a_2q|d_1+2a_3q|d_1+2a_4q|d_1$$
$$f_2|d_2=-2b_2|d_2+2a_2|d_2+2a_1q|d_2+2a_3q|d_2+2a_4q|d_2$$
$$f_3|d_3=-2b_3|d_3+2a_3|d_3+2a_1q|d_3+2a_2q|d_3+2a_4q|d_3 \qquad (14)$$
$$f_4|d_4=-2b_4|d_4+2a_4|d_4+2a_1q|d_4+2a_2q|d_4+2a_3q|d_4$$

Thus we have:

$$E(f_1|d_1)=-2E(b_1|d_1)+2\beta_1(d_1)+2qE[\beta_2(d_2)|d_1]+2qE[\beta_3(d_3)|d_1]+$$
$$2qE[\beta_4(d_4)|d_1]$$

$$E(f_2 \mid d_2) = -2E(b_2 \mid d_2) + 2\beta_2(d_2) + 2qE[\beta_1(d_1) \mid d_2] + \qquad (15)$$
$$2qE[\beta_3(d_3) \mid d_2] + 2qE[\beta_4(d_4) \mid d_2]$$
$$E(f_3 \mid d_3) = -2E(b_3 \mid d_3) + 2\beta_3(d_3) + 2qE[\beta_1(d_1) \mid d_3] + 2qE[\beta_2(d_2) \mid d_3] +$$
$$2qE[\beta_4(d_4) \mid d_3]$$
$$E(f_4 \mid d_4) = -2E(b_4 \mid d_4) + 2\beta_4(d_4) + 2qE[\beta_1(d_1) \mid d_4] + 2qE[\beta_2(d_2) \mid d_4] +$$
$$2qE[\beta_3(d_3) \mid d_4]$$

and finally:

$$\beta_1(d_1) + qE[\beta_2(d_2) \mid d_1] + qE[\beta_3(d_3) \mid d_1] + qE[\beta_4(d_4) \mid d_1] = E(b_1 \mid d_1)$$
$$\beta_2(d_2) + qE[\beta_1(d_1) \mid d_2] + qE[\beta_3(d_3) \mid d_2] + qE[\beta_4(d_4) \mid d_2] = E(b_2 \mid d_2)$$
$$\beta_3(d_3) + qE[\beta_1(d_1) \mid d_3] + qE[\beta_2(d_2) \mid d_3] + qE[\beta_4(d_4) \mid d_3] = E(b_3 \mid d_3) \quad (16)$$
$$\beta_4(d_4) + qE[\beta_1(d_1) \mid d_4] + qE[\beta_2(d_2) \mid d_4] + qE[\beta_3(d_3) \mid d_4] = E(b_4 \mid d_4)$$

System of equations given by (16) is the basis for the best decision functions β_1, β_2, β_3, and β_4 calculation and as such represents 4-person agent decision-making process. For n-person agent (using the above way of analysis) we have:

$$\beta_i(d_i) + \Sigma \, qE[\beta_j(d_j) \mid d_i] = E(b_i \mid d_i), \; j \neq I \qquad (17)$$
where i, j = 1, 2, ..., n.

Formalization of agent decision making process expressed by (17) is a tool necessary for modelling and evaluation of information flow in an autonomous system. Information flow connects agent members with the external environment described by random variables X. The connection is represented by information structure. This structure is modelled by matrix C in which $c_{ij}=1$ if the ith member has obtained (either by observation or communication) information about the jth variable X realization (if $c_{ij}=0$ he/she has not got it). The ith variable X realization can be observed only by the ith member of the agent. He/she can be informed about other realizations only when communication (information exchange) inside the agent is organized. The value of information structure defined above is given by the following:

$$VC = \min E[f(a, X) \mid C0] - \min E[f(a, X) \mid C], \qquad (18)$$

where $\min E[f(a, X) \mid C0]$ represents the utility of information structure C0 in which $c_{ij}=0$ for each i and j. Using (17) the VC can be represented by:

$$VC=E[b^T ß].\tag{19}$$

With the modelling tools given by (17) and (19) one can easily extract knowledge about autonomous systems functioning in various decision situations. In the next two Sections some samples of such a knowledge are specified for static and dynamic environments. This knowledge is easily codified and can be used in control, command, and management of autonomous systems.

3.   STATIC ENVIRONMENT

3.1   The role of correlation and interaction

Let us consider the following information structures for a two-person agent:

$$C1=\begin{bmatrix} 1 & 0 \\ 0 & 0 \end{bmatrix} \quad C2=\begin{bmatrix} 1 & 0 \\ 0 & 1 \end{bmatrix} \quad C3=\begin{bmatrix} 1 & 0 \\ 1 & 1 \end{bmatrix} \quad C4=\begin{bmatrix} 1 & 1 \\ 1 & 1 \end{bmatrix} \tag{20}$$

Information structures C1 and C2 are created only by observation. In C3 and C4 both observation and communication are involved. Using the tools introduced in the previous Section, it can be shown that:

$$VC1=s^2, \ VC2=2s^2/(1+qr), \ VC3=s^2[(1-qr)^2+1-q^2]/(1-q^2),$$
$$VC4=s^2 2(1-qr)/(1-q^2), \tag{21}$$

where $s^2=Var[X_1]=Var[X_2]$, q is the coefficient of interaction as introduced earlier, and r is the correlation coefficient between X_1 and X_2 random variables. Figures 4 through 7 describe two-person agent functioning and stress the role of correlation in the external environment and interaction in the internal one.

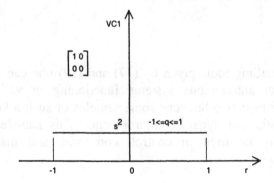

Figure 4-4. Value of a single piece of information modelled by information structure C1

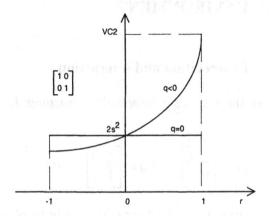

Figure 4-5. The value of information structure that represents observation (information structure C2)

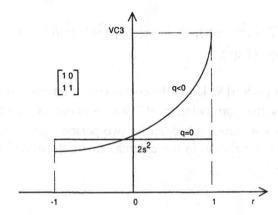

Figure 4-6. The value of information structure that represents observation and partial communication (information structure C3)

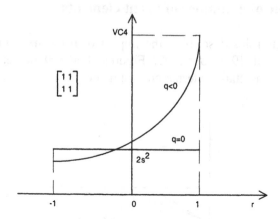

Figure 4-7. The value of information structure that represents full information (information structure C4)

The conclusions that can be extracted from the dependences given by (21) and Figures 4 through 7 are summed up as production rules 11 through 18 in Table 1 presented at the end of this Section. The production rules were developed applying the model solution for a two-person agent. The same rules hold for any value of n (number of agent elements). It is easy to notice that the rules in Table 1 are true for n-person agent and the following information structures:

$$C5 = \begin{bmatrix} 1 & 0 & 0 & \ldots & 0 \\ 0 & 0 & 0 & \ldots & 0 \\ & \cdot & & & \\ & \cdot & & & \\ & \cdot & & & \\ 0 & 0 & 0 & \ldots & 0 \end{bmatrix} \quad C6 = \begin{bmatrix} 1 & 0 & 0 & \ldots & 0 \\ 0 & 1 & 0 & \ldots & 0 \\ & \cdot & & & \\ & \cdot & & & \\ & \cdot & & & \\ 0 & 0 & 0 & \ldots & 1 \end{bmatrix} \quad C7 = \begin{bmatrix} 1 & 1 & 1 & \ldots & 1 \\ 1 & 1 & 1 & \ldots & 1 \\ & \cdot & & & \\ & \cdot & & & \\ & \cdot & & & \\ 1 & 1 & 1 & \ldots & 1 \end{bmatrix} \quad (22)$$

for which the corresponding values VC are given as:

$$VC5 = s^2, \quad VC6 = ns^2/[1+(n-1)qr],$$
$$VC7 = s^2\{n[1+(n-2)q]-(n-1)nqr\}/\{(1-q)[1+(n-1)q]\} \quad (23)$$

For example, for the above information structures we have IF r=1 THEN VC6=VC7 (RULE 16 in Table 1), IF q=0 THEN VC6=VC7 (RULE 14 in Table 1), and IF 0<qr<1 THEN VC7>VC6 (RULE 15 in Table 1).

3.2   The role of a number of agent elements

In Table 1 the rules describing the impact of n on the value of information flow are numbered 19 through 22. Figures 8 and 9 depict the relationship between VC and n in static external environment.

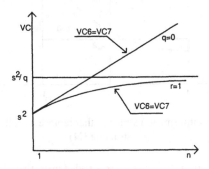

Figure 4-8. Relationship between VC and n for q=0 and r=1

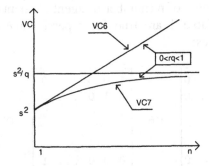

Figure 4-9. Relationship between VC and n for 0<qr<1

3.3   Losses caused by incompleteness

The impact of incomplete information on the value of information structure can be calculated as:

$$LVC\text{-}' = VC_{full} - Vc_{inc} \qquad (24)$$

where LVC' stands for losses caused by incompleteness, VC_{full} stands for the value of full information structure (in such a structure $c_{ij}=1$ for all i and j), and VC$_{inc}$ stands for value of information structure that is not complete. For information structures C1, C2, C3, and C4 we have:

$$LVC3' = VC4 - VC3 = [q^2(1-r^2)]/(1-q^2)$$
$$LVC2' = VC4 - VC2 = [2s^2q^2(1-r^2)]/[(1-q^2)(1+qr)] \quad\quad (25)$$
$$LVC1' = VC4 - VC1 = s^2(1-2qr+q^2)/(1-q^2)$$

The character of the above losses, for a given value of q, can be generally expressed as in Figure 10.

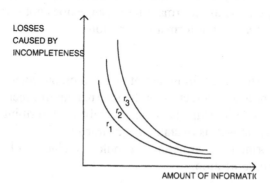

Figure 4-10. The character of the losses caused by incompleteness for a given q and different values of r ($r_1 < r_2 < r_3$)

As it can be seen in Figure 10, the smaller the correlation in the external environment the more desirable is the communication (information exchange) between the members of an agent (RULE 23 in Table 1).

Table 4-1. Production rules describing agents functioning in static environment

---

RULE 11
IF	an external environment of an autonomous agent is static,
AND	it is described by random variables,
THEN	the value of an information structure that represents the flow of information between the agent and its environment depends on interaction between agent members, correlation between random variables, and their variance.

RULE 12
IF	an external environment of an autonomous agent is static,
AND	it is described by a random variable,

THEN   the value of information about this variable realization is proportional to the value of its variance.

RULE 13
  IF   an external environment of an autonomous agent is static,
  AND   it is described by random variables,
  THEN   full information has the value that is always greater or equal to the value of any other information structure.

RULE 14
  IF   an external environment of an autonomous agent is static,
  AND   there is no interaction in the internal environment,
  THEN   it is enough to restrict the information flow only to observation; organizing an information exchange does not improve the value of a resulting information structure.

RULE 15
  IF   an external environment of an autonomous agent is static,
  AND   there is an interaction in the internal environment,
  AND   the relationship between variables describing the external environment is of statistical character,
  THEN   information structure should include observation and communication.

RULE 16
  IF   an external environment of an autonomous agent is static,
  AND   the relationship between variables describing the external environment is given by function dependence,
  THEN   communication between agent members does not affect the value of information structure; information flow should be restricted to observation.

RULE 17
  IF   an external environment of an autonomous agent is static,
  AND   interaction in the internal environment is of substitute character,
  THEN   positive correlation in the external environment is preferred.

RULE 18
  IF   an external environment of an autonomous agent is static,
  AND   interaction in the internal environment is of complementary character,
  THEN   negative correlation in the external environment is preferred.

RULE 19
  IF   an external environment of an autonomous agent is static,
  AND   the relationship between variables describing the external environment is given by function dependence,
  AND   there is an interaction in the internal environment,

THEN   it is easier to improve the value of information flow for small agents than for larger agents.

RULE 20

IF   an external environment of an autonomous agent is static,

AND   the relationship between variables describing the external environment is of statistical character,

AND   there is no interaction in the internal environment,

THEN   efficiency of an information flow increases with increasing n.

RULE 21

IF   an external environment of an autonomous agent is static,

AND   the relationship between variables describing the external environment is of statistical character,

AND   there is an interaction in the internal environment,

AND   there is no communication between agent members,

THEN   the increase in the value of information structure decreases with increasing n.

RULE 22

IF   an external environment of an autonomous agent is static,

AND   the relationship between variables describing the external environment is of statistical character,

AND   there is an interaction in the internal environment,

AND   there is communication between agent members,

THEN   efficiency of an information flow increases with increasing n.

RULE 23

IF   an external environment of an autonomous agent is static,

AND   there is an interaction in the internal environment,

THEN   the losses caused by incomplete information increase with decreasing correlation in the external environment.

---

4. DYNAMIC ENVIRONMENT

Let the external environment be described by the autoregressive process of the first order. The first order autoregressive process is given as [20,21,22]:

$$X(t) = wX(t-1) + \mu(t), \tag{26}$$

where $\mu(t)$ are uncorrelated random variables with zero mean and constant variance $Var[\mu]=\partial$, and w is the equation coefficient describing the dynamics of the process (the process is stable for $w<1$, explosive for $w>1$, and Brownian for $w=1$). The autoregressive process given by (26) can be used for the modelling purposes if the dependence X(t)=f[X(0)] is known. This dependence is as follows [20]:

$$X(t) = w^t X(0) + \sum_{m=0}^{t-1} w^m \mu(t-m), \qquad (27)$$

or more generally:

$$X(t) = w^{z+1} X(t-z-1) + \sum_{m=0}^{z} w^m \mu(z+1-m), \qquad (28)$$

where $1 \leq z \leq t-1$.

4.1   Nondelayed information

Using modelling platform introduced earlier, it can be shown that the values of information structures modelled by (20), i.e. C1, C2, C3, and C4 are given, for information that is not delayed, as:

$$VC1 = s^2 M, \; VC2 = 2s^2 M, \; VC3 = s^2 M(2-q^2)/(1-q^2), \; VC4 = s^2 M2/(1-q^2), (29)$$

where $M = \sum_{N=0}^{t} w^{2N}$, and the values of information structures

modelled by (22), i.e. C5, C6, and C7 are given as:

$$VC5 = s^2 M, \; VC6 = ns^2 M, \; VC7 = ns^2 M[1+(n-2)q]/[1+(n-2)q-(n-1)q^2], \; (30)$$

with the same value of M. General rules that can be formulated for dynamic environment using (29) and (30) are included in Table 2 placed at the end of this Section (rules 24 through 26).

Equations (29) and (30) also offer the opportunity to analyze the flow of information in various dynamic situations described by w. Such analysis allows us to formulate the rules for stable (w<1), Brownian (w=1), and explosive (w>1) character of the external environment (see rules 27 through 29 in Table 2).

Figure 10 shows the character of the relationship between t and VC for different values of w.

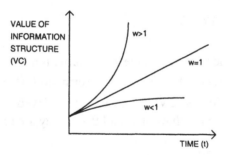

Figure 4-11. Character of the relationship between t and VC for different values of w

4.2   Delayed information

The values of information structures modelled by (22), i.e. C5, C6, and C7 are given for delayed information as:

$$VC5_\theta = s^2 w^{2\theta} \sum_{N=0}^{t-\theta} . w^{2N},$$
(31)

$$VC6_\theta = ns^2 w^{2\theta} \sum_{N=0}^{t-\theta} . w^{2N},$$
(32)

$$VC7_\theta = \{n[1+(n-2)q]/[1+(n-2)q-(n-1)q^2]\}s^2 w^{2\theta} \sum_{N=0}^{t-\theta} . w^{2N},$$
(33)

where θ stands for delay. It is easy to show that for $\theta=0$ (information is not delayed) the values of information structures given by (31), (32), and (33) become identical with the ones given by (30).

Independent stochastic process can be modelled by equation (27) for $w=0$. If $\theta \neq 0$ (information is delayed) and stochastic process describing the external environment of an agent is independent, the value of each information structure C5, C6, and C7 is equal zero. Delayed information in such a case can not be used for inferences about the actual state of the environment so it is useless (see rule 30 in Table 2).

For dependent stochastic process in the external environment delayed information causes some losses in its value. Such losses are given as:

$$LVC'' = VC_{\theta=0} - VC_{\theta\neq0}, \tag{34}$$

where $VC_{\theta=0}$ stands for the value of information structure without delay and $VC_{\theta\neq0}$ represents the value of information structure with delayed information. The losses LVC'' caused by delayed information can be calculated for different values of w and θ and they are expressed as follows:

$$LVC1'' = s^2[(1-w^{2\theta})/(1-w^2)], \tag{35}$$

$$LVC2'' = ns^2[(1-w^{2\theta})/(1-w^2)], \tag{36}$$

$$LVC3''=\{n[1+(n-2)q]s^2/[1+(n-2)q-(n-1)q^2]\}[(1-w^{2\theta})/(1-w^2)] \tag{37}$$

The rules concerning delayed information are presented in Table 2 (rules 31 through 33).

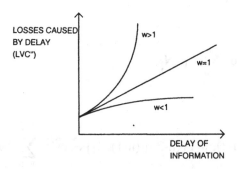

Figure 4-12. Character of losses in the value of information structure caused by delayed information

Table 4-2. Production rules describing agents functioning in dynamic environment

RULE 24

IF	an external environment of an autonomous agent is described by stochastic process,
AND	information is not delayed,
THEN	the value of full information is, for each decision situation, greater than the values of other possible information structures.

RULE 25

IF	an external environment of an autonomous agent is described by stochastic process,
AND	information is not delayed,
AND	there is no interaction in the internal environment,
THEN	there is no need for communication inside the agent.

RULE 26

IF	an external environment of an autonomous agent is described by stochastic process,
AND	information is not delayed,
THEN	the more uncertain the realizations in the external environment the bigger the value of the information about these realizations.

RULE 27

IF	an external environment of an autonomous agent is described by stochastic process,
AND	information is not delayed,
AND	the external environment is stable,
THEN	the value of information structures stabilizes with time.

RULE 28

IF	an external environment of an autonomous agent is described by stochastic process,
AND	information is not delayed,
AND	the external environment is described by Brownian movement,
THEN	the value of information structures increases proportionally with the increase of time.

RULE 29

IF	an external environment of an autonomous agent is described by stochastic process,
AND	information is not delayed,
AND	the external environment is of explosive character,
THEN	the value of information structures increases exponentially with time.

RULE 30

IF	an external environment of an autonomous agent is described by stochastic process,
AND	information is delayed,
AND	stochastic process is independent,
THEN	value of any information structure is equal zero.

RULE 31

IF	an external environment of an autonomous agent is described by stochastic process,
AND	information is delayed,

AND   stochastic process is dependent,
AND   the external environment is stable,
THEN   the losses caused by delayed information stabilize with
           increasing value of delay.

RULE 32
IF   an external environment of an autonomous agent is described
           by stochastic process,
AND   information is delayed,
AND   stochastic process is dependent,
AND   the external environment is described by Brownian movement,
THEN   the losses caused by delayed information increase
           proportionally with the increase of delay.

RULE 33
IF   an external environment of an autonomous agent is described
           by stochastic process,
AND   information is delayed,
AND   stochastic process is dependent,
AND   the external environment is of explosive character,
THEN   the losses caused by delayed information increase
           exponentially with delay.

---

5.   SOFT MODELLING IN ACQUISITION OF KNOWLEDGE FOR INFORMATION MANAGEMENT

A formal quantitative model as presented in the previous Sections can be helpful in creation of knowledge connected with an information flow evaluation in autonomous systems. Because of its complexity the model cannot be used for analysis and evaluation of an information flow in all possible decision situations. Qualitative modeling and reasoning, on the other hand, are areas of Artificial Intelligence (AI) that focus on reasoning about the behaviour of real life complex systems without relying on numbers. In the development of an information structure for a given system, Qualitative Reasoning (QR) tools can play a role similar to that of traditional analysis based on the mathematical model.

Next, some non-quantitative tools are discussed for addressing the problem of knowledge acquisition for an autonomous system (subsystem) in various decision situations.

5.1   Connectionist systems

Problem solving tasks, such as information structure development, may be considered pattern classification tasks. The system analyst learns mappings between input patterns, consisting of characteristics of system's external and internal environment, and output patterns, consisting of information structures to apply to these characteristics. Thus, neural networks (neural-based expert systems) offer a promising solution for automating the learning process of the analyst.

As we already know, systems analyst, while developing an information structure for a given system, transforms certain characteristics of a system into recommendations concerning the flow of information. These characteristics represent the input for the system and their full description (for both static and dynamic environments) includes 5 parameters: correlation in the external environment (r), dynamics (t), interaction in the internal environment (q), delay (d), and type of the process describing the external environment (w). Output consists of the following decisions (recommendations): (i) observation (or sensoring) should be present, and (ii) exchange of information should be present. An input portion together with an output portion of the data represents a training pair. The training pairs were used to train a 5-10-2 neural network [23].

The target values for each output node were normalised in such a way that the maximum target for each node received a value of 0.75 and the minimum target for each node received a value of 0.25. The training values for each input node were identically normalised. The learning rate and momentum term of 0.9 were used in the network. The network was trained using error back propagation procedure with a training tolerance of 5%. The network was considered trained if, for all training pairs and output nodes, |(desired output - actual output)/(desired output)| < tolerance.

After training, additional characteristics of a system were generated for use by the network. Five sets of characteristics were submitted to the network. In response, the network suggested five information flow recommendations. In all cases the recommendations agree with the IF ... AND ... THEN rules presented in Tables 1 and 2.

5.2   Decision tree classifiers

Decision tree classifiers are used successfully in many diverse areas. Their most important feature is the capability of capturing descriptive decisionmaking knowledge from the supplied data [24]. Decision tree can be generated from training sets. The procedure for such generation based on the set of objects (S), each belonging to one of the classes C_1, C_2, ..., C_k is as follows [25]:

Step 1.   If all the objects in **S** belong to the same class, for example
               C_i, the decision tree for **S** consists of a leaf labelled with this
               class.

Step 2.   Otherwise, let T be some test with possible outcomes O_1,
               O_2, ..., O_n. Each object in **S** has one outcome for T so the test
               partitions **S** into subsets S_1, S_2, ... S_n where each object in S_i
               has outcome O_i for T. T becomes the root of the decision
               tree and for each outcome O_i we build a subsidiary decision
               tree by invoking the same procedure recursively on the set
               S_i.

The above procedure is applied to training sets. The training sets are
delivered from the analysis based on the quantitative model presented
earlier.

Suppose, for illustration purposes, that we are interested in decision
making situations involving static environment only. For such cases the
following rules can be delivered using decision tree classifiers [23]:

Rule 1
IF   an external environment of a system is static
AND   it is described by random variables
AND   there is no interaction in the internal environment
THEN   communication (exchange of information) between system elements
is not necessary

Rule 2
IF   an external environment of a system is static
AND   it is described by random variables
AND   there is interaction in the internal environment
AND   the relationship between variables describing the external
          environment is of statistical character
THEN   exchange of information between system elements should be
organised

Rule 3
IF   an external environment of a system is static
AND   it is described by random variables
AND   there is interaction in the internal environment
AND   the relationship between variables describing the external
          environment is given by function dependence

THEN exchange of information between system elements is not necessary

The use of decision trees is simple and as effective as the analysis based on a rigorous mathematical model (the production rules formulated above are the same as the rules based on quantitative modelling given in Table 1).

5.3 Signed directed graphs

A directed graph, or digraph, is a graph in which all edges are directed [25]. A signed digraph is a digraph with either + or - associated with each edge. SDG nodes are chosen as variables relevant to or representative of the problem that is studied. There is an edge from variable A to variable B if a change in A has a significant direct effect on B. The sign of the edge is + if an increase in A leads to an increase in B, and a decrease in A leads to a decrease in B. The sign is - if the effect is opposite; an increase in A leads to a decrease in B, and a decrease in A leads to an increase in B.

According to the mathematical model presented in previous Sections, information flow depends on the following state parameters: delay of information (d), amount of information (a), dynamics in the external environment (w), variance in the external environment (s), and interaction in the internal environment (q). The above parameters influence the loss in the value of information caused by delay (L1), the loss in the value of information caused by incompleteness (L2), and total loss (LV). Based on relationships and dependencies described by mathematical model, the SDG can be developed and then simplified. Two principles are used for the simplification process. The first one is the principle of removal of intermediate nodes and the other one is the simplification of positive feedback loop.

The following logic rules can be written for the model after simplification [15]:

SDG Rule 1:
IF [d=+] .and. p[dLV]
THEN it is a possible solution pattern for a positive change in d

SDG Rule 2:
IF [a=+] .and. n[aLV]
THEN it is a possible solution pattern for a positive change in a

SDG Rule 3:

IF[w=+] .and. p[wLV]
         .and. p[wd]
         .and. p[dLV]
THEN it is a possible solution pattern for a positive change in w

Using the above logic rules, the qualitative behaviour of the SDG model can be found. It is easy to notice that the corresponding qualitative states (consistent patterns) for the parameters of our interest are given as follows:

(i) solution pattern for a positive change in d

d	a	w	LV
+	0	0	+

(ii) solution pattern for a positive change in w

d	a	w	LV
0	+	0	-

(iii) solution pattern for a positive change in a

d	a	w	LV
+	0	+	+

The above results of qualitative simulation are again the same as quantitative information flow modelling and evaluation. For example, they depict the adverse character of two contrary information attributes, i.e. delay and incompleteness. They also show clearly the effects of increasing dynamics in the external environment. More generally, the results show that as far as the analysis of overall directions of a system behaviour is concerned the simple qualitative model can be sufficient at a minimum level of complexity.

6.   CONCLUSION

This Chapter tries to discuss some of the emerging challenges and opportunities in the area of information flow modelling and simulation based on formal mathematical modelling platform. It also includes the preliminary results of some non-quantitative procedures applied in the process of knowledge acquisition for information management. The procedures show the potential for use in reasoning and retrieval of knowledge describing the flow of information between a system and its external environment as well as within a system. It was shown that the techniques applied are able to provide general knowledge about system functioning in static and dynamic external environments. The techniques presented illustrate the ease and appropriateness of such methods for dealing with implicit knowledge and also provide a model for extension into other expert domains.

REFERENCES

[1] T Morimoto, Application for communication agent, in *Knowledge-based Intelligent Information Engineering Systems and Allied Technologies*, Editors: Baba, Jain, Howlett, IOS Press: Amsterdam, pp. 1619-1621, 2001.

[2] A Tharumarajah, A self-organising model for scheduling distributed autonomous manufacturing agents, *Cybernetics and Systems: An International Journal*, Vol. 29, pp. 461-480, 1998.

[3] A Gunasekaran, M. Sarhadi, Planning and management issues in enterprise integration, *Concurrent Engineering: Research and Application*, Vol. 5, pp. 98-100, 1997.

[4] B Prakken, *Information, Organisation and Information Systems Design*, Kluwer: Boston, 2000.

[5] RI Mckay, R Sarker, X Yao, Intelligent and Evolutionary Systems, *International Journal of Knowledge-Based Intelligent Engineering Systems*, Vol. 4, pp. 141-143, 2000.

[6] A.K. Kamrani and P.R. Sferro, *Direct Engineering: Toward Intelligent Manufacturing*, Kluwer: London, 1999.

[7] P O'Grady, *The Age of Modularity*, Adams and Steele: Iowa, 1999.

[8] F C Morabito, *Advances in Intelligent Systems*, IOS Press: Amsterdam, 1997.

[9] J Wyzalek, *Systems Integration Success*, Auerbach: London, 1999.

[10] W Pedrycz, A Bargiela, Information Granulation, in *Knowledge-based Intelligent Information Engineering Systems and Allied Technologies*, Editors: Baba, Jain, Howlett, IOS Press: Amsterdam, pp. 1147-1152, 2001.

[11] N Bajgoric, Organizational Systems Integration: Management Information Systems Perspective, *Concurrent Engineering: Research and Application*, Vol. 5, pp. 113-123, 1997.

[12] E Szczerbicki, External environment of an autonomous manufacturing agent: dynamics and representation, *International Journal of Systems Science*, Vol. 27, pp. 1211-1218, 1996.

[13] E Szczerbicki, Simulation modelling for complex production systems, *Cybernetics and Systems: An International Journal* Vol. 31, No. 3, pp. 333-351, 2000.

[14] E Szczerbicki, Intelligent integration for autonomous manufacturing systems, *International Journal of Knowledge-Based Intelligent Engineering Systems*, Vol. 6, No. 4, pp. 214-219, 2002.

[15] E Szczerbicki, Soft modelling support for information management, *Cybernetics and Systems: An International Journal* , Vol.33, no 4, pp. 413-426, 2002.

[16] G Matsumoto, Brain Computing, *Artificial Life and Robotics*, Vol. 3, pp. 24-27, 1999.

[17] RJ Bogdan, *Minding Minds*, MIT Press: Boston, 2000.

[18] E Kreyszig, *Advanced engineering mathematics*, New York: Wiley 1983.

[19] J L Gersting, *Mathematical structures for computer science*, Freeman: New York, 1982.

[20] H Theil, *Principles of econometrics*, New York: Wiley 1971.

[21] R V Hogg, E A Tanis, *Probability and statistical inference*, Macmillan: New York, 1993.

[22] R V Hogg, J Ledolter, *Applied statistics for engineers and physical scientists*, Macmillan: New York, 1992.

[23] E Szczerbicki, Decision trees and neural networks for reasoning and knowledge acquisition for autonomous agents, *International Journal of Systems Science,* vol. 27, 233-239, 1996.

[24] S Safavian and Landgrebe D, A survey of decision tree classifier methodology. *IEEE Transactions on Systems, Man, and Cybernetics*, vol 21, 660-668, 1991.

[25] J R Quinlan, Decision trees and decision making. *IEEE Transactions on Systems, Man, and Cybernetics*, vol 20, pp. 339-346, 1990

[25] G Chartrand and O.R. Oellermann, *Applied and algorithmic graph theory*, New York: McGraw-Hill, 1993.

Chapter 5

SUMMARIZATION OF TEXTS FOUND ON THE WORLD WIDE WEB

Marie-Francine Moens, Roxana Angheluta and Rik De Busser
Katholieke Universiteit Leuven, Belgium

Abstract: Summaries of texts found on the World Wide Web are valuable. They help the user of a search engine to select information and are an aid for processing the vast amount of information found on the Web. This chapter describes the technologies that can be applied for summarizing the texts of Web pages. The focus is on technologies that currently generate the best results and are suited for the specific heterogeneous environment that makes up the World Wide Web. This chapter gives an overview of generic, query-biased and task-specific summarization, as well as single-document and multi-document summarization. Among the technologies that are discussed are semantic frame technologies, rhetorical structure analysis, learning discourse patterns, techniques relying upon lexical cohesion, and text clustering.

Key words: Information filtering, information extraction, summarization.

1.   INTRODUCTION

Summarization of text concerns the generation of a reduced representation of the content of a text. This representation can take different formats ranging from continuous, coherent text to a profile that extracts and structures certain information from the text. The idea and first attempts of automatic summarization go back to the end of the 1950s [Luhn 1958]. At that time, it seemed like a far-fetched theory, but during the last decade automatic summarization grew into an absolute necessity. We are confronted with ever expanding collections of textual documents that are accessible via the World Wide Web.

Searching for just the right information on the Web is not easy. This is because search engines allow little more than full text retrieval augmented by keyword searches based on manually added subject labels. When searching large databases such as the Web, subject labels - besides the huge cost of assigning them manually - are either found to be too general to be useful or too precise to be remembered by users. Many of the documents on the Web (i.e., Web pages) are often structured in HTML (HyperText Markup Language) or XML (Extensible Markup Language), but there are enormous variations in possible structures, making that simply searching for words on Web pages still remains the most convenient way. Moreover, natural language is immensely varied and often there is no easily discoverable relationship between the text that is actually used and the concepts that are searched for. A search query and a subject in a text can be treated and expressed in a large number of ways depending on the searcher or writer and on his context. For this problem information retrieval has provided technologies that expand query terms with synonyms and related terms to make it possible to find more relevant pages. There is, however, a second more pressing problem, that is only aggravated by solving the first one. It is well known that searching large databases such as the Web - either by a full text search or by selecting subject labels - results in a large number of potentially relevant documents. It is not possible to consult them all.

Consequently, we need other ways of selecting the relevant information on the Web. One way is by using summaries both of single pages and sets of pages. In addition, summarization of Web pages is sometimes a necessity. When displaying Web pages on small screens (e.g., of mobile phones or of PDAs), specific services often have to condense the text to its essentials (e.g., technologies used in the Wireless Application Protocol (WAP) or with i-mode (mobile Internet)). Furthermore, question-answering systems are becoming popular as a way of searching textual databases. They generate the answer to a natural language question, which is extracted and often summarized from the content of the texts.

This chapter describes technologies that can be applied for summarizing the texts of Web pages. It is organized as follows. We describe the kinds of texts found on the World Wide Web. We outline the types of summaries that are useful in a Web context. We go deeper into the suitable technologies for single- and multi-document summarization. Finally, we summarize the findings and give advise about the best techniques for summarizing Web pages.

2.   TEXTS FOUND ON THE WORLD WIDE WEB

Web pages cover all possible text genres and subject domains, and are written in all possible languages. They can be of any size and can display all kinds of structures and formats. The texts are volatile, change frequently, and are often redundant. Pages can be linked to other texts, which can be less or more similar in content or have very little relationships with the pages from which the links originate. Summarization systems have to cope with large volumes of data, different languages, distributed data and few classified training examples from which they can learn. Users have different backgrounds and interpretation capabilities of the summaries.

Texts on the Web have a number of formats, the most prominent currently being HTML, PDF (Portable Document Format) and PS (Postscript). Besides the text, a page can contain references to metadata (e.g., layout, attribute and content descriptors), imbedded objects (e.g., images and sound tracks), or to small programs to be executed (i.e., in the form of Java scripts). Web pages can be static or they can be dynamically generated from the content of databases.

The texts on the Web are mostly in *natural language*. Through a finite set of words and syntactic constructs, language offers an enormous potential of combinatorial expression possibilities and Web pages use language with all of the advantages and disadvantages of this flexibility. They contain common paradigms of words as found in ordinary language as well as domain-specific interpretations of terms. The public for which Web texts are written is also very varied and the writer of a text assumes a certain background knowledge on the side of the users, which implies that some content is often not made explicit. As we will further see, the large variation in text genres, subject domains, languages and the audience of the pages put a lot of constraints upon the technologies that can be used for summarization of texts found on the World Wide Web.

3.   TYPES AND USE OF SUMMARIES WHEN SEARCHING THE WORLD WIDE WEB

In a typical interaction with a Web search engine, the user enters a specific information need expressed as a query. For each of the documents presented in the answer list, its title, its location (URL), and possibly the first few sentences of the page or the sentences in which the query terms are found are shown to the user. These sentences act as a kind of rudimentary summary, which should help a user of the search engine to decide which of the retrieved pages are relevant to his information need. However, it is not always the case that the title and this rudimentary summary accurately reflect the content of the Web page. Moreover, even when the user is only skimming summaries, it is usually impossible for him to consult all the pages that are retrieved by a Web search engine. Multiple retrieved pages could be grouped and summaries of multiple pages could be very useful to help with the selection.

With respect to automatic summarization, the following types of summaries have proven their value both in single-document and multi-document summarization. A *generic summary* is a summary that truly reflects the main content of the original text. A *user-relevant* or *query-biased summary* is a summary that is customized to reflect the information need in the query. It has been shown that query-biased summaries assist users in performing relevance judgments more accurately and more quickly. This effect is especially attributed to the fact that they adequately indicate the context in which potentially ambiguous query terms are used [Tombros & Sanderson 1998]. A *task-specific summary* like a query-biased summary is tailored to a specific information need (e.g., extraction of specific information from documents that forms the summary), but the information need is more stable over a period of time than a query-biased summary.

Summaries generated by machines are often just *extracts*, i.e., a number of sentences or other text fragments are literally extracted without any modifications. One usually speaks of an *abstract* when a text is not a verbatim copy of part of its source text. However, summaries do not need to be coherent texts. A *profile* or template is a frame-like representation acting as a summary containing distinct slots of information each of which has a well-defined semantic meaning. The slots are filled with information extracted from the original text. The extracted information can be used in a variety of other applications (e.g., in e-commerce).

4.   THE TECHNOLOGIES

4.1   Requirements and constraints

One could assume that a summarization tool for Web pages should be as general as possible in order to cope with the heterogeneity of the Web. Ideally a Web summarization system should generate acceptable summaries for all languages, all types of pages and all kinds of contents. However, this is a utopian dream. In text summarization and information extraction the systems that have the best results are systems that rely upon a large amount of symbolic knowledge that is needed for "understanding" the content of the texts. This knowledge concerns both linguistic and domain-specific knowledge. Given the heterogeneity of the Web texts, the knowledge would be enormous to acquire, but also building algorithms that efficiently make use of it would be a hard task. However, information retrieval has a tradition of working with a limited amount of domain knowledge and of acquiring the additional knowledge through machine learning techniques, most of which are of statistical nature.

The summarization task consists of an *analysis of the text* to be summarized, a *selection of important information* in it, possibly a *generalization* of the information, and the *editing or generation* of a summary text from the selected information [cf. Sparck Jones 1993]. In linguistic terms the analysis is usually very shallow and the selection of information is in many systems restricted to a selection of sentences. For a generic summary, important information should reflect the main content of the text. For a query-biased or task-specific summary, the selected information should summarize the content of the text that is relevant for the query or task. The summarization task is similar to the generic summarization task, but the text to be summarized is often restricted to a number of relevant passages.

Consequently, issues are how to select and to extract specific information from a text and how to detect its main content. Information is selected and extracted by considering the *contextual patterns* by which it is signaled. The major indicators of the main content of a text are its *discourse structures* with corresponding discourse markers and *lexical cohesion* of the text [cf. Kintsch & van Dijk 1978]. The knowledge that is necessary to detect information extraction and discourse patterns can be implemented symbolically (e.g., in knowledge frames and ontologies) or can be learned from a training corpus with the help of machine learning techniques. *Supervised learning* automatically detects classification patterns in a training set of classified examples that can be used to classify previously unseen objects. In *unsupervised learning* patterns are inferred from the data as natural groupings or relationships of features. Learning might also be performed with parametric training methods, in which parameters are estimated from the training set by making an assumption about the mathematical functional form of the underlying population density distribution.

In text summarization different approaches originated from the field of natural language processing - including the Message Understanding Conferences (MUC) organized by the Defense Advance Research Projects Agency, USA -, but there are also statistical machine learning techniques which were originally developed in information retrieval [e.g., Luhn 1958]. Currently, the yearly Document Understanding Conferences (DUC), which is part of the DARPA program and is organized by the National Institute of Standards and Technology (NIST), USA, is a benchmark for testing text summarization systems.

In the next sections we will discuss the techniques in detail. The focus is on technologies that currently generate the best results and are suited for the specific heterogeneous environment that makes up the World Wide Web [for an exhaustive overview of the technologies: see Mani & Maybury 1999, Moens 2000, DUC 2001, DUC 2002]. We will start with the oldest approaches that rely on symbolic knowledge and will gradually move to current machine learning techniques. We sometimes include recall, precision or coverage values obtained by the techniques as compared to ideal summaries by experts. These values are merely an illustration since ideal summaries are very hard to build as different human abstractors produce different summaries from the same text. Moreover, the techniques are often difficult to compare because they are tested and evaluated on different corpora. We refer to the DUC Web site for the most comprehensive assessment of different systems and technologies that are evaluated on the same text corpora.

4.2   Information extraction techniques

When one knows a priori the types of texts, their language and the information to be included in the summary, you can define template patterns that describe the linguistic (e.g., syntactic) and lexical contexts of the information. The most popular techniques rely on frame theory, which originated with Schank's famous conceptual dependency (CD) theory [Schank 1972]. Fully developed CD scripts are supposed to contain all the information about any event, which could possibly occur in a given situation. The majority of the information extraction and summarization systems that were influenced by Schank's theory did not use fully developed CD scripts, but made use of so-called *sketchy scripts*, which only contain the most crucial or most relevant conceptualizations. An example is the FRUMP system, which summarizes typical newspaper stories (kidnappings, acts of terrorism, diplomatic negotiations, etc.) [DeJong 1982]. It accurately extracts specific information (e.g., the nature and location of an event) from stories in the pre-selected topic areas and generates a summary based on the extracted information. The sketchy script describes sequences of events and thus imposes a kind of structure on the stories and inferences about additional events that may occur. A parser skims through texts looking for words signaling a known script, only interprets those parts of the text that directly relate to elements of the script, and ignores the rest of the text. Specific information from the text is extracted by considering the contextual patterns of this information (e.g., the weapon of an attack is found in a sentence clause after the infinitive form of "kill" and is introduced with the preposition "with").

The symbolic knowledge that is necessary for script-based analysis of texts and for the analysis of the information context in sentences is often stored in knowledge frames. A frame or template is a knowledge representation that not only guides the analysis of the texts, but also prevails as a target representation structure of a text that maps a class of entities or situations onto a limited set of relevant features that are expressed as type-value pairs. Feature values are empty slots on which certain constraints or rules are placed. An information extraction algorithm will try to match linguistic representations of real-world occurrences with particular templates by filling out the slots in accordance with the constraints or rules placed on them. The text is syntactically analyzed, if this is required by the frame constraints. A part-of-speech (POS) tagger assigns a tag to each word that indicates its syntactic class (e.g., noun) and verb sub-categorization allows detecting simple syntactic structures such as detecting the subject, verb, object and prepositional phrases (e.g., the subject of the verb "kill" might indicate the perpetrator in an attack).

There are many ways of using frames, scripts and their constraints when analyzing texts. In cases in which the constraints or rules can be expressed with regular expressions, the analysis is restricted to pattern matching the expressions with the text. This procedure can be implemented as a finite state automaton. Often, the analysis of the text occurs in different steps, which might be implemented as a cascade of finite state automata in which the output of one automaton forms the input of the next one. A famous example is the FASTUS system [Hobbs et al. 1996].

The frame- or template-based approach is successful for text summarization as it results in a superior performance at the yearly DUC conference [e.g., Harabagiu & Lăcătuşu 2002].

A bottleneck is the manual construction of frames, which forces developers to restrict the information extraction systems to very limited subject domains. This has led to the idea that the required symbolic knowledge can be automatically learned from annotated example texts. For instance, when the information to be extracted is annotated or classified, the correct extraction patterns can be learned based on a set of lexical and syntactical features. Research experiments have demonstrated that learning techniques produce results that are comparable to systems that use handcrafted patterns (e.g., Riloff [1996], Soderland [1999]). Research of Craven et al. [2000] demonstrates that first-order predicate logic provides a powerful representation for learning and classifying Web pages, hypertext links and page text fields.

The performance of hand-coded and learned extraction patterns depends upon the difficulty of the extraction task. When processing strongly structured texts with little textual variation in the extraction patterns, high recall and precision values can be obtained (e.g., rental ads: 70% recall at 97% precision); however, in free text the results are often much worse (e.g., in the management succession domain: 46% recall at 69% precision) [Soderland, 1999].

Another problem is the acquisition of the frame knowledge that is necessary to extract the information *without* or with *less annotations*. Annotations present a serious knowledge-engineering bottleneck that is especially detrimental for the summarization of Web pages. Harabagiu and Lăcătuşu [2002] have defined an ad-hoc method for automatically acquiring the frames of a certain topic domain. Given a large set of example texts of the domain, typical information can be identified as frequently signaled in syntactical constructs of the type Subject-Verb-Object (SVO) + Prepositional attachments. The terms of these syntactical constructs are related to a conceptual category with the help of thesauri such as WordNet or, in case of proper names, categorized (e.g., as person name) with the help of named entity recognition tools. In this way a domain-specific template can be constructed (e.g., for the topic "natural disaster", it might contain the following slots: natural phenomenon, amount of damage, number of victims, location and date). In a second step, the rules that map these slots to real texts and extract the information from them are also automatically acquired [Harabagiu & Maiorano 2000] by retrieving text fragments that contain any of the slot values of the template (again by using a thesaurus and named entity recognizer) and parsing them in their SVO patterns. The patterns that are found in this way and in which terms are replaced by their conceptual category form the mapping rules. For instance the clause:

"Armco[ORGANIZATION] named John Haley[PERSON] chairman [POSITION]"
generates the following rule:
[*Subject* = ORGANIZATION] [*Verb* = name][*Object1* = Person] [*Object2* = Position]

Another approach investigates whether less domain-specific semantic roles for frames can be learned from lexical and syntactic properties of texts and studies their usefulness in information extraction [De Busser et al., 2002]. These semantic roles are of the type introduced by Fillmore [1976 ; see also Gildea & Jurafsky, 2002], which describes abstract actions or relationships, along with their participants (e.g., a STATEMENT frame contains the semantic roles SPEAKER, ADDRESSEE and MESSAGE). Domain-independent semantic frames have the advantage that they do not require a complete new set of frame slots for each new application domain.

In the following sections we discuss techniques for selecting important content from a text. Unless the summary has the form of a profile or is of a very task-specific nature, summarization usually comes down to selecting important content. One of the technologies that is useful here is by using rhetorical structure analysis.

4.3   Rhetorical structure analysis

The rhetorical structure of a text is a main indicator of how information in that text is ordered into a coherent informational structure. Rhetorical Structure Theory (RST) assumes a text to have a hierarchical organization based on asymmetrical nucleus-satellite relationships. A nucleus segment can exist in itself, but its satellite creates a motivating framework around it, which means that pairs of elementary textual units combine into parent units - *text spans* - which are again recursively merged until at a certain point a unit spanning the entire text - the *root* - is reached. The constituent halves of any text span are linked together by a text structuring relation, which typically holds between a more central unit - the nucleus - and a more peripheral one - the satellite (although there also is a small set of multi-nuclear relations). The rhetorical relationship of "purpose" between a nucleus (N) and satellite (S) is illustrated in the following example:

[S In order to have some more space S] [N we will have to rent another building. N]

Although in theory the set of discourse relations is open, Mann and Thompson [1988] consider it to be a relatively fixed set of highly recurrent relations (e.g., that express evidence, elaboration, contrast, etc.). A recursive application of the relations on the consecutive levels of pairs of units makes it possible to parse a text into its rhetorical structure, which allows one to determine the relative importance of any unit based on its nucleus-satellite properties. Marcu [2000] provides algorithms for computing the text units' salience and uses this approach in text summarization.

The main problem is to determine the RST structure automatically. Linguistic surface phenomena that signal rhetorical relations are lexical cues, pronouns and other forms of phoric reference, and tense and aspect [Hovy 1993]. The most prominent indicators are the lexical cues, most typically expressed by conjunctions and by certain kinds of adverbial groups (e.g., "in order to", "however"). However, rhetorical cue phrases are often ambiguous and not all discourse relations are indicated by explicit cues in the text.

Rhetorical structure analysis has introduced the importance of learning discourse cues on which we will further elaborate in the next section.

4.4   Learning discourse patterns

The communicative function in any natural language text is realized as a set of *discourse patterns*. Discourse patterns often signal important content in texts. Among the discourse patterns that are used in text summarization are sentence position (e.g., first sentence of a paragraph), sentence length, cue phrases (e.g., rhetorical cues mentioned above), named entities, the position of a certain word in a text, and the presence of pronouns (cf. biographies). Their appearance or non-appearance allows for scoring the sentences of a text for inclusion in a summary.

Discourse patterns, including the distribution and linguistic signaling of highly topical sentences, and their importance may vary according to the document corpus, subject domain and text type, or to the task the summary is intended for. It is possible to learn the weight of a discourse pattern from an example corpus with summaries, which is very valuable when for a specific text corpus the machine simulates the summaries made by a professional abstractor [van Halteren 2002].

Most commonly, a simple *naïve Bayes classifier* is used [Kupiec, 1995]. In a naïve Bayes classifier, each sentence is described by a number of discourse patterns or features and the probability of summary inclusion is computed based on estimates of the probabilities of the individual features in the example summaries and example source texts. The computation of summary inclusion is simplified by assuming feature independence.

Other pattern classification methods have also proven their usefulness, although they are more complicated to compute. Among them are *support vector machines* [Hirao et al. 2002]. Given the positive and negative examples of a class (sentences that belong or not belong to the summary) that are linearly separable, a support vector machine finds the hyperplane with maximum margins in the t-dimensional feature space that best separates these positive and negative examples. The resulting function can be used to classify previously unseen sentences. Support vector machines can be generalized to examples that are not linearly separable.

4.5   Techniques relying upon lexical cohesion

Another strong indicator of the content of a text is *lexical cohesion*. Humans perceive a text as a coherent unity, i.e. as exhibiting a certain form of semantic continuity [Halliday 1994 p. 309 ff.]. This semantic continuity is to a considerable extent accomplished by lexical cohesion, i.e., semantically related words signal cohesive relations in a text. Lexical cohesion implies the existence of sequences of related words that recur with a significant frequency over a certain stretch of text. Relationships between the words include relationships of reiteration and collocation. Reiteration comprises all relations in which words are connected because they express identical or similar semantic concepts, the most common being repetition, synonymy, hypernymy (hypernym = more general term) and hyponymy (hyponym = more specific term). Two or more lexical items form a collocation if they exhibit a tendency to co-occur in a specific semantic pattern. The probability of co-occurrence of items should be higher than random (e.g., the collocational bond between *smoking* and *pipe*). Lexical cohesion has been exploited in various techniques for text summarization. Techniques of topic segmentation and techniques that cluster related sentences or passages are based on lexical cohesion. One of the most obvious examples is the technique of constructing lexical chains.

In text summarization, *lexical chains* can be used for detecting important sentences in a text [e.g., Barzilay & Elhadad 1999]. The first step of a lexical chain-building algorithm is the selection of words to be involved in the analysis. The simplest strategy only takes into account nouns (detected with a POS tagger), but theoretically all words with a certain information density could be included (a considerable part of the verbs and adjectives in the text). Words that have a strong semantic relationship (e.g., synonymy) are put in the same chain. These relationships are detected with the help of a thesaurus (e.g., WordNet). Different algorithms have been proposed that deal with the problem of word sense disambiguation [e.g., Morris & Hirst 1991; Barzilay & Elhadad 1999]. The summarization algorithms rely upon several heuristics to identify the important sentences. For instance, the system of Barzilay and Elhadad [1999] locates the first appearance of the representative word of the strongest chains and extracts the sentences containing it. A chain's strength is computed as a function of the length of the chain and the frequency of its members.

Lexical chain construction is useful for languages like English, for which extensive thesauri with word relationships are developed. Most of the algorithms used in text summarization rely on reiteration, while linguistic analysis shows that most cohesive ties are collocational. However, research of Lin and Hovy [2002] shows that lexical cohesion detected by collocational relationships between words (e.g., words that often co-occur) is a good indicator of textual content and consequently is valuable in text summarization.

4.6   Techniques of topic identification and segmentation

Identification of the topics and subtopics is very useful in text summarization, as important topics can be selected for inclusion in the summary. The TOPIC system of Hahn [1990] is a good example of a system that exploits the thematic structure of a text for summarization. Hahn implemented three basic patterns of thematic progression in texts: The elaboration of one specific topic within a text passage, the detection of topic shifts within a sentence, and the derivation of a topic, which is composed of different subtopics across text passages. Although this approach is very valuable, topic recognition in TOPIC strongly relies on specific domain knowledge that is embodied in lexical frames.

The simplest techniques that use topic identification in text summarization extract sentences with the highest weighted terms, which possibly occur in close proximity [Luhn 1958]. A term is selected based on its syntactic class (e.g., noun, verb) or on its non-belonging to a stoplist. It is weighted with classical functions such as the multiplication of the term's frequency in the text and the inverse of its frequency in a text collection (*tf x idf*).

Topic segmentation concerns the detection of the overall organization of the text into themes or topics and the identification of text segments that correspond to general and more specific topics. Once segments are found, they can be described by key terms, headlines or sentences that form the summary. Topic segmentation is often accomplished by grouping "similar" sentences, paragraphs or text blocks with a fixed size that share common terms [Salton et al. 1994]. The text fragments to be grouped are mainly represented as term vectors with *p* components where *p* is the number of unique content terms in the document text that is segmented. Different similarity functions can be applied for the grouping. The problem is that it is difficult to define similarity in content between sentences or passages (see below computation of similarity) and to identify when they are sufficiently dissimilar to speak of a topic shift or break.

The most famous algorithm for topic segmentation is TextTiling, which computes the similarity of each two adjacent text units [Hearst 1997]. The resulting sequence is placed in a smoothed graph with valleys identifying ruptures in the topic structure. Other linear segmenters are Segmenter from Columbia University, NY [Kan et al. 1998] and C99 of Choi [2000]. The linear segmenters lack a hierarchical discrimination of the topics, which is useful if one wants to zoom in and out the content. Moens and De Busser [2001] have developed a hierarchical topic segmentation algorithm that produces a table of content of a text. Their algorithm relies on word distributions, on discourse markers of term position in sentences and on persistency of terms across subsequent sentences. These discourse cues are typical for SVO languages such as English, French and Dutch. The following is an example of a topic tree constructed for document AP880911-0016.S, set d061j of the DUC-2002 corpus (the numbers refer to character pointers in the text):

> *Hurricane Gilbert rains storm   0   1949*
> *storm mph   180   405*
> *need   275   405*
> *Civil Defense Director Eugenio Cabral Hurricane Gilbert   406   1432*
> *people   498   628*
> *National Hurricane Center   734   943*
> *National Hurricane Center storm   944   1252*
> *weather   1137   1252*
> *winds 1253   1432*
> *reports   1396   1432*
> *San Juan coast   1433   1658*
> *Saturday   1535   1658*
> *Residents   1659   1749*
> *Hurricane Florence hurricane   1750   1949*
> *Debby   1843   1949*

This table of content is used in summarization by selecting the first sentence of each topical segment at a chosen level of detail yielding the following summary [Angheluta et al. 2002]:

Hurricane Gilbert swept toward the Dominican Republic Sunday, and the Civil Defense alerted its heavily populated south coast to prepare for high winds, heavy rains and high seas. The storm was approaching from the southeast with sustained winds of 75 mph gusting to 92 mph. Cabral said residents of the province of Barahona should closely follow Gilbert's movement. San Juan, on the north coast, had heavy rains and gusts Saturday, but they subsided during the night. Residents returned home, happy to find little damage from 80 mph winds and sheets of rain. Florence, the sixth named storm of the 1998 Atlantic storm, was the second hurricane.

4.7   Clustering of sentences or passages

Similar to the foregoing are the summarization techniques that cluster sentences or text passages. The aim of the clustering algorithm is to group similar sentences or text passages into one cluster. A cluster should ideally cover one topic of the Web page and contain sentences or passages related to that topic. After clusters are created, one representative sentence from each cluster can be selected to be included in the summary.

Clustering algorithms [e.g., Kaufman & Rousseeuw 1990] are typically hierarchical algorithms (e.g., group average and complete link) and partitioning algorithms (e.g., *k*-means and *k*-medoid). In case of hierarchical methods, the clustering stops when a target number of seed clusters is reached, i.e., a number that can be inferred from a predefined length of the summary or can be estimated as $\log_2 N$ (where N = number of documents).

For summarization, it is important to detect a natural grouping of the sentences or passages, so that each topic cluster can have a representative in the summary. Such algorithms are often computationally expensive. They search for a best or very good clustering by considering a large number of possible groupings and choose the one that minimizes the similarity between objects of different clusters and maximizes the similarity between objects of the same cluster. Because the number of sentences or passages is often fairly limited in a text to be summarized, this is often computationally feasible. Such a clustering approach was implemented by Moens [2000, p. 173 ff.] and Angheluta et al. [2002].

The clustering requires that sentences or text passages are represented as term vectors and that their pairwise similarity is computed (see below). From each cluster a *representative sentence* can be extracted. It can be the medoid (i.e., the sentence that is on average the most similar to all the other sentences of the cluster), or it can be selected with the help of discourse patterns that signal important content, such as selecting a sentence that appears as the first sentence of a paragraph (see above).

4.8   Computation of the similarity

Approaches of topic segmentation and clustering require techniques for comparing the content of sentences or passages and computing the similarity between them. The most common similarity functions are the *inner product* and the *cosine function* applied on the term vectors of sentences. Another variation is considering *n*-gram matching instead of single-term overlap for the similarity measure.

These popular similarity functions are the basis for more sophisticated metrics, which, for instance, measure the novelty of the information when the summary already contains a number of sentences such as the *Maximal Marginal Relevance* metric (MMR) [Goldstein 1999]. One can incorporate all kinds of restrictions into the similarity functions, which take into account linguistic indications of content similarity. The matching can be restricted to words with corresponding part-of-speech, to words in a specific order, to identical phrases or phrases that share the same head word, or to words that occur in the same semantic role. Equally, the similarity criteria can be relaxed by allowing to match semantically related terms (e.g., synonyms) or even words belonging to the same entity class (e.g., organization, location).

Considering the large variety of natural language utterances expressing the same content, of text types, of author styles and of summary types, defining useful similarity criteria is difficult. Ideally, when examples of similar sentences in a training corpus are available, the weight or importance of a similarity criterion can be learned [Hatzivassiloglou et al., 1999].

5. MULTI-DOCUMENT SUMMARIZATION

A particular challenge is the summarization of the similarities and differences in the information content of several Web pages. Given the large number of potentially relevant Web pages that search engines retrieve *multi-document summarization* techniques are very valuable. Pages can be clustered according to the different meanings and contexts that the query terms represent, and for each cluster of pages a summary is generated. The technologies discussed in the previous sections are also applicable for multi-document summarization. However, multi-document summarization has extra requirements and problems.

When summarizing multiple documents or Web pages, the texts should be condensed in a very sizeable way. Consequently, selecting the most important content and eliminating redundancies are very important. This explains why anti-redundancy techniques (e.g., MMR) have become very popular and why first summarizing the single texts and than summarizing these summaries into one summary yields good results [Hardy et al. 2001, Angheluta et al. 2002].

It is known that in a set of texts, the vocabulary is much more diverse than within a single text, and problems of synonymy and ambiguity are more prominent. Consequently, when terms are replaced by standard synonym terms across multiple texts, the contexts of the texts in which the source and target terms occur should be similar. Other smaller problems might occur. For instance, the same word can have different spellings (e.g., proper name).

When making summaries of multiple pages, it is often useful to identify similarities and differences in content. This is a particularly difficult task, which did not receive a lot of attention yet. Simple heuristics such as preferring sentences for a summary that are extracted from many documents over sentences that only appear in a few pages can help. The importance of sentences that reflect the similarity of the documents in a set and of sentences that reflect the individual character of a document in the set can be modeled probabilistically with language modeling techniques [Kraaij et al. 2002]. In addition, the information extracted from different documents might be inconsistent or might represent different points of view. This can be compared by means of additional knowledge rules as illustrated by the SUMMONS system [McKeown & Radev 1999]. In this system, text fragments are compared for a change of perspective, contradictory statements, gaps in the information, additions, confirmations, and refinements of the information.

Compared to single-document summarization, it is more difficult to generate the right logical order of the sentences or the information extracted in multi-document summarization. For instance, the correct temporal order should be followed in the summary (e.g., a person can not first die and than become sick). The logical order also regards other rhetorical relationships such as a causal order. This problem did not receive a lot of attention yet. An exception is the *Majority Ordening Strategy* developed by Barzilay et al. [2001]. Their method finds the best possible ordering between sentences by grouping related sentences from different texts (themes), by relying on the majority of orderings between two sentences of different themes in the original texts, and by ordering sentences of the same theme close to each other in the summary.

A final challenging problem in multi-document summarization, which is not treated here, is *cross-language summarization*, i.e., constructing a summary in one language from multiple Web pages in different languages.

6. TEXT GENERATION

A final (often optional) task is to generate a summary that forms a complete, coherent, and comprehensible text, which is comparable to manually created abstracts. For instance, from a template that summarizes the information in a text, grammatically well-formed sentences are generated. *Text generation* has a lot of facets, including the selection of information to be communicated, text organization and the generation of linguistically well-formed surface expressions such as sentences and the lexical choice of the words employed. Making a summary with text generation techniques requires many additional knowledge sources that are of linguistic and of domain-specific nature [McKeown et al. 1999]. Summary generation imposes an additional constraint: The content has to fit into a minimum of text lines.

A simple form of *text editing* replaces often text generation, which includes the removal or resolution of dangling referents (e.g., resolution of anaphors based on the original text), the removal of rhetorical connectives and merging sentences with repetitious structure.

7. CONCLUSIONS: WHAT TECHNOLOGIES DO WE RECOMMEND?

Texts on the Web are very heterogeneous with regard to their content and language. They are volatile, change frequently, and are often redundant. Summarization systems have to cope with these limitations.

Information extraction techniques that rely on symbolic knowledge of the contextual patterns have proven their usefulness for automatic text summarization. When summarizing texts on the World Wide Web, it is useful that contextual patterns are learned automatically. Supervised learning from texts in which important information is annotated has its own shortcoming. A substantial manual effort is needed for the annotations and a large number of training examples is required in order to cover all variant expressions in natural language. External knowledge sources (such as WordNet for English) is very useful in order to learn variant contextual patterns.

A primary task in generic text summarization - including the summarization of Web pages - is the *detection of important content*. In query-biased and task-specific summarization, this problem is less severe, but it is still present. The most promising approaches rely on surface linguistic properties of the texts, such as the use of rhetorical structure and lexical cohesion. Other discourse markers (e.g., the length of a sentence, the position of a sentence in a paragraph) prove to be valuable in text summarization, but are less convenient in a heterogeneous environment such as the Web, because their use might depend on the style of the author, the text genre and the subject domain. The heterogeneity of Web texts also makes it very difficult to automatically learn a comprehensive set of good cues. In addition, representative example summaries of Web pages made by professional abstractors are hard to find.

Techniques that rely on lexical cohesion seem to be the most promising ones for summarizing texts on the World Wide Web. Techniques of building lexical chains are useful for languages that are backed with extensive term relationship thesauri, but care must be taken to correctly disambiguate the words of a text when building chains of related words. Simple topic segmentation algorithms that rely on content terms are also very useful for summarizing Web pages. Finally, clustering the content of one Web page or of multiple pages is especially convenient for selecting the most relevant pages that are retrieved by a search engine and for detecting redundancies in the texts. The challenge here is to define suitable similarity functions that correctly compute when sentences have a similar content and to build tools that extract a suitable description of each cluster. Lexical cohesion has not yet been fully exploited. In the context of text summarization, it is specifically interesting to investigate collocational patterns and thematic progression in subsequent sentences. Moreover, cohesive patterns that are useful for multi-document summarization should further be explored.

There are a number of aspects in text summarization that uptil now did not receive a lot of attention. Very little effort has been made to present a summary text that contains more *abstract concepts* than the ones found in the texts. This could be very useful for multi-document summarization, e.g., describing a cluster of related documents with concepts. Such as task is considered as text classification. Furthermore, we do not know of any substantial research that exploits the *linking structure* of Web pages in summarizing a set of pages.

Summarization of Web pages poses a lot of challenges. This chapter has discussed a number of techniques that are very valuable for summarizing single and multiple Web pages. Completely generic techniques that can be used across the different languages on the Web are the most practical ones, but they do not yield the best summaries. We therefore plead for using shallow natural language processing and taking advantage of surface linguistic features such as discourse structure and lexical cohesion to identify important content in texts. Statistical techniques such as clustering are useful for detecting similar content once important sentences have been selected and molded into correct representations.

REFERENCES

[Angheluta et al. 2002] R. Angheluta, M.-F. Moens & R. De Busser, "The Use of Topic Segmentation for Automatic Summarization", in *Proceedings of the Workshop on Automatic Summarization*, Philadelphia, PA, 2002, pp. 66-70.

[Barzilay & Elhadad 1999] R. Barzilay & M. Elhadad, "Using Lexical Chains for Text Summarization", in I. Mani & M.T. Maybury (Eds.), *Advances in Automatic Text Summarization*, Cambridge, MA, MIT Press, 1999, pp. 111-121.

[Barzilay et al. 2001] R. Barzilay, N. Elhadad & K. McKeown, "Sentence Ordering in Multi-document Summarization", in *Proceedings of the Human Language Technology (HLT) 2001 Conference*, San Diego, http://www.cs.columbia.edu/~regina/.

[Choi 2000] F. Choi, "Advances in Domain Independent Linear Text Segmentation", in *Proceedings of the ANLP/NAACL-00*, 2000, pp. 26-33.

[Craven et al. 2000] M. Craven, D. DiPasquo, D. Freitag, A. McCallum, T. Mitchell, K. Nigam & S. Slattery. "Learning to Construct Knowledge Bases from the World Wide Web", *Artificial Intelligence*, 118, 2000, pp. 69-113

[De Busser 2002] R. De Busser, R. Angheluta & M.-F. Moens, "Semantic Case Role Detection for Information Extraction", in *COLING 2002 - Proceedings of the Main Conference*, New Brunswick, ACL, 2002, pp. 1198-1202.

[DeJong, 1982] G. DeJong, "An Overview of the FRUMP System", in W.G. Lehnert & M.H. Ringle (Eds.), *Strategies for Natural Language Processing*, Hillsdale, Lawrence Erlbaum, 1982, pp. 149-176.

[DUC 2001] *Proceedings of the Document Understanding Conference*, 2001, http://www-nlpir.nist.gov/projects/duc/.

[DUC 2002] *Proceedings of the Document Understanding Conference*, 2002, http://www-nlpir.nist.gov/projects/duc/.

[Fillmore 1976] C.J. Fillmore, "Frame Semantics and the Nature of Language", in *Annals of the New York Academy of Sciences: Conference on the Origin and Development of Speech*, 280, 1976, New York, Academy of Sciences, pp. 20-32.

[Gildea & Jurafsky 2002] D. Gildea & D. Jurafsky, "Automatic Labeling of Semantic Roles", *Computational Linguistics*, 28 (3), 2002, pp. 245-288.

[Goldstein 1999] J. Goldstein, "Automatic Text Summarization of Multiple Documents", 1999, http://citeseer.nj.nec.com/goldstein99automatic.html.

[Hahn 1990] U. Hahn, "Topic Parsing: Accounting for Text Macro Structures in Full-text Analysis", *Information Processing and Management*, 26 (1), 1990, pp. 135-170.

[Halliday 1994] M.A.K. Halliday, *An Introduction to Functional Grammar*, London, Arnold, 1994.

[Harabagiu & Lăcătuşu 2002] S. Harabagiu & F. Lăcătuşu, "Generating Single and Multi-Document Summaries with GISTexter", in *Proceedings of the Workshop on Automatic Summarization*, Philadelphia, PA, 2002, pp. 30-38.

[Harabagiu & Maiorano 2000] S.M. Harabagiu & S.J. Maiorano, "Acquisition of Linguistic Patterns for Knowledge-based Information Extraction", in *Proceedings on the Second International Conference on Language Resources and Evaluation (LREC)*, Athens Greece, 2000, http://engr.smu.edu/~sanda/papers.html.

[Hardy et al. 2001] H. Hardy, N. Shimizu, T. Strzalkowski, L. Ting & X. Zhang, "Cross-Document Summarization by Concept Classification", in *Proceedings of the Document Understanding Conference 2001*, 2001, pp. 65-70.

[Hatzivassiloglou et al. 1999] V. Hatzivassiloglou, J. Klavans & E. Eskin, "Detecting Text Similarity over Short Passages: Exploring Linguistic Feature Combinations via Machine Learning", in *Proceedings of the Joint SIGDAT Conference on Empirical Methods in Natural Language Processing and Very Large Corpora (EMNLP/VLC-1999)*, College Park, MD, 1999, http://www.cs.huji.ac.il/~eeskin/papers/.

[Hearst 1997] M.A. Hearst, "TextTiling: Segmenting Text into Multi-paragraph Subtopic Passages", *Computational Linguistics*, 23 (1), 1997, pp. 33-64.

[Hirao et al. 2002] T. Hirao, Y. Sasaki, H. Isozaki & E. Maeda, "NTT's Text Summarization System for DUC-2002", in *Proceedings of the Workshop on Automatic Summarization*, Philadelphia, PA, 2002, pp. 104-107.

[Hobbs et al. 1996] J. Hobbs, D. Appelt, J. Bear, D. Israel, M. Kameyama, M. Stickel & M. Tyson, "FASTUS: A Cascaded Finite-state Transducer for Extracting Information from Natural-language Text", in E. Roche & Y. Schabes (Eds.), *Finite State Devices for Natural Language Processing*, MIT Press, Cambridge, MA, 1996, http://www.ai.sri.com/pubs/files/356.pdf.

[Hovy 1993] E.H. Hovy, "Automated discourse generation using discourse structure relations", *Artificial Intelligence*, 63, 1993, pp. 341-385.

[Kan et al. 1998] M.-Y. Kan, J.L. Klavans & K.R. McKeown, "Linear Segmentation and Segment Relevance", in *Proceedings of 6th International Workshop of Very Large Corpora* (WVLC-6), Montréal, Québec, Canada, 1998, pp. 197-205.

[Kaufman & Rousseeuw 1990] L. Kaufman & P.J. Rousseeuw, *Finding Groups in Data: An Introduction to Cluster Analysis*, New York, John Wiley & Sons, 1990.

[Kintsch & van Dijk 1978] W. Kintsch & T.A. van Dijk, "Toward a model of text comprehension and production", *Psychological Review*, 85 (5), 1978, pp. 363-394.

[Kraaij et al. 2002] W. Kraaij, M. Spitters & A. Hulth, "Headline Extraction Based on a Combination of Uni- and Multidocument Summarization Techniques", in *Proceedings of the ACL-2002 Post-Conference Workshop on Automatic Summarization*, 2002, pp. 95-104.

[Kupiec et al. 1995] J. Kupiec, J. Pedersen & F. Chen, "A Trainable Document Summarizer", in E.A. Fox, P. Ingwersen & R. Fidel (Eds.), *Proceedings of the 18th Annual International ACM SIGIR Conference on Research and Development in Information Retrieval*, New York, ACM, 1995, pp. 68-73.

[Lin & Hovy 2002] C.-Y. Lin & E. Hovy, "Neats in DUC 2002", in *Proceedings of the Workshop on Automatic Summarization*, Philadelphia, PA, 2002, pp. 99-103.

[Luhn 1958] H.P. Luhn, "The automatic creation of literature abstracts", *IBM Journal of Research and Development,* 2 (2), 1958, pp. 159-165.

[Mani & Maybury 1999] I. Mani & M.T. Maybury (Eds.), *Advances in Automatic Text Summarization,* Cambridge, MA, MIT Press, 1999.

[Mann & Thompson 1988] W.C. Mann & S.A. Thompson, " Rhetorical Structure Theory: Toward a Functional Theory of Text Organization", *Text,* 8 (3), 1988, pp. 243-281.

[Marcu 2000] D. Marcu, *The Theory and Practice of Discourse Parsing and Summarization,* Cambridge, MA, MIT Press, 2000.

[McKeown et al. 1999] K.R. McKeown, J.L. Klavans, V. Hatzivassiloglou, R. Barzilay & E. Eskin, "Towards Multi-document Summarization by Reformulation: Progress and Prospects", in *Proceedings of AAAI'99,* San Francisco, Morgan Kaufmann 1999, pp. 453-460

[McKeown & Radev 1999]. K. McKeown & D. Radev, "Generating Summaries of Multiple News Articles", in I. Mani & M.T. Maybury (Eds.), *Advances in Automatic Text Summarization,* Cambridge, MA, MIT Press, 1999, pp. 381-389.

[Moens 2000] M.-F. Moens, *Automatic Indexing and Abstracting of Document Texts (The Kluwer International Series on Information Retrieval* 6). Kluwer Academic Publishers, Boston, 2000.

[Moens & De Busser 2001] M.-F. Moens & R. De Busser, "Generic Topic Segmentation of Document Texts", in *Proceedings of the 24th Annual International ACM SIGIR Conference on Research and Development in Information Retrieval,* ACM, New York, 2001, pp. 418-419.

[Morris & Hirst 1991] J. Morris & G. Hirst, "Lexical Cohesion Computed by Thesaural Relations as an Indicator of the Structure of Text", *Computational Linguistics* 17 (1), 1991, pp. 21-43.

[Riloff 1996] E. Riloff, "An Empirical Study for Automated Dictionary Construction for Information Extraction in Three Domains", *Artificial Intelligence,* 85, 1996, pp. 101-134.

[Salton et al. 1994] G. Salton, J. Allan, C. Buckley & A. Singhal, "Automatic Analysis, Theme Generation, and Summarization of Machine-readable Texts", *Science,* 264, 1994, pp. 1421-1426.

[Schank 1972] R.C. Schank, "Conceptual Dependency: A Theory of Natural Language Understanding", *Cognitive Psychology* 3, 1972, pp. 552-631.

[Soderland 1999] S. Soderland, "Learning Information Extraction Rules for Semi-structured and Free Text", *Machine Learning,* 34 (1-3), 1999, pp. 233-272.

[Sparck Jones 1993] K. Sparck Jones, "What Might Be in a Summary?" in G. Knorz, J. Krause, & C. Womser-Hacker (Eds.), *Information Retrieval '93: Von der Modellierung zur Anwendung,* Konstanz, Universitätsverlag, 1993, pp. 9-26.

[Tombros & Sanderson 1998] A. Tombros & M. Sanderson, "Advantages of Query Biased Summaries in Information Retrieval", in W.B. Croft, A. Moffat, C.J. van Rijsbergen, R. Wilkinson & J. Zobel (Eds.), *Proceedings of the 21ˢᵗ Annual International ACM SIGIR Conference on Research and Development in Information Retrieval,* New York, ACM, 1998, pp. 2-10.

[van Halteren 2002] H. van Halteren, "Writing Style Recognition and Sentence Extraction", in *Proceedings of the Workshop on Automatic Summarization,* Philadelphia, PA, 2002, pp. 50-63.

Chapter 6

MODEL OF USER PROFILES AND PERSONALIZATION FOR WEB-BASED INFORMATION RETRIEVAL SYSTEM

Czesław Daniłowicz, Huy Cuong Nguyen, Ngoc Thanh Nguyen
Department of Information Systems, Wrocław University of Technology, str. Wyspiańskiego 27, 50-370 Wroclaw, Poland
Email: {danilowicz, cuong, thanh}@zsi.pwr.wroc.pl

Abstract: In this chapter a model of user profiles and personalization for web-based information retrieval system is presented. The authors show that this model satisfies postulates for intelligent information retrieval system formulated in Section 3.1. In particular, owing to this model a user should be satisfied with search results without necessity of understanding search methods.

Key words: user profile, personalization, information retrieval system

1.   INTRODUCTION

The classical model of information retrieval has been worked out by Boolean. In this model a document is represented by means of key words and a query – by means of a Boolean expression. In a system based on Boolean model for a given query documents belonging to the database are often divided into two groups, one of which consists of consistent and the other consists of inconsistent documents with the query. From the point of view of a user these groups consist of relevant and non-relevant documents, respectively. If an answer for given query includes only consistent documents then it often happens that this answer contains a lot of non-relevant documents and their elimination is practically impossible.

    In case of large databases and imprecise queries (such queries are most often formulated by users) answers include so many documents that users are not able to make an overview and choose relevant documents. Although it is possible to decrease the number of documents in an answer by introducing an additional term and joining it to the earlier Boolean query by operator AND, but such procedure is most often "forced" on a user and is not consistent with his (her) real information needs. Besides, although in this way one can achieve small document number in the new answer but generally many relevant documents may be lost. One can improve the quality of information retrieval by increasing the precision of document indexing [baeza_99],[salton_87],[danilowicz_83], for example by adding new terms to the dictionary with their classifications, hierarchies (thesaurus) etc. but it is not possible to move the disadvantages of information retrieval systems based on Boolean model.

Another aspect of Boolean information retrieval systems is that there is not any order of consistent documents in an answer. Therefore, determining document orders in answers is one of the main problems which have been investigated since the first computer information systems based on Boolean model arose [danilowicz_94]. Ordering documents is one of the most important problems in information retrieval field and has been considered in all later models: vector model, fuzzy model and probabilistic model [danilowicz_00], [danilowicz_01], [salton_87], .

New problems referring to information retrieval which require solutions are supplied by Internet, particularly by Web-based systems. An enormous number and very big diversity of documents (pages) in WWW resources are the biggest difficulties to which one often meets in retrieving information.

The most dominant element of the structure of WWW systems is so called *links* which point at pages connected with the page, on which they are placed. Using links one can perform retrieval process by moving from one page to the other. The advantage of this method is that it enables the full control of users. But the disadvantages are bigger. It is a very time-consuming method because after a few moves it often happens that the content of current page is in a little degree consistent with the information needs included in the first page. So it is needed to go back to the begin page. Besides a Web-based system is often a collection of disjoint sets which are connected with each other by links. Therefore it is practically impossible to hit these sets which include the major of relevant documents [danilowicz_00].

For facilitating retrieval in WWW resources many tools have been worked out. The most important tools are: *catalogs* or *subject directory catalogs*; *indexes* or *search engines indexes*. These tools are distinct information systems in the sense that each of them has its database (consisting of selected pages from the WWW resources) and an interface for serving users. For securing the largest information complexity catalogs and indexes offer to users a very large numbers of pages: from several millions to over 100 millions.

The information retrieval systems in which the orders of documents in answers reflect the degrees of their consistency with queries, are undoubtedly nearer to user awaiting than Boolean model based systems. However, these systems have in common a disadvantage which is "objectivity". The consequence of this feature is the fact that the valuation of document revelation is often agreed with the valuation of the consistency with queries. Thus the most relevant documents not always appear in the beginning of answers. Elimination of this disadvantage is impossible without taking into account the individual preferences of users in information retrieval processes. One of solutions of this problem is based on personalizing retrieval by introducing so called user profiles. Usually using this method one can take as the basic one of typical retrieval models and extends it by introducing user profile model. This chapter presents the description and analysis of this kind of models. The authors pay particular attention to these solutions which come from their original results.

2. USER PROFILE AS A REPRESENTATION OF USER PREFERENCES IN INFORMATION RETRIEVAL SYSTEMS

2.1 Personalized Information Systems

As mentioned above, the expansion of digital information and Internet has caused that the systems, which are built on basis of classic approaches, are not able to fulfill the user information needs. These systems often have to coupe with problems, which are connected with the specification and the size of the document database, such as:
– Users still have troubles in formulating their own information needs in chosen query language and the query modification mechanisms are still not perfect. In the consequence, using methods based on user feedback requires multiple repetitions of retrieval, which are very time-consuming.
– There is usually large difference between document rankings given by a search engine and the one that a user would like to receive. In other words, it is widely recognized that irrelevant documents are often among top items of the system recommendation.

- The system answer for a given query often contains hundreds items and only several of them are relevant. Checking all items is impossible to realize in practice.

Therefore, it is needed to build an information system model in which it is possible to realize the following tasks:

- During query formulation, the user does not have to realize all aspects of his (her) information needs, which should affect the relevance of system answers;
- The effectiveness of system should be independent from the user knowledge about the mechanism of the search engines, the organization of the database etc.;
- There is no necessity for query modification by the user in purpose to get better results;
- The document ranking in the system answer should be consistent with the user information needs, such that the most relevant documents should be in the beginning of the ranking. Owing to this, the user does not waste time for downloading and reading irrelevant documents, appearing in the end of the ranking.

In order to realize the above mentioned targets, an intelligent information system should suite to the end user, that means it should have information selectively followed to the user instead of making the user go after information. In particular, there is a need for personalizing the system to deliver really relevant information to the user. Since information preferences vary greatly across users, information systems must be highly personalized to serve the individual interests of the user.

The realization of systems satisfying the mentioned above requirements is rather very hard on the basis of conventional approaches in information retrieval. It is then necessary to define new tools within the intelligent information retrieval technology, which should be capable to make decisions on automatic query modification.

The capability of making decisions can be realized by introducing a software agent that determines preferences of an individual user and utilizes them in searching process. In personalized information retrieval systems, an information agent is a computer program, which should save information about user interests in the form of so called *user profiles*. A user profile is used to rank items in the document space not only according to a query formed by the user, but also referring to his preferences. User profiles should be created in an independent way such that the participation of users is minimal. There are different approaches for constructing user profiles, however, all of them are based on feedback model. In section 3.2 an overview of user modeling will be presented.

2.2   User Profile as a Representation of User Preference

A profile of a user is understood as the representation of his (her) information needs, which are assumed to be relatively stable in some period of time [danilowicz_92]. In traditional information retrieval systems, a user expresses his (her) temporary information needs only by means of queries, which often are insufficient to establish the relevance degree of documents in a database. Experiments have proved that different users may expect different answers for the same query, and the same user for the same query may expect different answers in different periods of time. This means that the information preferences (or profile) of a user should be changeable in retrieval processes [myaeng_90]. It implies that the abilities of creation and modification of user profiles should be the most important feature of an information agent.

The main task of an information agent is to establish profile structures and to learn algorithms that adapt to changes of user interests. The agent usually gathers information about user interests from implicit and explicit feedback: the user can either explicitly evaluate documents or the system can observe some implicit evidence about the user's preferences in each document. Implicit feedback is based on user behavior and is determined by observing the user's actions in using the system, usually without user's involvement. For examples, if a user selects an article, it can be inferred implicitly that in some degree he (she) is interested in the content of this article [stadnyk_92]. According to Liebeman [liebeman_95], one of the strongest behaviors is for the user to save a reference to a document, explicitly indicating interest. Following the link can indicate several things. First, the decision to follow a link can indicate interest in the topic of the link. However, because the user does not know what is referenced by the link at the time the decision to follow it has been made. If the user returns immediately without having either saved the target document, or followed further links, an indication of disinterest can be assumed. Liebeman [liebeman_95] built an information agent called Letizia, which assisted a user in Web browsing. Letizia monitors the user's browning behavior, develops a user profile, and searches for potentially interesting pages for recommendations. An important aspect of Letizia's judgment of "interest" in a document is that it is not trying to determine some measure of how interesting the document is in the abstract, but instead, a preference ordering of interest among a set of links. In [young_00] several factors (*time for reading, bookmark, following up*) are used with appropriate weights to count the total score of implicit feedback in a Web filtering system called WAIR. In their reinforcement learning approach, actions are defined as the picking up of terms that participate in estimating the relevance between documents and the profile. Information about the user can be then gathered from an interaction process, during which the user is given some queries, and his profile is built on the basis of his (her) answers [kok_88]. In [danilowicz_92] the author has introduced a method, which enables to construct the user profile from queries given to the system by the user. Chan [chan_99] has developed a non-invasive learning approach for constructing Web user profile, which monitors the user's access behavior and captures his (her) interest in a user profile.

The advantage of implicit feedback is that it makes the information agent more user-friendly. However, the ambiguity in the interpretation of user interests may bring about imprecise results in retrieval processes. For examples, an unread document could be treated by a search engine as irrelevant to the user profile, or the factor *"time of reading"* makes sense if only it is assumed that the user never takes a break during reading an article. Therefore, accurate interpretation of user interests through implicit feedback is a very difficult task and requires sophisticated tools for observing user behaviors.

On the contrary, although explicit feedback methods involve the user's cooperation, they are easier to realize in practice. The advantage of explicit feedback is that information from users is unambiguous and more confident than implicit feedback. Strong positive or negative feedback should result in a significant change of profiles, which makes profile more dynamic. If the feedback indicates that a user really does not like a piece of information from the system's answer, then similar information should not appear in future answers. In contrast, a high-rating document should make similar documents to be presented in top ranking among others documents. After analyzing the system's recommendation, the user indicates documents, which he (she) is interested in, and his (her) profile is constructed as an average of those documents [danilowicz_94] or by consensus methods [nguyennt_02]. Chen [chen_98] developed WebMate, an agent that helps users to effectively browse and search the Web. WebMate keeps tracks of user interests in different domains through multiple weighted vectors. The domains become a subject of information agents' learning automatically as users give positive feedback. In Chen's system, a new domain category is created for user feedback if the number of domains is still below its upper limit. If the number of domains has reached its maximum limit, the document to be learned should be used to modify the vector with the greatest similarity. McElligot and Sorensen in [mcelligot_94] developed a neural network approach employing two-layer connectionist model to filter news article on the Internet. In addition to keywords, their system uses the context in which it occurs to present a user profile. This system operates in two modes. The first mode consists of the learning phase, where sample documents are presented on input. The second mode consists of the comparison phase, where retrieved documents are filtered out to the user. Owing to this the system can enter the learning phase to learn additional interesting documents. Pazzani et al., Syskill and Webert [pazzani_97] ask the user to rank pages in a specific topic. Based on the content and ratings of pages, the system learns a user profile that predicts if pages are of interest to the user. They investigated a number of topics and a different user profile is learned for each topic. Pages are recommended from pre-selected web sites. Similar to Syskill & Webert, Balabanovic's Fab [balabanovic_97] requires the user to rank pages and learns a user profile based on the rankings and content of pages. However, Fab considers recommendation based on profiles of all the other users on the system (though Fab does not identify users of similar interests). Fab's collection agent performs an off-line best-first search of the web for interesting pages.

Although explicit feedback employs the user's involvements, it is widely used in personalized information systems as a confident information source for building a user profile. In this paper, we concentrate on the personalized information retrieval system, in which the representation of user preferences is defined and modified on base of user feedbacks, then it is used together with the user query to rank documents according to his information needs and preferences.

2.3   User Profile in Retrieval Processes

As the representation of user interests, a user profile may be used in different ways in retrieval processes. In personalized information systems there are four methods for using user profiles, which can be formulated as follows:
- Using user profiles for information filtering: the user does not need to give queries to the system, only system recommendations are regularly delivered to him (her). This approach is usually used in personalized news services or information filtering systems, where information sources are updated regularly.
- Modifying user queries: because a user query is more or less inaccurate and incomplete, it seems desirable to adjust the representation of the query by the representation of the profile. As a result, we have a new modified query that affects the retrieval process.
- Reordering the output: the user profile is treated as a post-filter to the system answer for the user query.
- Modeling with two focal points: a profile and a query can be considered as the same kind of entity directing in the retrieval process.

Widyantoro [widyantoro_99] has developed a model of information filtering system using so called a *personalized news agent*. The user profile is composed of different interest categories; each of them contains a positive descriptor, a negative descriptor and a long-term descriptor. The positive and negative descriptors maintain a feature vector learned from documents with positive and negative feedback respectively, while the long-term descriptor maintains the feature vector of documents obtained from both types of feedback. Each descriptor has also a weight to present the interest level of the corresponding descriptor's interest category. The information filtering process is performed as follows: Given a document feature vector, the system finds out the most relevant category in the user profile, and the document score is determined as the difference between positive similarity (similarity of the positive descriptor and the document vector) and negative similarity (similarity of the negative descriptor and the document vector). The greater a document score is, the better is the document. The set of first n documents with greatest scores will be given to the user as system's recommendation. The disadvantage of this approach is that the user can not use the query as the expression of his (her) temporary information need, which is not the same as user interests.

Myaeng and Korfhage [myaeng_90] have proposed some methods for modifying queries using user profiles in a vector space model. In their approach, the two original entities (query and profile) are no longer considered, and only the modified query affects the retrieval process. Different linear dependences of queries and profiles were studied for their simplicity and intuitive appeal.

Daniłowicz [danilowicz_94] has introduced a model based on Boolean information retrieval model, a well-known model for its simplicity and intuitive query forming. For given query the system's answer consists of a set of documents. A user profile is created on the basis of queries formed by the user or on the basis of documents marked by the user as relevant. The user profile is used to rank documents according to ascending order of distances from them to the profile.

In order to formulate a more complex and flexible shell in the vector space model, a concept of two focal points has been introduced [myaeng_94], where a user query and a user profile are used at the same time to judge documents. The document score is depended on two variables: the distance from the document to the query and the distance from the document to the user profile. A number of methods for combination of two distances have been investigated. Korfhage [korfhage_97] assumed that the judgment of a document may depend on more than two reference points, which need not be queries or profiles but other documents, key terms or other entities. Based on this assumption, a multiple reference point model has been presented.

In above mentioned approaches, the user profile is used in order to deliver to the user information with regards to his (her) preferences. However, in all models, the non-linear dependence between a query and a user profile, i.e. the dynamic relation between user stable interests and his (her) temporary information needs, has not been considered.

3. MODEL OF INFORMATION RETRIEVAL SYSTEM

In this section, we present a model of information retrieval system which is based on conventional vector space model. We show how to introduce a user profile into the system, which affects the retrieval process in the form of a retrieval function. We also propose an algorithm for profiles creation and modification. Some properties of the system are presented and discussed.

Let's make some assumptions for this model:

Assumption 1. The system's answer to a user query is an order of documents, in which the first document is suggested as the most relevant to the query and the user preferences. The user after examining the system's answer may accept it or make some changes, then send it back to the system as the user feedback.

Assumption 2. Every user feedback might (but needn't) have some influence on later retrieval processes of this user.

3.1. INFORMATION RETRIEVAL BASED ON VECTOR SPACE MODEL

The basic element of classic vector space model is n-dimensional vector space V_n. In a information retrieval system, documents and queries are represented by vectors such that the i-th component of a vector is a real number indicating the weight of i-th index term describing a document or a query. Vectors are usually described by expression $u=(w_{u1},w_{u2},....,w_{un})$ or $u=((u_1,w_{u1}), (u_2,w_{u2}),....,(u_n,w_{un}))$. For each pair $u,v \in V_n$, a distance function $d(u,v)$ or a similarity function $s(u,v)$ should be defined. In addition, in information retrieval system based on vector space model, for given query q and document x, a retrieval function $f(q,x)$ should be established.

The retrieval function in the vector space model is defined on basis of a similarity function or a distance function between vectors [wong_87]. Generally the dependence between similarity function and distance function can be expressed by the following formula:

$$s(u,v) = M_V - d(u,v), \text{ where } M_V = \underset{a,b \in V, a \neq b.}{\text{MAX}} d(a,b) \tag{1}$$

If the vector space V_n is normalized, then $M_V = 1$, so that $s(u,v) = 1 - d(u,v)$. Apart from it $f(q,d) = d(q,d)$. Conventional vector space model then can be presented as a triple $\langle X, Q, d \rangle$, where X is the set of documents, Q – set of queries and d – distance function.

One of the serious constraints of the classical vector space model is that the user queries, which are in the vector form, consist of the weighted terms. For an end-user of the system, constructing such a query would be far more difficult than for instance an intuitive Boolean query, in which index terms (keywords) are connected with logical operators such as AND, OR, NOT etc. Moreover, assigning a weight to a term is a task for experts. This problem is solved in the Generalized Vector Space Model [wong_87], In which the authors proposed an unique transformation of every Boolean query to a vector in the vector space. Owing to that, the user may send a Boolean query to an information retrieval system based on vector space model. In the model proposed in this article, we do not introduce the using of mentioned transformation, but we only assume that queries, like documents and user profiles, are described by vectors in the vector space.

In the purpose to integrate user profiles in retrieval processes, it seems desirable to introduce the extended vector space model, which allows introducing the set of user profiles P and the retrieval function f. The role of the retrieval function f is assigning a retrieval value to each document, which is depended on the relative positions of this document, given query and user profiles. We can present the extended vector space model for information retrieval as a quintuple $\langle X, Q, P, d, f \rangle$, where P is the set of users' profiles and f is the retrieval function.

3.2. USER PROFILE IN INFORMATION RETRIEVAL SYSTEM

In the model of information retrieval system proposed in [danilowicz_01] and in the later modifications [danilowicz_02], the user interest is represented by one user profile, which is constructed after the first user feedback, and is modified after the later ones. In this model, we propose that after every user feedback, one user piecemeal profile is constructed, and the user interest is represented by a sequence of all his piecemeal profiles. Therefore, if we denote by $p_{u_k}^i$ a piecemeal profile of user u_k after his i-th feedback, then after t-th feedback, the interest of user u_k in the system is represented by a sequence of his piecemeal profiles $(p_{u_k}^i, p_{u_k}^{ii}, \ldots, p_{u_k}^t)$. Hereafter we denote by t the number of feedbacks, which have been given by a user at the moment.

The information retrieval and user profile constructing process is described as following:

1. The user sends query q^1 to the information retrieval system.
2. In the beginning, $t=1$ (user does not have his own profile yet), system ranks documents according to ascending values of distance function $f^1(q^1,x_i) = d(q^1,x_i)$. As a result the order $o^1 = (x_1^1, x_2^1..., x_n^1)$ is displayed on the output as the system's answer for query q^1.
3. On base of the order o^1 proposed by the system, the user reorders documents according to his own justification in new order $o^{u^1} = (x_1^{u^1}, x_2^{u^1}..., x_n^{u^1})$ and sends it to the system as the user feedback.
4. The piecemeal profile p^1 is created from ranking o^{u^1} in the following way: If we ranks the documents set according to the distance from the documents to the profile p^1, we should get in result order o^{u^1}. In other words, for any pair of documents $x_i^{u^1}$ and $x_j^{u^1}$, if $x_i^{u^1} > x_j^{u^1}$ (i.e. $x_i^{u^1}$ precedes $x_j^{u^1}$) in the order o^{u^1} where $i<j$, then $d(p^1,x_i^{u^1}) \le d(p^1,x_j^{u^1})$. Generally, profile p^1 can be calculated as following:

$$p^1 = \frac{\sum_{i=1}^{n} \omega_i . x_i^{u^1}}{\sum_{i=1}^{n} \omega_i} \qquad (2)$$

where $\omega_1,...,\omega_n$ – parameters denoting parts of particular documents in profile vector, which are set by system to fulfill the following condition: $i<j \Rightarrow d(p',x_i^u) \le d(p',x_j^u)$.

We do not present the algorithm for the calculation of $\omega_1,...,\omega_n$ because of the limited size of this paper. The mechanism for the user profile creation is based on linear adding of vectors, which is used in algorithms worked out by Rocchio [chen_00] and other authors [chen_01] for updating retrieval queries.

5. In the second query session, let the user send the query q^2 to the system. This time the system ranks the document set on base of the query q^2 and the piecemeal profile p^1 according to the following function:

$$f^2(q^2, p^1, x_i) = \alpha_1.d(p^1, x_i) + \beta.d(q^2, x_i) \qquad (3)$$

where a_1, β $(a_1 < \beta)$ – parameters denoting parts of influences of the query and the user profile in the retrieval function. In result, the user should get the output order as the system's answer $o^2 = (x_1^2, x_2^2 ..., x_n^2)$.

6. The process of creating the piecemeal profile p^2 is identical to the process of creating the profile p^1 in steps 3 and 4.

7. By induction, at the moment t, the retrieval process is described as following: The user has already on his account t piecemeal profiles p^1, $p^2, ..., p^t$, and he sends the query q^{t+1} to the system. The system ranks the document set according to the retrieval function:

$$f'(q^{t+1}, p^1, p^2, ..., p^t, x_i) = \sum_{k=1}^{t} \alpha_k . d(p^k, x_i) + \beta . d(q^{t+1}, x_i) \qquad (4)$$

where $\alpha_1, \alpha_2, .., \alpha_t, \beta$ $(\alpha_1 < \alpha_2 < .. < \alpha_t; \sum_{i}^{t} \alpha_i < \beta)$ – parameters denoting parts of influences of particular uset profiles and the query in the retrieval function. In result, the system displays the answer order at the output $o^{t+1} = (x_1^{t+1}, x_2^{t+1} ..., x_n^{t+1})$. The user judges the answer and sends back the order $o^{u^{t+1}}$, from which the $(t+1)$-th piecemeal profile is created.

Example 1.

Given three documents represented by the following vectors:

x1={0.7; 0.5; 0.9}; x2={0.9; 0.5; 0.7}; x3={0.7; 0.9; 0.5};

Assume that after giving the first query q^1, a user ranks these items in order (x_1, x_2, x_3), that means the user is interested in the first term and third term, but the third term is a little more important, what explains why x_1 exceeds x_2 in the order. The system sets values of parameters $\omega_1 = 1$; $\omega_2 = 0.9$; $\omega_3 = 0$; therefore we can compute the profile as $p^1 = \{0.795; 0.500; 0.805\}$, which confirms the prediction about user preference.

Suppose that after some period of time, at t-th retrieval process, the user would rank documents in other order (x_2, x_3, x_1), what means his preference has changed to the first term and the second term (but the first term is the most important), his modified profile would be $p^t = \{0.805; 0.689; 0.605\}$, which represents his current interests.

The class of retrieval functions $f'(q^{t+1}, p^1, p^2, ..., p^t, x_i)$ can be an interesting subject for further researches on extended vector space model, because every function of this class possesses some characteristic properties expected from an intuitive retrieval function, such as:

Function f' takes into account all the feedbacks the user has done before, that means the document ranking proposed by the system considers not only the query but all the preferences that user showed in the past.

The later user feedback has more influence in the retrieval process, because of $\alpha_1 < \alpha_2 < .. < \alpha_t$.

In each time, the user query always has priority above all the piecemeal profile ($\sum \alpha_t < \beta$).

Accotding to the presented method for profile creation, in the feedback process, the user has to reorder whole set of documents, which seems to be impossible in practice. However, in such case, a acceptable ranking strategy can be employed [chen_01],[wong_88]: If a user has no preference of two documents, then he (she) is really not interested in how these documents should be ranked. The user can put a few documents in an order as a feedback portion, then the system should regard that these documents are most interesting for the user and they should be moved to the top of ranking in the reordering process (step 3). All other documents may remain in the same order as the system's recommendation.

Example 2.

Suppose that the documents set contains 100 documents $\{x_1, x_2,.., x_{100}\}$. On base of system's order $(x_1, x_2,.., x_{100})$, the user reorders according to his preference $x_4 > x_2 > x_{90} > x_8$. We assume that the following order: $(x_4, x_2, x_{90}, x_8, x_1, x_3, x_5, x_6, x_7, x_9, x_{10},.., x_{89}, x_{91},.., x_{99}, x_{100})$ is an acceptable ranking for this user, which can represent his preferences.

The following theorem shows that calculated user profile should represent long-term interests of its owner.

Suppose after t ($t \geq 1$) user feedbacks, the user has on his account t piecemeal profiles $p^1, p^2,.., p^t$, and a query q^{t+1} is given to the system. After studying the system answer o^{t+1}, the user corrects it and sends back a new order o''^{t+1}. On the basis of o''^{t+1}, the new piecemeal profile is created as p^{t+1}. Now the user does all things once again, that means he gives to the system the same query q^{t+1}, the system displays as an answer the order o^{t+2}. Let's denote by $x_i > x_j$ the fact that the document x_i precedes the document x_j in the order o^k. We prove the following theorem:

Theorem 1.

The following inequality is true

$$\forall i, j; i, j \leq n \in N: \quad x_i \overset{o^{t+1}}{>} x_j \ \wedge \ x_i \overset{o''^{t+1}}{>} x_j \ \Rightarrow \ x_i \overset{o''^{t+2}}{>} x_j. \tag{5}$$

Proof. We can write the implication in (5) in another way:

$$d(p'^{+1},x_i) \le d(p'^{+1},x_j) \wedge f'^{+1}(q'^{+1},p^1,...,p',x_i) \le f'^{+1}(q'^{+1},p^1,...,p',x_j) \Rightarrow$$

$$\Rightarrow f'^{+2}(q'^{+1},p^1,...,p',p'^{+1},x_i) \le f'^{+2}(q'^{+1},p^1,...,p',p'^{+1},x_j)$$

$$\leftrightarrow d(p'^{+1},x_i) \le d(p'^{+1},x_j)$$

$$\wedge \sum_{k=1}^{l} \alpha_k.d(p^k,x_i) + \beta.d(q'^{+1},x_i) \le \sum_{k=1}^{l} \alpha_k.d(p^k,x_j) + \beta.d(q'^{+1},x_j) \Rightarrow$$

$$\Rightarrow \sum_{k=1}^{l+1} \alpha_k.d(p^k,x_i) + \beta.d(q'^{+1},x_i) \le \sum_{k=1}^{l+1} \alpha_k.d(p^k,x_j) + \beta.d(q'^{+1},x_j)$$

$$\leftrightarrow d(p'^{+1},x_i) \le d(p'^{+1},x_j)$$

$$\wedge \sum_{k=1}^{l} \alpha_k.d(p^k,x_i) + \beta.d(q'^{+1},x_i) \le \sum_{k=1}^{l} \alpha_k.d(p^k,x_j) + \beta.d(q'^{+1},x_j) \Rightarrow$$

$$\Rightarrow \sum_{k=1}^{l} \alpha_k.d(p^k,x_i) + \beta.d(q'^{+1},x_i) + \alpha_{l+1}.d(p'^{+1},x_i) \le$$

$$\sum_{k=1}^{l} \alpha_k.d(p^k,x_j) + \beta.d(q'^{+1},x_j) + \alpha_{l+1}.d(p'^{+1},x_j).$$

The last implication is always true because the right side is a linear adding of two inequalities present in the left side, then it causes that (5) is always true.

Theorem 1 shows very important feature of this model, that is the system's answer should be changed to adapt the user preferences. The interpretation of this theorem is the following: If the user gives twice the same query and judges the same order of documents as his preferences, then at the second time, the system should propose better or the same answer than at the first time, that means the document order should be more similar to that one which the user expects. This is an important property of user profile, which is a necessary condition for correct representation of user preferences.

4. CONCLUSIONS

This paper is devoted to user profiles and personalization models with focus on applications in WWW information retrieval systems. The models we have presented in this work satisfy postulates for intelligent information retrieval system, which were formulated in Section 3.1. In particular, a user should be satisfied with search results without necessity of understanding search methods, document indexing or query modification rules etc., which are usually elements of knowledge of an expert in information retrieval domain. The effectiveness of the system is due to introducing users' profiles and exploring the retrieval functions, which aggregate in one formula the distance between queries and documents with the distance between profiles and documents. The future works should concern verification of retrieval functions and profile modifying methods in terms of maximizing the retrieval effectiveness.

REFERENCES

[baeza_99] Baeza-Yates R., Ribeiro-Neto B. *Modern Information Retrieval.* ACM Press, New York 1999.

[balabanovic_97] Balabanovic M., *An Adaptive Web Page Recommendation Service.* Proceedings of 1ˢᵗ International Conference on Autonomous Agents, 1997, 378-385.

[chan_99] Chan P.K., *A Non-invasive Learning Approach to Building Web User Profile.* KDD-99 Workshop on Web Usage Analysis and User Profiling, 1999.

[chen_98] Chen L., Sycara K., *Webmate - Personal Agent for Browsing and Searching.* In: Proceedings of the Second International Conference on Autonomous Agents, St. Paul, MN, May, ACM Press, New York (1998) 132-139.

[chen_00] Chen Z., Zhu B., *Some Formal Analysis of Rocchio's Similarity-Based Relevance Feedback Algorithm.* Lecture Notes in Computer Science 1969 (2000) 108-119.

[chen_01] Chen Z., *Multiplicative adaptive algorithms for user preference retrieval.* Proceedings of the Seventh Annual International Computing and Combinatorics Conference, Springer-Verlag (2001).

[danilowicz_83] Daniłowicz C., *Relative indexing on the basis of users' profiles.* Information Processing and Management 19 (3), 1983, 159-163.

[danilowicz_92] Daniłowicz C., *Models of Information Retrieval Systems with Special Regard to Users' Preferences.* Scientific Papers of the Main Library and Scientific Information Center of the Wrocław University of Technology No.6, Monographs No.3, Wrocław (1992).

[danilowicz_94] Daniłowicz C., *Modeling of User Preferences and Needs in Boolean Retrieval Systems.* Information Processing & Management, 30 (1994) 363-378.

[danilowicz_00] Daniłowicz, C., Baliński J., *Ordering documents using Markov chains.* Reports of Wrocław University of Technology, Department of Information Systems. No. 28, 2000. (in Polish).

[danilowicz_01] Daniłowicz C., Nguyen H.C., *User Profile in Information retrieval Systems.* Proceedings of the 23ʳᵈ International Scientific School ISAT 2001, PWr Press (2001) 117-124.

[danilowicz_02] Daniłowicz C., Nguyen H.C., *Using User Profiles in Intelligent Information Retrieval.* Proceedings of the ISMIS 2002 Conference, LNAI 2366, Springer (2002) 223-231.

[kok_88] Kok A.J., Botman A.M., *Retrieval Based on User Behavior.* In: Proceedings of the 11ᵗʰ ACM Annual International Conference SIGIR, France (1988) 343-357.

[korfhage_97] Korfhage R.R., *Information Storage and Retrieval.* Wiley computer Publishing, 1997.

[lieberman_95] Lieberman H., *Letizia: An Agent that Assists Web Browsing.* Proceedings of International Joint Conference on Artificial Intelligence, Montreal, 1995.

[mcelligot_94] McElligot M., Sorensen H., *An Evolutionary Connectionist Approach to Personal Information Filtering*. In: Proceeding of the Fourth Irish Neural Network Conference, Dublin, Ireland (1994) 141-146.

[myaeng_90] Myaeng S.H., Korfhage R.R., *Integration of User Profiles: Models and Experiments in Information Retrieval*. Information Processing & Management 26 (1990) 719-738.

[nguyennt_02] Nguyen N.T., *Consensus System for Conflict Solving in Distributed Systems*. Information Sciences 147 (2002) 91-122.

[pazzani_97] Pazzani M., Billsus D., *Learning and Revising User Profile: The Identification of Interesting Web Sites*. Machine Learning 27, 1997 313-331.

[salton_87] Salton G., *Historical note: The past thirty years in information retrieval*. Journal of the American Society for Information Science, 38(5), 1987, 375-380.

[stadnyk_92] Stadnyk I., Kass R.: Modeling Users' Interests in Information Filters. Communications of the ACM 35 (1992) 49-50

[widyantoro_99] Widyantoro D.H.: Dynamic Modeling and Learning User Profile in Personal News Agent. Master Thesis, Dept. of Computer Science, Texas A&M University (1999).

[willett_85] Willett P., *An algorithm for the calculation of exact term discrimination values*. Information Processing and Management 21, 3 (1985), 225-232.

[wong_87] Wong S.K.M., Ziarko W., *On Modeling of Information Retrieval Concepts in Vector Spaces*. ACM Transactions on Database Systems, 12 (1987) 299-321.

[wong_88] Wong S.K.M., Yao Y.Y., Bollmann P., *Linear structures in information retrieval*. Proceedings of the 1988 ACM-SIGIR Conference on Information Retrieval (1988) 219-232.

[young_00] Young W.S., Byoung T.Z.: A Reinforcement Learning Agent for Personalized Information Filtering. In: Proceedings of the 2000 ACM International Conference on Intelligent User Interfaces (2000) 248-251.

Chapter 7

AN OPEN, DECENTRALISED ARCHITECTURE FOR SEARCHING FOR, AND PUBLISHING, INFORMATION IN DISTRIBUTED SYSTEMS

Harald Häuschen
Department of Information Technology, University of Zuerich, haeusche@ifi.unizh.ch

Abstract: The range of information that can be obtained via the Internet continues to grow significantly. New sources of information are being added daily. This information is available in various formats (amongst others HTML, XML, PDF, catalogues, and industry-specific databases). Even with the help of search engines, it can still be impossible or very difficult to find much of the information. In addition, different programs are usually required to access the information. This article presents a distributed search architecture, known as "DiSA", which enables information from a variety of existing sources to be published in a structured manner, and in such a way that they can be found quickly. In essence, the solution is based on an approach which links the globally distributed information sources into a search architecture by means of a simple standardised interface. The solution is decentralised and to a large extent neutral in terms of language, and it facilitates both standardised and individualised information, product and service offerings. The architecture is simple enough for existing information sources to be linked in very quickly.

Keywords: Distributed Search, Architecture, Publishing Information, E -Commerce

1.   INTRODUCTION

1.1   Sources of Information

The range of information that can be obtained via the Internet continues to grow significantly. Every day, new servers, databases, and applications are being added. An immense variety of information is available. However, much of this information is never found and many offers remain untouched. The reasons for this are easy to list:

- Despite the wide range of search engines which is available, there is no longer anyone with an overview of what is available from where, and in what format.
- The information is stored in a variety of formats (HTML, XML, PDF, catalogues, and industry-specific databases, amongst others).
- Different programs are usually required to access the information.
- It is easy to spend hours, even days, searching in vain, even though the enquiry appears to be straightforward and many seemingly relevant pages are found.
- Despite the existence of standards such as HTML, XML, and RDF, the information pages themselves are not standardized.
- Information is often provided in only one language.
- Co-operation between the suppliers of different platforms is almost non-existent.
- A standardized method for the automation of enterprise-independent processes (e.g. search, evaluate, compare etc.) is only achievable with great difficulty.
- Information providers invest more time in designing the navigation and the presentation (multimedia presentations, advertising etc.) than in the specific structure of their information [12].

The above statements apply not only to the Internet, but frequently also to Intranets. Here, too, large quantities of information can be found and users complain about the lack of an overview and a lack of transparency when accessing the various sources of information.

1.2   Search for Information

The search for information, and its organisation, have been topics for discussion for some time now. The research is broad and the results of this research are being applied to a variety of applications and systems.

- In the Internet, search engines are especially popular. These maintain lists of millions of search terms, and the associated links to relevant Internet pages, in one or more databases. Users can find the information they require by using appropriate expressions or else with the help of categorised listings. A search is often based on a simple text string and does not support any structured refinements.
- Meta search engines often have no database of their own, relying instead on various other search engines to find the information and collecting together the results.

- In the Business-to-Business sector, catalogues and industry-specific databases have become particularly predominant. The advantage of these is that the information can be stored and searched in a structured manner. This means, however, that a standardisation process must first take place and a common basis established in respect of access to different catalogues.
- In some industries, companies have collaborated in order to agree a standard by which information can be retrieved. The so-called "Information Resource Locators" can be helpful in finding the required information.
- In areas where a search is very time-consuming, and access to information is difficult, various information brokers have become established. For a fee, these will search for, and deliver, the required information.
- Search Agents are autonomous individual software components which, when required by a user to do so, are able to search for information in the Internet, automatically, and in a user-oriented manner, thereby carrying out specific actions.
- In certain environments, such as astronomy and physics, where exceptionally large quantities of information are accumulated and processed, a specific architecture is being prepared within the international "Grid" project, in order to deal with the flood of information [6].

Each of these systems has advantages and disadvantages. The one common feature is that each of them can only find a small percentage of the available information, and that the information that is being sought cannot be defined with sufficient accuracy because too few criteria with respect to how it is structured are available [14].

Thus many suggestions from groups and conferences with an interest in Information Retrieval are concerned with the need to find, and to define, a standard organisational structure for data. Similar activities are also being undertaken within individual enterprises. Organisations are making data warehouses available, in which all the important data that accrue within the organisation can be found. But one should not strive too hard for this, because standardisation is difficult to achieve and converting information sources into new formats demands significant resources. Neither is it always economic.

RDF [11] and other new description facilities for describing knowledge pieces [4] constitute a newly emerging standard for metadata that is about to turn the World Wide Web into a machine-understandable knowledge base, called semantic web [1]. Thus, it might turn up as a natural choice for a widely-useable ontology description language [13]. However, RDF defines and describes Information Objects but it is not possible to publish individually information. However, the semantic web can profit from the proposed new search architecture.

Thus there is a broad selection of tools, applications and systems available to the user, but these cannot be used simultaneously in a uniform and straightforward manner when searching for information.

1.3   Summary

Until now, there have been no satisfactory solutions available, nor are there any in prospect, and this in spite of the fact that searching for and locating information are core activities for the Information Society; that the costs of searching and the quality of the results are becoming increasingly relevant; and that at present, searching involves considerable interactive effort.

This paper therefore proposes a different approach. The sources of information and descriptions can be left exactly as they are. Only the search methods and the structure of the information are made publicly accessible. This is achieved by means of a simple architecture that consists of middleware, a few interface APIs and some common search services. No proposals are made in respect of new database search techniques, new standards for the storage of information, new data management systems or replacements for existing information formats.

2.   PREREQUISITES

2.1   Examples

The general requirements for a search facility are self-evident. It must be possible to find information (e.g.: about products and services) quickly, on a global or regional basis, and in accordance with individual requirements. Furthermore, the user would like to receive just a few results, albeit precisely in accordance with his/her enquiry. This is illustrated by the following examples.

– Example 1: there are products (e.g. CDs, books) that one can search for on a global basis and which can be purchased anywhere. The product frequently has a clear specification (there is only one edition, one quality and only one producer). It would therefore be sufficient for the user to formulate his/her wishes and then for the appropriate prices/sources/offers of supply to be displayed on his/her desktop.

- Example 2: if one is looking for a piece of classical music but on no particular CD, then already the enquiry is no longer so clearly defined and the person searching must use be able to enter differentiated search terms (e.g.: recording, conductor, soloist and orchestra) and expect a detailed overview. In this example, the user must be able to enter and receive more information, such as further pieces on the CD, audio samples, etc. It could also be useful to provide him with an indication that a new product is in preparation.
- Example 3: there are products (e.g. hotels) that one can search for globally, but only use locally. The price and the quality comparisons are limited to the locality. In addition, the availability of rooms on a particular date and the suitability of the facilities for individual requirements are key factors.
- Example 4: there are products (e.g. clothing, computers) that must first be adapted / configured. In this example, it is important that the supplier receives as much information as possible about the user, in order to be able to restrict the number of proposals that can be sent to him.

As these simple examples demonstrate, from the user's point of view, an enquiry can be simple and clear, and ideally the answer will reflect the context of the enquiry. It can also be useful to have information about the person who is searching (preferences, location, etc.), in order to provide a tailored response.

2.2 Requirements

It follows that a new strategy can only be successful if the following criteria, which reflect the user's viewpoint, are taken into consideration:
- Simplicity: operation must be intuitive and appropriate to the user.
- Culture / language independent: whether the user is searching in English, German or French, the language used must have no significant influence on the results, unless the user explicitly wants this.
- Multimedia: the individual preparation and presentation of the information is of great importance.
- Personalisable: the user must be able to set up and manage his/her own profiles, which contain his/her preferences and conditions.
- Anonymity: the person searching should be able to remain anonymous.
- Reusable: search filters and results should be re-usable.
- Security: availability, integrity and confidentiality must be guaranteed.
- Automatable: search processes must be capable of being automated.

From the information provider's viewpoint, attention should be paid to the following:

- Integration: the overhead required to connect existing systems should not be excessive.
- Standards: existing standards should be integrated and made use of (HTML, SQL, XML).
- Scalability: information and processes should be capable of being distributed as necessary.
- Transactions: the overall quality of the transaction must be high.
- Synchronicity: it must be possible to process asynchronous as well as synchronous enquiries.
- Access: Pull and Push principles must be supported.
- Flexibility: it must be possible to manage the versions of Information Objects.

The architecture as suggested attempts to fulfil these requirements. A central objective is to provide the user with just the information that he/she is actually looking for, rather than with as many hits and as much information as possible. The focus is therefore on the individual user, with his/her particular preferences and behaviour patterns, which are to be taken into account for every enquiry.

3.   DISTRIBUTED SEARCH ARCHITECTURE

3.1   Architecture

The "DiSA" (Distributed Search Architecture) defines an architecture in support of the search for and publishing of information (*Figure 7-1*). The architecture includes:
- Applications and services, which simplify organisation and searching,
- Basic services and libraries for networks and interfaces, and
- Middleware, for the purpose of linking services with each other in a platform-independent manner.

The architecture is designed to support any required expansion.

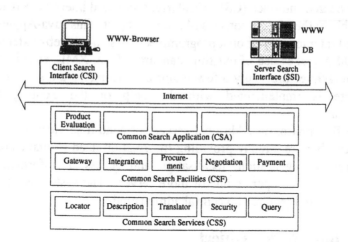

Figure 7-1. DiSA architecture

- Common Search Services (CSS): the CSS services form the basis of the architecture. They serve to describe information, products and services, to transform information, to implement security requirements, to localise information and to define complex enquiries. The user does not come into contact with these services. They are designed to simplify the creation of complex services.
- Common Search Facilities (CSF): the main purpose of the facilities is to make those services available that have applications in e/m-Business. These include gateways to other search systems, integration services, mediation services and payment services.
- Common Search Application (CSA): by building on the basic services and facilities, it is possible to define typical applications. An example could be an application in the field of market research. Here, information is collected, filtered, formatted and supplied, in exchange for a payment. The user of such a service receives detailed information in response to his/her enquiry, for which he/she is prepared to pay. For example: an enquiry for the "number of Internet users" does not simply deliver a sequence of WWW pages on which this term can be found, but precise facts concerning this question.
- Server Search Interface (SSI): in order that the existing sources of information are linked in and can make use of the services that are provided, and can also make them available, a standard interface is established. This makes all the functions available, so that the CSS, CSF and CSA services can be used.

- Client Search Interface (CSI): similarly, a standard interface is made available to the user. It consists of a Java-Applet. This Java-Applet can be used interactively or on a programmed basis and thereby extended.

The DiSA makes use of existing standards (Java, XML, etc.) in order to define the architecture. Only a few minor enhancements are suggested. The architecture is implemented with the help of the existing Internet infrastructure.

In the first phase, no additional servers or central services are required. The servers that are already providing information need to implement three basic services: registration, localisation and access of information (see below). Anyone can operate one or more servers. The system is completely de-centralised and requires no central administration.

3.2   Information Object

At the centre of the architecture is the Information Object. It describes a class of information with similar characteristics. For example: the class of hotels, with the number of rooms and categories (amongst others) being attributes. The user can call up the Information Objects from a registration server and thereby formulate his/her enquiries. The Information Object is fully described by means of XML [15]. The definition of an Information Object is highly flexible and leaves room for considerable creative freedom. The following is already predefined:

- Attributes, which are possessed by every Information Object of this type.
- Information Objects can consist of other Information Objects.
- Versions of Information Objects.
- Rules about how an Information Object can be transformed into the next highest version. This happens by means of XSLT.
- Hints about the translation of attributes and information.
- Description of the layout.
- Information about the originator.

An Information Object which can be used for a simple CD search enquiry is shown in *Figure 7-2*.

```
<Information-Object >
    <Name>CD</Name>
    <Version>1.0</Version>
    <Create>
        <Name>Harald Häuschen</Name>
        <Mail>haeuschen@haeuschen.ch</Mail>
    </Create>
    <Standard>
        <Attribute> <Name>Gruppe</Name>
            <Typ>string</Typ><Size>50</Size></Attribute>
        <Attribute><Name>Titel</Name>
            <Typ>string</Typ></Attribute>
        <Attribute ><Name>Preis</Name>
            <Typ>float</Typ></Attribute></Standard>
    <Dictionary>
        <us>"Gruppe" "Group";"Titel" "Title"</us>
        <uk><like>us</like></uk></Dictionary>
</Information-Object>
```

Figure 7-2. Example of the definition of an Information Object

3.3   Registration

Before a user can make use of an Information Object, it must be registered by one or more servers that offer registration services (*Figure 7-3*). This registration is performed by the transmission of the name of Information Object, URI, and version number. The URI guarantees that a definition is stored and managed externally. As long as the object with this Name, version number, and URI does not exist, the server adds the object definition to its database and responds with a hash value as confirmation. If such an object with the same version number and URI already exists, then the definition of this object is provided by way of a reply and no entry is made. The supplier now has the opportunity to provide another version number and at the same time to describe how the existing similar objects can be transformed into his/her object. In this way there is an assurance that changes and different definitions can be implemented at any time but that the person searching still only needs to complete one Information Object in order to find the information required.

Servers that offer a registration service distribute Information Objects to other servers that are also known to offer a registration service (replication).

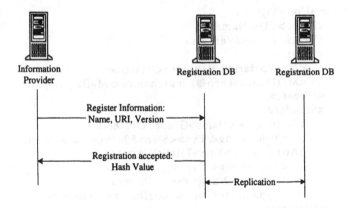

Figure 7-3. Registration service from the viewpoint of the information provider

3.4   Localisation

For each Information Object, it is necessary on the one hand to record where sources of information are to be found which contain relevant data, and on the other, the information providers must declare which Information Objects they support. For this purpose, a server is used which offers a localisation service. The information provider sends his/her address (URI) and the hash value of the supported Information Object to the server (*Figure 7-4*). The server registers this and sends the data on to further localisation services of which it is aware (replication).

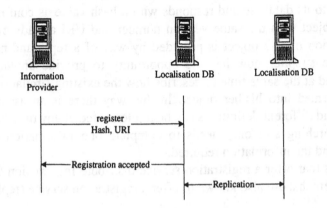

Figure 7-4. Localisation service from the viewpoint of the information provider

3.5   Searching for Information

If the user now wishes to find some specific information on the Internet, then he/she will first look for a matching Information Object (*Figure 7-5*). Next, he/she inserts the desired values into the enquiry fields. Now the localisation service is asked which servers support the desired Information Object. The named servers then receive the enquiry. At this point, the user can determine for himself which servers should be included or excluded from the enquiry. The enquiries can be simultaneously transmitted and processed. All the answers from all of the servers are collected together in a common list.

The response from an information server can include any amount of information that is appropriate to the enquiry. At this point, the response can be enhanced dynamically with additional features. In this way, it is always possible for the information provider to deliver more information than is required.

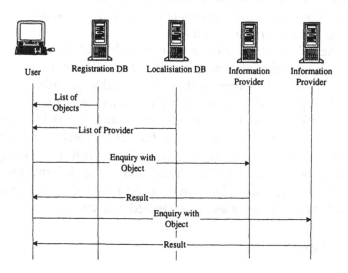

Figure 7-5. Process of searching for information from the viewpoint of the person looking for it

3.6   Evaluation

It is apparent that one cannot force information providers to supply only the data that has been requested. Furthermore, the context of the enquiry is not always known. For that reason, the evaluation of the responses is always carried out at the client computer. As a first step, the client interface filters the information supplied once according to the nature of the enquiry, and in so doing takes into account the personal profile of the user. The user can now filter, sort and compare all the responses in any way that he/she wishes, without the need for further communication with the servers. The enquiry will only need to be resent if he/she changes the enquiry.

3.7   Profile

The client interface interprets the user's input criteria. These could include, amongst other things, priorities concerning servers that are to be interrogated, filter criteria and sort criteria. This input data is stored locally. The user can review his/her profile at any time and change it as necessary. But he/she can also forward parts of his/her profile so that information providers can evaluate this in order to provide tailored responses.

All enquiries can be saved by the client. In this way it is not necessary for the user to reformulate his/her enquiry every time. Alternatively, he/she can very quickly modify an existing enquiry. With the help of his/her profile, he/she can now obtain useful results in less time. It is also possible to create simple time / results oriented enquiries.

With the help of the Profile and the re-usable Information Objects, it is now possible to implement a simple push service. The user now has a means of leaving his/her instructions with the information provider so that he/she can receive regular information on a push basis. For example: the user is looking for information about scientific literature in the field of robotics. At the same time he/she has a preference for publications in German and for those that deal with autonomous robots. Since such articles appear only infrequently, he/she sends his/her Profile and his/her Information Object to the information providers. These in turn can now supply the enquirer with individually tailored responses at any desired time interval.

3.8   Agents

Until now it has always been assumed that the user is permanently online and that he/she receives and evaluates all the information himself. This is not always the case. It would be useful therefore if one could search for information in mobile situations, when one cannot always be online. For example: an external worker flies from Zurich to Denver. Before departing, he/she starts an enquiry for a hotel. After he/she has landed, he/she would like to see the results of his/her search. This can be achieved by one of two means. Either he/she can leave his/her enquiry with a broker, who takes over the search on his/her behalf (see below), or he/she uses a software agent for this purpose. An agent is a software component that independently carries out a service on behalf of the originator [8]. Further features of agents are:

- Autonomous: decides for itself about how it runs.
- Goal oriented: works towards a pre-determined goal, adapting its behaviour to the achievement of this goal.
- Reactive: can react to external events and adapt its behaviour accordingly.
- Intelligent: makes decisions.
- Mobile: can migrate between different systems.

The Agent needs to have the Information Object and certain parts of the user's Profile. With these, the Agent is in a position to migrate into the network and to collect the information. Agents can be designed in such a way as to execute complex queries efficiently. For this to be possible, there need to be some suppliers or brokers that provide an agent platform.

3.9 Information Brokers

As previously mentioned, the user is not always able or willing to undertake the search or the evaluation himself. Thus an opportunity opens up for brokers to obtain specific information on behalf of third parties. This activity is easy to support with the existing architecture. The broker simply has to declare which Information Objects he/she is able to offer. Then when he/she receives an enquiry, he/she himself can start an appropriate search and evaluate the responses. For a set fee the results can then be made available to the person who needs the information. All the necessary services are already provided for in the architecture.

4. AN INFORMATION NETWORK IS CREATED

So far, our description has been mainly confined to the essential technical issues concerning the construction of such a search network. What now follows will show how, over time, people and companies will work together to form associations. The process is similar to information distribution process in a peer-to-peer environment.

4.1 Step-by-step Construction

As already revealed, there is no central administration for the system. As a result, there is no requirement for initial standards or committees to define the structure of Information Objects or infrastructures. Rather, the idea is far more that, as a first step, existing information providers supply the registration, localisation and access services for their own Information Objects. At the same time, they can have newly created Information Objects sent to them from other registration servers. Even this first step represents a major step forward for the information seekers and information brokers, because information can now be searched for within many servers in a structured manner. Initially, however, the person searching for the information must make the server addresses known to the system himself. This will however only be necessary for a short while, as history has shown that when a new service is successfully introduced, central servers are soon established.

4.2   Islands of Information

Of course, not all information providers will be keen to co-operate in establishing a network with others, as there may be a fear of creating a certain transparency and therefore also of promoting unwanted competition. Nevertheless, over time, small and large independent information associations will be created. Within such associations there will also be a willingness to agree how Information Objects for specific types of information should be structured. Then, as already mentioned, the providers will not have to change everything; rather, they will be able to bring their definition in line with the generally acknowledged format through the use of a transformation description. The effort required for the transformation is small.

Over time, the islands of information will merge, since the information seeker will in any case be able to interrogate each of the islands independently.

4.3   Conflicts

As there is no central point for establishing the definition of an information type (e.g.: Hotel Offer) it can happen that there are different definitions for one and the same information type. A conflict can therefore arise as a result of the automatic distribution of definitions. There is a plan for an automatic conflict resolution to address this problem. In effect, each registration server can accept any definition, because every definition with name, URI, and version is unique. But the originators are informed by e-mail after the same name is registered with different URI or version number. They then have the opportunity either to describe a transformation (*Figure 7-6*), or to get in touch with each other in order to agree on a particular version. In this way, over time, a certain uniformity will emerge. This can already be seen in the existing XML definitions for certain industry branches as published in virtual catalogues.

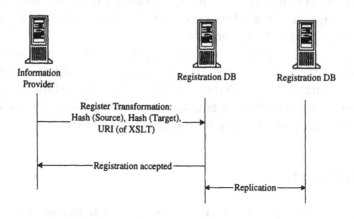

Figure 7-6. Process of defining transformations for two Information Objects

5. SUMMARY

The system presented here does not replace existing systems, neither does it threaten them. Rather, it shows how existing information databases can be linked with each other in a simple manner. In this way, the system integrates and simplifies the work of both the information seeker and the information provider. No suggestions are made within this architecture as to how information is to be structured and organised in order that they can be efficiently administered. The architecture is deliberately restricted to the management of Information Objects and their localisation in the Internet. In addition, the information seeker benefits from special extra support to help him evaluate the information for himself, locally, according to his/her own preferences. The proposed architecture strengthens the efforts to homogenize the search process in a heterogeneous infrastructure.

6. OUTLOOK

It is apparent that the architecture proposed here can be used not just for the search for information, but above all also in e/mCommerce for the rapid location of products and services. The advantage here is that the supplier only needs to link his/her product catalogue into the search system rather than having to develop a complete shop. In this way, many SMEs that would not otherwise be in a position to open a virtual shop of adequate quality are still able to publish details of their products and services. Furthermore, there are always situations where a virtual shopping experience on especially impressive pages is not at all necessary, the speedy execution of the desired action being of far greater importance.

Electronic shopping could therefore acquire a whole new dimension. Instead of visiting virtual shops, the user would formulate an enquiry and shortly afterwards receive individual offers on his/her desktop. These offers would be from different organisations, would reflect the individual requirements of the user but still be as detailed as necessary.

REFERENCES

1. Berners-Lee T., Hendler J., Lassila O.: The Semantic Web. In: Scientific American, May 2001.
2. Binder W: Design and Implementation of the JSEAL2 Mobile Agent Kernel.In: Proceedings of the 6th ECOOP Workshop on Mobile Object Systems, Cannes, June 2000.
3. Foster I., Kesselmann C.: The Grid: Blueprint for a New Computing Infrastructure. Morgan Kaufmann Publisher San Francisco, 1999.
4. Gil Y., Ratnakar V.: Markup Languages: Comparison and Examples - XML Schema, RDF Schema and DAML+OIL, Trellis Project, 2001.
5. Guarina N.: Formal Ontology and Information Systems. In: Proceedings of FOIS'98, Trenta, June 1998.
6. Moore R.W. et al.: Data-Intensive Computing. In: The Grid: Blueprint for a New Computing Infrastructure (Ed.: Foster I., Kesselmann C.), Morgan Kaufmann Publisher San Francisco, 1999, S. 105-130.
7. Mucha et al.: Standards im E-Business. Bundesministerium für Wirtschaft, 2002.
8. Nwana H.S., Ndumu D.T.: A Brief Introduction to Software Agent Technology. In: Agent Technology: Foundation, Application, and Markets (Ed.: Jennings N.R., Wooldrigde M.J.), Springer-Verlag Berlin Heidelberg New York, 1998, S. 29-48.
9. Oram A.: Peer-to-peer: Hernessing the power of disruptive technologies. O'Reilly, 2001.
10. Patel-Schneider P. F., Siméon J.: Building the Semantic Web on XML. In: Proceeding of The Semantic Web ISWC 2002, First International Semantic Web Conference, Ed.: Horrocks I., Hendler J., Sardinia, June 2002.
11. Manola F., Miller E.: RDF Primer. W3C Working Draft, Jan. 2003, available at http://www.w3.org/TR/rdf-primer.
12. Schneider B., Lederbogen K.: Navigationskonzepte für Internet Anwendungen. In: Information Management and Consulting, Bd. 14, 1999, S. 103-109.
13. Staab St., Erdmann M., Maedche A., Decker St.: An Extensible Approach for Modeling Ontologies in RDF(S), ECDL 2000, Workshop on the Semantic Web, 2000
14. Stanoevska-Slabeva K., Hombrecher A.: Vor- und Nachteile verschiedener Suchmethoden und das Beispiel eines Attributbasierten Suchsystems, HSG St. Gallen, 1998.
15. Bray T., Paoli J., et al.: Extensible Markup Language (XML) 1.0 (Second Edition). W3C Recommendation, 2000, available at http://www.w3.org/TR/REC-xml.

Chapter 8

INFORMATION RETRIEVAL UNDER CONSTRICTED BANDWIDTH
Information Extraction

Hakikur Rahman
SDNP

Abstract: Information filtering systems are designed to examine a stream of dynamically generated documents and display only those which are relevant to a user's interests. Information retrieval systems, by contrast, are designed to respond once to each query based on the contents of a relatively static set of contents.

Most significant distinction between filtering and retrieval is the duration over which the users' need to settled in for desire of information must be remodeled for rapid access. Users may have many interests, and the lifetime of a particular interest is widely variable in relatively dislocated environments.

In an interactive information retrieval architecture, intelligent agents can be utilized to route queries and update documents to relative locations. Between the "user-agents" (the interactive queries) and the "back-ends" (the information provider), a kernel is needed to be proactive, adaptive, wide spread, heterogeneous, dynamic and able to manage immensely huge interactivities, and to be able to react either gradually or abruptly.

On the other hand, information filtering systems must operate over relatively long time scales, and hence, the ability to observe, model and adapt to their persistence, variation and interaction of interests are important. Some progress has already been made in this direction. Utilizing query recall and modification methods of many information retrieval systems, some explicitly continuing information interests have been identified including the modifications that those interests have undergone.

Although the structure of the resulting search space is becoming more complex, machine learning techniques should obtain benefit from information systems related issues of constraints observed in actual demands/ interests. The richer vocabulary of concepts about those interests can also be used to enhance the quality of user participation in the filter design processes. Several ongoing processes in these aspects have been reviewed with follow-ups and suggestions to improve algorithms by accommodating provision of intelligent dynamic updates.

Key words: interactive information retrieval

1. BACKGROUND

There may be four types of information need- visceral, conscious, formalized, and compromised [1]. In recent years research in automatic mediation of access to networked information has exploded in many aspects. Information filtering and retrieval techniques with emphasis on performance evaluation for very large collection of contents with multilingual contexts including images and graphics under restricted bandwidth has been made the main focus of interest of this chapter.

With advances in information infrastructures, importance of information retrieval from large databases with increased storage capacity is becoming popular. Though cost of bandwidth is decreasing continuously, but affordability is still restricted only in specialized regions, thus leading to constricted bandwidth in most part of the globe. Apart from storage capacity and bandwidth, there arises a need to establish an efficient information extraction system. This can be achieved through fair use of algorithms, computationally efficient search engines and intelligent user interfaces.

In information retrieval, user's queries may vary significantly during a single session, while the collection of information to be searched is relatively static. In information filtering, a user's interests are relatively static, but those interests are matched against a dynamic information stream [2].

Majority of retrieval systems depends on exact pattern matching of terms in queries, with terms in text requiring queries ranging from simple Boolean expressions to complex pattern matching expressions, utilizing proximity operators, nested expressions, feedback compensations, dynamic updates, etc. in addition to effective user interfaces. There has been improvement in retrieval systems with input of natural language statements, with sentences, or phrases, and retrieval through a ranked output of relevance. However, there need some expression of interest for dynamically changing documents with multilingual approach.

Information retrieval is used expansively to include information filtering as selective information dissemination or data mining, while information filtering is associated with passive collection of information. Data mining can be referred as a technique of availing vast quantities of information that are available simultaneously.

Information retrieval is sometimes used expansively to include information filtering, an alternate form of "Selective Dissemination of Information", while information filtering is associated with passive collection of information. In information filtering system, the system's representation of the information need is commonly referred to as a "profile." Because the profile fills the same role as what is commonly called a "query" in information retrieval and database systems, sometimes the term "query" is used instead of "profile" in information filtering as well. [3]

Content-based filtering allows the user to operate independently by utilizing information deriving from document contents. Collaborative filtering associates critical mass of users with overlapping interests. Criteria of a text selection process is shown in the following table:

Table 8-1. Text selection process

Content	Selection	
	Relevant	Not Relevant
Relevant	Found	Wrong Content
Not Relevant	Missed Partially	Rejected Rightaway
Redundant	Missed Completely	Rejected Exponentially

A few terms can be defined from the above table:

Extraction = (Found / (Found + Wrong Content))
Feedback = (Found / (Found + Missed Partially))
Rejection = (Wrong Content / (Wrong Content + Rejected Rightaway))

2. INTRODUCTION

Information filtering systems are typically designed to sort through large volumes of dynamically generated information and present the user with sources of information that are likely to satisfy the user's requirement. Rather than simply removing unwanted information, information filtering actually gives the ability to reorganize the information space [4].

The information contents can be text, audio, video, images, or moving objects. Information filtering can be termed as a personal intermediary service. Like a library, a text filtering system can collect information from multiple sources and produce in some useful format to the user. Figure 8-1 illustrates a sequence diagram for typical information retrieval and filtering system.

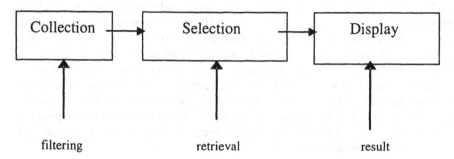

Figure 8-1. Information retrieval and filtering in a sequence diagram.

Database retrieval, information extraction, and alerting techniques are the three benefits of advance text filtering researches. In text filtering systems, term-frequency or inverse document frequency can not be defined clearly, but, estimates based on sampling earlier documents can produce acceptable inverse document frequency values for domains where term usage patterns are relatively stable. The objective is to automate the process of examining documents by computing comparisons between the representations of the information need and the representations of the contents. The automated process can be termed as successful when it appears to produce outputs similar to those by human interaction of the documents with actual information requirement. A text filtering model is portrayed in the figure below:

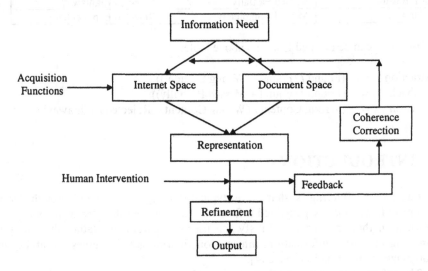

Figure 8-2. Text filtering model

A traditional information retrieval system can be used to perform an information filtering process by repeatedly accumulating newly arrived documents for a short period, issuing an unchanging query against those documents and then flushing the unselected documents. Dynamic information can be collected actively, passively or combination of two. In integrated information filtering system, some aspects of user model design are common to the two modules. The commonality may provide a basis for sharing information about user needs across the inter-module interface.

By allowing the human to adaptively choose to terminate their information seeking activity based in part on the observed density of useful documents, human and machine synergistically achieve better performance than either could achieve alone [3]. In interactive applications an imperfectly ranked output can be superior to an imperfectly selected set of matching documents. Figure 8-3 offers the oversight of an information processing system.

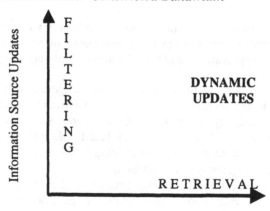

Information Requirement Updates

Figure 8-3. Information acquiring processes for information requisition

Information systems that represent the information content of an object on the basis of feedback provided by users of that object are now often referred to as recommender systems [5]. Recommender systems are associated with information filtering; a term used to describe so-called "push" services designed to find new information on pre-specified topics. Information filtering systems can be classified into two forms: content-based and collaborative. Recommender systems can be contrasted to "content-based" systems, where information content is represented on the basis of the terms that they contain.

Implicit feedback can be referred to set an indirect relationship to the user's assessment of the usefulness of any individual document. Kim et al. [6] conducted experiments with two user groups, examining how observations of reading time and printing behavior for journal articles might be used jointly to build a better user model than could be built using either source alone. Oard, D.W. [7] produces a framework for modeling the content of information objects.

3. METHODOLOGIES

Collaborative filtering systems are relatively more flexible in dynamic domain as participating users draw different inferences from the same observations as if they do not share a common set of objectives. On the other hand, collaborative filtering systems using the static strategy are more context based and locally available for interpreting observations available at other points in the network.

In small-scale applications, it may be possible to perform all computations on a single server. But scaling these techniques to a regional / global network will clearly call for a distributed implementation in which the context needed to support inference exists partially at one server and partially at another depending on the relevance factor. In such cases, it might be worth considering a hybrid approach in which some preliminary interpretation is performed locally when the observation is made, additional changes might be made at other points in the network (to conserve bandwidth through aggregation), and then the ultimate inference is performed in the user's server.

Due to the increased use of the Internet, the staggering volume of available material has led to the scenario where users have difficulty in attaining relevant information. The difficulty in attaining relevant information has been termed as information overload. With respect to web-based information, the problem of information overload stems from a few underlying factors:

- huge explosion in quantity of information;
- dynamic nature of information (information available on the web is of a transient nature with information published, modified and removed in a completely adhoc manner); and
- relatively unstructured nature of the web (information is added to the web in an unstructured manner with no adherence to a consistent structure).

Several methods on information extraction are highlighted in this section:

3.1 Collaborative Filtering

Collaborative filtering uses a database about user preferences to predict additional products a new user may prefer. These techniques are based on correlation coefficients, vector-based similarity calculations and statistical Bayesian methods. Sometimes, estimating the probability that a document can satisfy the information need at a particular sequence can be represented as a profile by availing probabilistic approach. This method generates a ranked order documents rather than extracting exact information requirement in a particular session.

To develop this probability approach, term frequency information is treated as an observation, and the distribution of the binary event "document matches profile" conditioned by that observation is computed [8]

Automated search is based on a query identifying intrinsic features of the items sought. Search for text documents uses queries containing words that are resided in the returned documents to match a query describing the content with the individual items for presenting to the user with a ranked list of suggestions. These systems do not use any information regarding the actual content, but are rather based on usage or preference patterns of other users by building on the assumption that a good way to find interesting content is to find other people who have similar interest and recommend titles of similar interests.

A simple approach can be to study the existing users (human users with desire of information collection), attempt to provide the user with desirable contents, measure them relating to their satisfaction, and constricting the gap of desire and expectation gradually. This may involve explicit feedback on the interaction during extraction of information. However, to reduce complicacies in assembling sufficiently large number of participants, implicit feedback can be introduced with inclusion of a measuring factor for better choice of the set of dynamically dependent variables.

Collaborative filtering systems are often characterized by their operation as implicit or explicit selection. Explicit selection refers to a user consciously expressing the preference for an item, in a ranked list. Implicit selection refers to interpreting user selection to impute a preference and regardless the type of data availability, the algorithm needed to take care of missing data. Users will choose the items that have been accessed, and are likely to access in future.

By interpretation through positive preferences and making different assumption about nature of missing data, performance of collaborative filtering algorithms can be improved. Memory-based algorithms operate over the entire database for making predictions. While Model-based collaborative filtering, uses database to estimate a model used for prediction.

Collaborative filtering techniques guided by humans are always preferred than other systems as the user usually does not be overloaded with undesired information. These techniques can be improved substantially by including some automated algorithm in association of latest computing facilities and advanced programming languages. Content-based systems can also assist in reducing volume of information at manageable level. Hence, content-based collaborative filtering could be a homogeneous integrated system of filtering with more reliability and simplicity. However, providing services to a critical mass of enquirer may impose expensive operational procedures; like enormous memory size, recursive algorithm, complicated procedures, etc.

Sometimes there arise some difficulties in constructing suitable indicators for measuring the effectiveness of the collaborative filtering systems in comparison to content-based filtering techniques. Collaborative filtering techniques has advantage over the content-based filtering as it is non-reliant on normative judgments for document relevance and does not suppress the individual variations.

Adoptive algorithms can be implemented in this system of filtering as the learning rates and variability in learning behavior across large heterogeneous populations can be investigated with mass collections of simulated users with diversified redundancies in information requirements. A total solution can be thought of with collaborative filtering including web-based information through easy-to-use, effective, high-precision filtering.

The collaborative filtering module may also be used to increase the user's productivity while browsing the web, by advising query modifications and by re-ordering results based on collaborative recommendations. The browsing agent (profiler) can create databases of user-ratings. These ratings can be gathered in restrained manner with almost no explicit user interventions.

3.2 Vector similarity

Similarity between two documents is often measured by treating each document as a vector of word frequencies and computing the cosine of the angle formed by the two frequency vectors [9]. Under this algorithm, selection is based on positive preference and there is no negative selection. Unselected items receive a zero rank.

Vector space method can be improved substantially by transforming the raw term-frequency vector in ways, which amplify the influence of words which occur often in a document but rarely in the whole document. The term-frequency can be related as tfidf$_{ik}$ = Occurrences of term i in document k*log$_2$ (Number of documents/Number

of documents with term i)

where,   tfidf   =   term frequency inverse document frequency,
           i   =   term, and
           k   =   document.

3.3 Bayesian Network model

Effectiveness of a collaborative filtering algorithm depends on manner in which recommendations will be presented to the user. Collaborative filtering applications present the user with an ordered list of recommended items and utilizes two methodologies; one appropriate for individual item-to-item recommendations, and other appropriate for ranked lists.

Predictive accuracy is probably the most important aspect in gauging the efficacy of a collaborative filtering algorithm, including size of model, sampling, and runtime performance. There are possibilities to construct a Bayesian inference net as cosine of the angle between two vectors, the vector space method can be interpreted as a special case of probabilistic method.

Sometimes, both exact match and ranked output techniques can be introduced to produce multiple-valued result. A linux based server can filter specific contents from the mailserver and then rank the remaining documents in order of preference accepted by the demand of the user. Combination of these techniques in a ranked output text filtering can specify a landing point in the document space. Eventually, multiple rank orderings can be accommodated to produce richer display by combining multiple viewpoints, terming it as a visual information retrieval interface.

3.4 Retrieving information from a database

Using a library catalog to find the title of a book can be a good example of database access process and database systems can be applied to information filtering processes. Information extraction process is similar to database access for providing information to the user. It is differentiated from the database access process by the nature of the sources from which the information is being obtained.

In database access process information is obtained from some type of database, while in information extraction the information is less well structured. Information extraction techniques are sometimes found in the selection module of a text filtering process, assisting to represent texts in a way that facilitates selection. [3].

3.5 Browsing

Browsing is another information seeking process and can be performed on either static or dynamic information sources. Browsing is similar to both information filtering and information retrieval. Searching the Web in browsing mode is related to relatively static content and searching for online newspapers is more dynamic.

However, in browsing the users' interests remain broader than in information filtering and retrieval processes, which need to be specified at narrow spaces.

3.6 Search engines

Search engines works as black boxes by accepting query strings, and returns ranked lists of URLs. Typically a search engine comprises of three parts: a crawler, an index, and search software. The crawler is a program that visits each site on the web, and examines the contents of the pages on that site. It pays special attention to the text in a page's title, as well as the first few paragraphs of text in the page. The crawler places the words found in the title and initial text into the second part of the search engine: the index. The index is a catalog of pages/keywords for the entire web. Finally, when the user submits a query to the search engine, the search software searches the index for pages with keywords that match the user's input. The search software then generates a ranked output based on the location and frequency of the keywords in the page.

This strategy has two common flaws. Firstly, the data for any site in the engine's index is not continuously updated; it is updated only when a crawler revisits the site. Therefore, the index may contain out of date information for a site, or more logically, it may contain data for pages that no longer exist. Secondly, the keyword match performed by the search software does not take into account the context in which the keywords are used in a particular page.

3.7 Web caching

The architecture of a Web caching mesh is highly dependent on the network topology and creates cost factors for the installation and expansion of the network.

Caching is used in two forms in the Web. The first is a local cache, which is built into the Web browser. A Web client with caching stores not only the contents currently displayed in browser windows, but also documents requested in the past. The local cache is also used for (temporary) storage of the browsing history.

There are two forms of client caches: persistent and non-persistent. A persistent client cache retains its documents between invocations of the Web browser. Netscape uses persistent cache. A non-persistent client cache (used in Mosaic) reallocates any memory or disk used for caching when the user quits the browser.

The second form of caching is in the network used by the Web. The cache is located on a machine on the path from multiple clients to multiple servers. A caching proxy can be on a machine serving as a Web client or an HTTP server. The caching proxy caches URLs generated by multiple clients. It is possible to use caching proxies hierarchically, so that caching proxies cache URLs from other caching proxies.

3.8 Web rings

Web rings are simple and effective method of reducing time and effort in locating desired information interest on the web. Linear Rings are comprises of a series of pages, all with a common theme, that are linked to one another. Generated Rings have one central location for the ring and those who want to attach simply put a line of code into their page with a JavaScript, or some other type of interface. While dynamically updated web rings are becoming popular with the advance of distributed databases, widely available resource materials on the web, and increasing processing power.

3.9 Dynamic approach

Depending on relevance factor within an extracting algorithm a repetition argument can be introduced with optimum caching. This technique can improve intelligence accumulation of content during repeated search at congested bandwidth and can also be used in locating contents in dynamically distributed databases. A very sketchy algorithm is provided below:

Algorithm-   "word search, w1"
          first lookup table =>   n contents
          first screen   =>   10 contents
          first hit (fh)   => refined search (rs)=>(n-x $_{argument}$) content
          where, argument =   "w1" + rs f(fh)

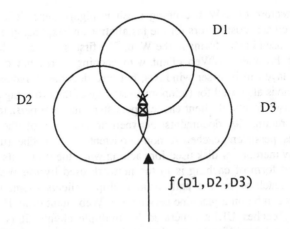

Figure 8-4. Commonality function in distributed databases.

As f(D1,D2,D3) extends, caching increases, and searching time may reduce with content refinement as shown in Figure 8-4.

Automated search depends on query identifying intrinsic features of items sought. Search for text documents uses queries containing words inside the returned documents. Major content retrieval methodologies adopt a similarity score to match queries describing the content with individual items to be presented in a ranked list. Multiple query searching among distributed databases should generate a common element of content which can be utilized in similar future searches. Dynamically accumulated caching reduces searching time on the web by increasing relevant contents at the proxy of requesting server.

4. PREFERENCES

Several advantages are included below to recognize advances in collaborative filtering methodologies with other instruments to support:

- Collaborative filtering automates the informal cohesive system where one person recommends material to another, by recognizing shared interests and recommending material based on shared interests.
- Evolution of Relational Database Management Systems (RDBMS) has given the facilities of easier image retrieval, relational data modeling and multilingual searching ability.
- Ranked output text retrieval system offers further improvement by adjusting system parameters to maximize the match between system's document order and user's desire order with relevance feedback and dynamic update.
- Latent Semantic Indexing (LSI) has been applied to improve access to available textual materials in comparison to other available word-matching techniques.
- Mobile Agents for Web Searching (MAWS) technique utilizes mobile agents to reduce the volume of irrelevant links returned by a typical search engine.

5. DRAWBACKS

Due to increased processing power and storage capacity for images, audio and video have became important in addition to text and multilingual contents that lead to complicated algorithms for retrieval processes and aggravating errors, like typographical, optical character recognition, wrong choice of words, wrong image calibration, etc.

Immense amount of retrieved information may often mislead, frustrate and complicates the user/ the inquirer. The situation aggravates further with constricted bandwidth.

6. CONCLUSIONS

Networked information retrieval systems are needed to be language-independent, corruption-tolerant, automatically-generated, with scalable meta-data for use in making routing decisions, able to update dynamically through relevant feedback. Monolingual information retrieval systems sometimes produce useful results due to fortuitous matches between words in different languages, and proper names that are rendered in the same way in different languages.

Cross-language information retrieval, an imperative for access to information written in many languages is becoming increasingly demanding, which applies detection of relevant documents in one natural language using queries expressed in another. Earlier cross-language information retrieval evaluations have been hampered by inadequate test collections, but the Text REtrieval Conference (TREC-6) has developed the first large-scale multi-language collection that is designed specifically to support cross-language information retrieval experiments [10].

With meta-search capabilities, multiple search engines can be treated as a single entity and with improved filtering processes volume of useless data may be reduced drastically. Perhaps at some point in the near future, there will be free of the crushing weight of information overload that burdens the information seeker.

REFERENCES

[1] Robert S. Taylor, *The process of asking questions, American Documentation*, 13(4):391-396, October 1962.

[2] Nicholas DeClaris (Moderator), *Information Filtering and Retrieval: Overview, Issues and Directions*, Basis for a Panel Discussion, 1997.

[3] Douglas W. Oard & Gary Marchionini, *A Conceptual Framework for Text Filtering*, EE-TR-96-25, May 1996.

[4] Curt Stevens, *Knowledge-based Assistance for Accessing Large, Poorly Structured Information Spaces*, PhD Thesis, University of Colorado, Department of Computer Science, Boulder, 1972.

[5] CACM, 1997, *Special Issue on Recommender Systems, Communications of the ACM*, 40(3), March 1997.

[6] Kim et al, 2000, Kim, J., Oard, D.W., & Romanik, K. (2000), *User modeling for information access based on implicit feedback*, Technical Report: HCIL-TR-2000-11/UMIACS-TR-2000-29/CS-TR-4136, University of Maryland.

[7] Oard, D.W. & Kim, J., (1997), *Modeling Information Content using Observable Behavior*, Institute for Advanced Computer Studies, University of Maryland.

[8] Howard Turtle & W. Bruce Croft, *Inference networks for document retrieval, Proceedings of the 13th International Conference on Research and Development in Information Retrieval*, pages 1-24, ACM SIGIR, September 1990.

[9] Salton, G., & McGill, M., (1983). *Introduction to Modern Information Retrieval*. McGraw-Hill, New York.

[10] Oard, D.W., *A Comparison Study of Query and Document Translation for Cross-Language Information Retrieval*, College of Library and Information Services, University of Maryland.

Chapter 9

MULTILINGUAL WWW
Modern Multilingual and Cross-lingual Information Access Technologies

Feiyu Xu
DFKI LT Lab, Saarbrücken, Germany

Abstract: In this chapter, we describe the state of the art cross-lingual and multilingual strategies and their related areas. In particular, we show a WWW-based information system called MIETTA, which allows uniform and multilingual access to heterogeneous data sources in the tourism domain. The design of the search engine is based on a new cross-lingual framework. The framework integrates a cross-lingual retrieval strategy with natural language techniques: information extraction and multilingual generation. The combination of information extraction and multilingual generation enables on the one hand, multilingual presentation of the database content, and on the other hand, free text cross-lingual information retrieval of the structured data entries. We will demonstrate that the framework is useful for domain specific and multilingual applications and provides strategies for the future question answering systems, which should be able to deal with heterogeneous data sources in a multilingual environment.

Key words: multilingual and crosslingual information access technologies, information extraction/retrieval, multilingual generation, internet

1. INTRODUCTION

World Wide Web (WWW) plays more and more an important role as a global knowledge base and an international comfortable communication, information and business network. Above all, huge amount of business-to-business and business-to-consumer transactions will take place in the near future online and internationally. Although the major online transactions are still in USA and North America, it is predicated that the Internet Marketing will soon spread to Asia and European nations.

The growth of Non-English users and content on the web in the recent years is impressive. Various approaches are developed to estimate its multilingual characteristics [Nunberg, 1996; Crystal, 1997; Grefenstette and Nioche, 2000; Grefenstette, 2001; Xu, 2000a].

In 1998, the statistical data provided by an OCLC Web Characterization Project[1] and GVU's WWW user surveys[2] showed that English had a dominant role on both the content and the user sites: GVU's WWW user surveys found out that 92.2% users were primary English-speakers, while OCLC reported that English occupied more than 70% of the web content (Table 9-1):

Table 9-1: content distribution in 1998

Language	%	Language	%
English	71	Portuguese	2
German	7	Dutch	1
Japanse	4	Italian	1
French	3	Chinese	1
Spanish	3	Korean	1

According to the newest data in 2002 provided by Global Internet Statistics[3], the English-speaking users are only 36.5%, while the Non-English users play now a dominant role with 63.5%, in which the European languages contain 35.5% and Chinese-speaking people are 10.8% and Japanese 9.7% (more information can be found in Table 9-2).

Table 9-2: distribution of users

Language	%	Language	%
English	36.5	Italian	3.8
Chinese	10.8	French	3.5
Japanese	9.7	Portuguese	3.0
Spanish	7.2	Russian	2.9
German	6.7	Dutch	2.0

At the same time, the content distribution has changed too: the Asian languages Japanese and Chinese grow at faster space than other languages (see Table 9-3), although English still plays a dominant role.

Table 3: content distribution in 2002

Language	%	Language	%
English	68.4	Spanish	2.4
Japanese	5.9	Russian	1.9
German	5.8	Italian	1.6
Chinese	3.9	Portuguese	3.4
French	3.0	Korean	1.3

---

[1] http://www.w3.org/1998/11/05/WC-workshop/Papers/oneill.htm
[2] http://www.cc.gatech.edu/gvu/user_surveys/survey-1998-10/graphs/general/q11.htm
[3] http://global-reach.biz/globstats/index.php3

Parallel to the multilingual development on the web, there are a series of conferences and competitions organized by governments, research institutions and industries in the last few years to push idea exchange and further development of the multilingual and cross-lingual information access technologies.

Text Retrieval Conference[4] (TREC), sponsored by American government institutions NIST and DARPA, was started in 1992 as part of the TIPSTER Text program. Its purpose was to support research within the information retrieval community including government, industry and academia from all over of the world. TREC develops tasks and provides training corpora and performs evaluation. In TREC-5, Multilingual Information Retrieval task in TREC was integrated, focusing on information retrieval in non-English languages Spanish and Chinese. Cross-Lingual Information Retrieval (CIIR) was a new task since TREC-6. In contrast to the multilingual task, CIIR allows users to send a query in a different language than the document language [Schäuble and Sheridan, 1997].

EU is faced with the multilingual problem in her everyday life. Therefore, EU has provided and is going to provide big funding for research and development of multilingual and cross-lingual information access technologies. Human Language Technologies (HLT) RTD[5] is part of the *Information Society Technologies* (IST) program founded by EU, addressing on multilingual communication and cross-lingual information management

http://www.ee.umd.edu/medlab/mlir/conferences.html has collected a list of conferences related to multilingual IR and CLIR. In addition to the main conferences like TREC, SIGIR, ACL, there have been also special workshops for Asian languages like IRAL and for Arabic language within the ACL context active in the past years.

[Weikum, 2002] assumed that the current Web contains about 1 Billion (10^9) documents, while the so-called "deep Web" can potentially have 500 Billion documents containing databases and other digital libraries and archives behind Intranet and other portals. Most information retrieval approaches deal either with unstructured textual information like web documents [Braschler and Schäuble, 1999; Davis and Ogden, 1997; Erbach et al., 1997; Oard, 1999a; Oard, 1999b; Busemann, 1998] or with structured information like relational database information [Weikum, 2002]. Systems capable of handling both kinds of information are rare. However, in real world applications, information providers in many domains, often have to provide access to heterogeneous data sources. Systems suitable of dealing with them are very important for future Web [Burger et al., 2001; Lin, 2002].

---

[4] http://trec.nist.gov/
[5] http://www.hltcentral.org/page-842.0.shtml

The framework described here has been developed within the project MIETTA (Multilingual Information Extraction for Tourism and Travel Assistance), a project in the Language Engineering Sector of the Telematics Application Program of the European Commission[6] [Xu et al., 2000b].

The tourism domain is by its very nature multilingual [Tschanz and Klein, 1996], and its information is typically maintained as web documents or as database information by institutions like national or regional tourism offices.

The main objective of MIETTA is to facilitate multilingual information access in a number of languages (English, Finnish, French, German, Italian) to the tourist information provided by three different geographical regions: the German federal state of Saarland, the Finnish region around Turku and the Italian city of Rome.

In many applications, structured database information is accessed by means of forms, unstructured information through free text retrieval. In our approach, we attempt to overcome such correlations by making it completely transparent to the user whether they are searching in a database or a document collection, leaving it open to them what kind of query they formulate. Free text queries, form-based queries and their combination can yield documents and structured database information. The retrieved results are presented in a uniform textual representation in the user language.

We use automatic document translation to handle web documents, because it allows the user to access the content without knowledge of the document language and provides good retrieval performance within our limited domain. At the same time, multilingual access to the database information is supported by the combination of information extraction (IE) and multilingual generation (MG). IE identifies domain-relevant templates from unstructured texts stored in databases and normalizes them in a language-independent format, while MG produces natural language descriptions from templates. As a result, the database content becomes multilingually available for the result presentation, and natural language descriptions can be handled in the same way as web documents, namely, we can apply the advanced free text retrieval methods to them. The challenge of the approach is to merge the technologies of CLIR and natural language processing to achieve the following goals:

---

[6] The MIETTA consortium consists of following institutions: The technical partners are DFKI (Deutsches Forschungszentrum für künstliche Intelligenz), CELI (Centro per l'Elaborazione del Linguaggio e dell'Informazione), Unidata S.p.A., the University of Helsinki and Politecnico di Torin. The user partners are the city of Rome, Staatskanzlei des Saarlandes and city of Turku and Turku TourRing.

- Provide full access to all information independent of the language in which the information was originally encoded and independent of the query language;
- Provide transparent natural language access to structured database information;
- Provide hybrid and flexible query options to enable users to obtain maximally precise information.

In the following sections we describe how these goals can be achieved in the MIETTA framework. The chapter is organized as follows: Section 2 discusses various CLIR approaches. Section 3 and section 4 show how MIETTA combines different cross-lingual strategies to achieve its ambitious goal and describe the overall MIETTA system. Section 5 discusses how much effort has to be paid to adapt the framework to new domains and new languages. Section 6 describes some evaluation issues for the MIETTA System. Section 7 summarizes the whole approach and discusses future work.

2. STATE OF THE ART

2.1 Monolingual Information Retrieval

In the traditional and classical information retrieval praxis, a user of a search engine sends a query in the same language as the document language [Salton and McGill, 1983]. The primary data structure of IR is the so-called inverted-index. Each index entry encodes the word and a list of texts, possibly with locations within the text, where the word occurs. The match between index words and the query helps to find out which documents are relevant to the query. In a monolingual environment, the best match is that the index and the query share the most common words. Vector Space Model (VSM) and Latent Semantic Indexing (LSI) [DeerWest et al., 1990] are two widely used IR techniques.

2.2 Cross-lingual Information Retrieval

In contrast to monolingual information retrieval, CLIR aims to find documents written in a different language than the query language. A useful application of CLIR is as follows: a user is capable of reading in a foreign language, but prefers to write a query in the native language. The search engine can find documents in the foreign language in spite of the query in another language.

CLIR is an intersected area between classic information retrieval and machine translation. Therefore, natural language processing tools are needed, e.g., language identification, multilingual dictionaries, morphological stemming, part of speech tagging, and terminology translation.

Typical CLIR strategies are based on query translation, document translation or a combination of both. We will discuss their advantages and disadvantages in the following.

2.2.1 Query Translation

The main goal of query translation is to help users to formulate their query in another language, such that the translated query can then be used as a search term (see Figure 9-1).

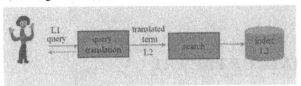

Figure 9-1: query translation in IR

Early experiments found in [Salton, 1971] showed that CLIR could work as well as monolingual information retrieval if a good transfer dictionary is available.

[Grefenstette, 1998] has summarized three problems concerning the query translation strategy:
- Finding translations
- Pruning translation alternatives
- Weighting the document relevance given translation alternatives

If a dictionary is available, the biggest problem is the poor coverage of the dictionary because of "missing word forms", "spelling mismatches", "compound", etc. Some systems used the parallel corpora to construct dictionaries automatically [Chen and Nie, 2000]. To achieve reliably results, the parallel corpora should be large enough. In comparison to machine translation, in CLIR, the exact translation of a given word in a given context is not always needed in order to find the relevant documents. Some experiments have been done with LSI [Littman et al., 1998].

The primary problem of query translation is that short queries provide less context for word sense disambiguation, and inaccurate translations can lead to bad recall and precision of the search results [Carbonell et al., 1997].

The MULINEX system [Erbach et al., 1997] provides a kind of user interaction for the sense disambiguation of translated terms. However, this kind of approach is only feasible in a specific scenario, namely, if the user has enough knowledge of the target language in order to select the right sense. Retranslating possible translations back into the original query language can solve this problem to a limited degree.

The third problem is concerned with weighting the document relevance given the alternative translations of the query, e.g., if a query contains two terms with each term owning different translations, whether a document contains one translation of each term should be more relevant than a document contains many translations of a term.

2.3   Document Translation

In a document translation approach, the search index is built from automatically translated documents, such that the search becomes similar to a monolingual search, i.e., the user query can be used directly as the search term (see Figure 9-2).

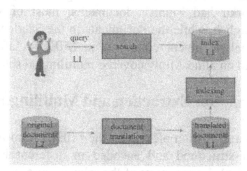

Figure 9-2: document translation in IR

The strategy would result in a higher translation and retrieval accuracy, since the full original document provides more contexts for disambiguation. Although retrieval performance still heavily depends on the quality of the underlying MT system, the word sense disambiguation problem is less severe.   Therefore, this option is often preferred compared to query translation [Carbonell et al., 1997; Dumais et al., 1996]. The main limitation is, of course, that under this approach at least the indices have to be duplicated, and in the offline translation the translated documents also need to be stored. Thus, for a global search engine, this approach is practically not viable due to massive cost of computation and storage. However, the approach is quite suitable in a restricted domain where the number of documents is limited.

3.   A UNIFORM FRAME FOR MULTILINGUAL ACCESS TO HETEROGENEOUS INFORMATION

3.1   Document Translation in MIETTA

In MIETTA, document translation was preferred, as it allows for direct access to the content, and provides better performance within a restricted domain. MIETTA web documents are limited to regional servers for the tourist domain, such that we do not face big storage problems. To translate the documents, the LOGOS system was employed, which covers the following directions:

German $\Rightarrow$ English, French, Italian

English $\Rightarrow$ French, German, Italian, Spanish

The situation to start from in MIETTA was as follows: Rome could provide documents manually translated into English, French, German, Italian and Spanish; Turku had Finnish documents, most of which were also translated into English, while the documents in the Saarland were mainly in German. The final document collection in MIETTA after the document translation yielded an almost fully covered multilingual setup.

3.2   Information Extraction and Multilingual Generation

The database information offered by the MIETTA information providers was mostly semi-structured and encoded in different languages (Italian, German and Finnish). Hence, most of the relevant information could only be found in the comment fields, mixed with other information. In order to make the database content more structured and multilingually accessible, we pursued an approach that combines IE and MG [Busemann, 1998]. The objective of IE in MIETTA is thus twofold:

- extraction of the domain relevant information (templates) from the unstructured data so that the user can access large amount of facts more accurately;
- normalization of the extracted data in a language-independent format to facilitate the MG.

MG takes a template provided by the IE component as input and generates a natural language description from it. The interaction of IE and MG is depicted in the Figure 9-3.

Figure 9-3: combination of IE and MG

A desired side effect of this strategy is that we can apply the same free text retrieval methods to generated descriptions as to web documents.

3.2.1 Information Extraction

The main task of IE is to analyze unstructured text and identify the relevant pieces of information [Cowie and Lehnert, 1996; Grishman and Sundheim, 1996; Appelt and Israel, 1997; Xu and Krieger, 2003]. One of its application areas is to detect the domain-relevant information from unstructured texts and convert it into database entries. The relevance of the information is determined by templates, which are predefined for the domain. We describe our usage of IE with the help of some examples.

The following German example text comes from the description field in an event calendar from the Saarland:

(1)
St. Ingbert: -Sanfte Gymnastik- für Seniorinnen und Senioren, montags von 10 bis 11 Uhr im Clubraum, Kirchengasse 11.

St. Ingbert: -Gentle Gymnastics for seniors, every Monday from 10:00 to 11:00 am, in Club room, Kirchengasse 11

The above text contains three pieces of information about the event, namely, event name, its location and its temporal duration:

<event> <city> St. Ingbert </city>: <name> -Sanfte Gymnastik- für Seniorinnen und Senioren </name>, <time> montags von 10 bis 11 Uhr: </time> <location> im Clubraum, Kirchengasse 11 </location>. </event>

To extract the relevant pieces of information contained in texts like the above example, we designed three steps:
- **NL shallow processing**:
     Identifying the relevant chunks of the text; for example, noun phrases and named entities (date, time, location, geographic names, phone no. and addresses).

- **Normalization**
  Converting information into a language-independent format;
  for example, date, time, location, addresses and phone no.
- **Template Filling**
  Mapping the extracted information into the database fields
  by employing specific template filler rules.

We applied SPPC [Piskorski and Neumann, 2000] for German shallow processing and IUTA[7] for Italian text analysis. For the "normalization", uniform formats are defined for date and time expressions, phone numbers, addresses, etc. E.g., "montags von 10 bis 11 Uhr" (*Every Monday from 10:00 to 11:00*) is normalized as follows:

Start time:	10:00
End time:	11:00
Weekday:	1
Weekly:	Yes

For our tourist domain, a specific set of templates was defined, corresponding to concepts like "event", "accommodation", "tours" etc. These concepts were organized in a three level concept hierarchy, drawing on the expertise of the MIETTA user partners in the tourism sector. Even if the hierarchy was designed for the MIETTA users, it can be easily adapted and generalized to other regions of tourism interest. The underlying format of the concept hierarchy is language independent. Each general concept can have several daughters, e.g., "event" has "theatre", "exhibition", "cinema" and "sports" as its sub-events. Templates in the same concept hierarchy inherit all attributes from their parents. For example, all the event templates have location, time and title as their attributes.

3.2.2   Multilingual Generation

In recent years, shallow natural language generation approaches have been shown to be quite useful for real-world applications within limited domains [Busemann and Horacek, 1998]. In particular, the combination of IE and MG provides a useful approach to a multilingual information presentation of structured information into a textual format. The basis for shallow text generation applied in MIETTA is the system TG/2. This system was developed in the TEMSIS project [Busemann, 1998], whose objective was to generate summaries of environmental data in German and French from database information. We use a JAVA implementation of TG/2, called

---

[7] http://celi.sns.it/~celi/projects/Iuta/iuta-top.html

JTG/2[8]. JTG/2 takes some language-independent input, applies language specific grammar rules and morphological lexicon, and returns some language-specific description. In MIETTA, five language-specific grammars were developed for the template generation. Because the JTG/2 rule formalism supports shallow grammar rules, construction new language-specific rule sets requires comparatively little effort. We illustrate the approach through a simple example from a MIETTA template. An event, such as a theater play, is encoded in a corresponding template as follows:

(2)

Level1:	Event
Level2:	Theater
Level3:	–
Event-Name:	Faust
StartDate:	21.10.99
PlaceName:	Staatstheater
Address:	Schillerplatz 1, 66111 Saarbrücken
Phone:	06 81-32204

The above template is used as the input for generation into five languages, resulting for example in the following texts:

(3)

English:
The theater show Faust will take place at the Staatstheater in Schillerplatz 1, 66111 Saarbrücken (in the downtown area). The scheduled date is Thursday, October 21, 1999. Phone: 06 81-32204

(4)

Finnish:
Teatteriesitys Faust järjestetään Staatstheaterissa, osoitteessa Schillerplatz 1, 66111 Saarbrücken (keskustan alueella). Tapahtuman päivämäärä on 21. lokakuuta 1999. Puhelin: 06 81-32204.

Texts like above are employed in two forms: as result presentation of the template content, and as input for free text indexing to allow advanced free text retrieval.

---

[8] JTG/2 is a Java implementation of DFKI's TG/2, developed by CELI, the Centro per l'Elaborazione del Linguaggio e dell'Informazione, for more information see http://www.celi.it.

To summarize, the combination of information extraction and multilingual generation is useful w.r.t. the following issues: It can make the translation of textual information in a database unnecessary, thus saving the duplication of the same piece of information in different languages. It greatly facilitates the maintenance of such data and ensures a higher degree of consistency across different languages. At the same time, it allows for an integrated or hybrid free text retrieval to both structured database and document information with the added dimension of multilinguality.

4. THE MIETTA SYSTEM

The user requirements of a tourism information system are quite varied with respect to the content. The needs for information range, on the one hand, from fairly structured information and precise facts (such as the opening times of a museum or the price of hotel accommodation), to some more general background information, as it is typically described on web pages concerning certain regions, towns, or vacation facilities. While the former type of information will be typically stored in a structured format (as a relational database), the latter is mostly available only in an unstructured format (as text documents). In order to allow the user to access these two different sorts of information in a uniform way, we provided hybrid search options:

- **Free text retrieval**
  Users can enter several words or phrases to find both web documents and descriptions generated from templates.
- **Concept based navigation**
  Users can navigate through web documents and templates according to the MIETTA concept hierarchy.
- **Form-based search**
  Users can select fields in a search form to access templates.

Our motivation is to make it completely transparent to users which source of information they are searching in, and to allow them to formulate their query as precise as they desired. In order to realize our goal, we developed our framework which integrated intelligently the existing techniques occurred in the cross-lingual free text retrieval and natural language processing communities. The implementation of the framework is our MIETTA system, which contains following three main components:

- **Data Capturing**
  collecting web documents and recording document information such as the title, URL, manual and automatic classifications, etc.

- **Data Profiling**
  document translation, IE, offline MG of templates, free text indexing.
- **Search Engine**
  search and visualization of the search result.

The interaction of the three components is illustrated in Figure 9-4.

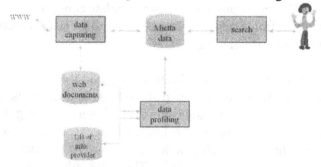

Figure 9-4: MIETTA overall system.

4.1   Data Capturing

A large part of the basic material provided by the MIETTA user partners comes in the form of web documents. To make this information accessible through the MIETTA search tools, they must be registered, gathered and indexed. The data-capturing tool provides a convenient user interface, which allows the information providers to register their web pages. The registration user interface provides a broad range of facilities: The user can enter the URL of the page or the site, the depth to be disclosed, and to enter the address of a potential document translation. Furthermore, he can also classify the page content based on the MIETTA concept hierarchy. Besides the URL registration and manual classification, the data capturing tool also integrates the JumboScan Web crawler package provided by UNIDATA[9] for downloading and indexing the document information like the URL name, title etc.

---

[9] See http://www.unidata.it/.

4.2   Data Profiling

The aim of the data-profiling component in the MIETTA system is to disclose the data sources in such a way that access through different search options becomes possible. It contains

- Document translation, based on the LOGOS machine translation system;
- IE from database entries for template construction;
- MG from templates to obtain natural language descriptions;
- Free text indexing

The first three aspects have been discussed in the last section. The result of applying these processes is that both web documents and template information becomes available in the different languages covered by MIETTA. We will focus on the free indexing work here. We employ an existing indexing and search tool developed by TNO[10] [Hiemstra and Kraaij, 1998] for the free text retrieval task. The TNO indexing tool generates two kinds of indexes:

- A lemma-based fuzzy index based on tri-grams (ISM);
- A Vector Space Model (VSM) index based on lemmatas.

These free-text indexing components are applied to web documents, translations and descriptions generated from templates, see the following Figure 9-5.

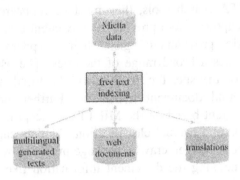

Figure 9-5: free text indexing

The indexing of the automatically generated descriptions adds a specific functionality to the MIETTA search engine, as the template content becomes accessible for fuzzy search and the vector space model search, which are normally not supported by relational database. As a result, both web

---

[10] See http://twentyone.tpd.tno.nl/.

documents and database information becomes available in a textual format in different languages, disclosed through classifications and a free text indexes.

4.3   Search Engine

We describe here the hybrid search options provided by MIETTA and how they are realized. With the help of data capturing and data profiling, the MIETTA search engine allows for standard free text retrieval as well as the following advanced search capabilities: concept-based navigation, and form-based query (template search).

The architecture of the search engine is described in Figure 9-6.

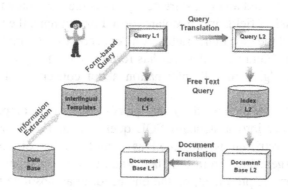

Figure 9-6: search architecture

As mentioned above, MIETTA uses the existing TNO ISM/VSM search engine for free text retrieval. The ISM part makes use of a kind of a fuzzy matching algorithm based on tri-grams. It allows the match of index terms with query words or phrases containing spelling errors or morphological variants. For example, the user can enter "baroque palaces" and find documents and template descriptions containing the phrase "baroque styled palace". In addition to the free text retrieval, the user can also navigate through the concept hierarchy to search for information in a certain category. In contrast to many other search engines, the MIETTA user can also combine the free text retrieval with the concept-based navigation by formulating a query with constrains such as "find all documents containing the word *colosseo* belonging to the category *Art and Culture*", see Figure 9-7.

 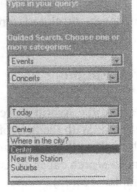

Figure 9-7: search menu   *Figure 9-8: form based query*

A more restricted and goal-directed query is the form-based query, where the user can select fields in a template form. For example, the user can select the "time" and the "location" fields of a "concert" event template by using a query form. In Figure 9-8, the user has formulated a query corresponding to the constraint "give me all information about concerts in the city center today".

All queries are processed by the query- processing component and are converted either into a standard SQL query or an ISM/VSM query. The result of the retrieval is presented as a uniform list of links to textual descriptions (generated from templates) and to web documents. Both types of information are presented, on the one hand, in an absolute ranking order, where only the relevance of the document plays a role, and on the other hand, sorted according to the different categories. If the user clicks on a link, they receive either a web document or a generated text as in the examples (3) and (4).

To summarize, the MIETTA search engine represents a flexible way of combining cross-lingual free text retrieval with standard database access. The hybrid query options and their interaction provide the user with a highly versatile range of options to express their different search requirements, which is also reflected in the presentation of the results and the further navigation options.

4.4   Scalability of the Framework

Our framework can be easily adapted to other domains. The domain modeling consists mainly of the definition of domain specific templates and the concept hierarchy. With respect to the IE task, the major part of the effort needs to be spent on the new definition of the template filler rules, since the natural processing and the normalization steps are domain independent. The MIETTA MG tool has already been proven to be reusable, as it has been applied in both the TEMSIS environmental and the MIETTA tourist domains.

When it comes to adding a new language, three language dependent components would be involved in the MIETTA system: natural language generation (JTG/2), document translation and natural language processing. As mentioned in section 2, our natural language generation tool requires less effort for the development of a grammar rule set in a new language. It supports also easy integration of a morphological component. In addition to the five generation-grammars developed within MIETTA, we also carried out some successful experiments with a Chinese grammar. Thus, integrating a new language outside the Western language family into JTG/2 also appears to be quite easy. Document translation is clearly dependent on the language pairs supported by the machine translation system employed, i.e., essentially independently from the MIETTA system itself. However, to deal with the problem of unavailable translation pairs, a statistical translation model, as proposed in [Chen and Nie, 2000] could be employed. Such translation models are much easier to establish than MT systems, and it would be sensitive to the domain of the training corpus. Similar to the scalability of the machine translation, the shallow language processing components are dependent on the developments for a certain language. In the recent years, the natural language processing society in Asia is very active, in particular, as far as Chinese, Japanese and Korean are concerned. Hence, the integration of one of these languages is realistic.

4.5 Evaluating MIETTA

Because of the broad variety of search strategies and the heterogeneous data sources, the standard relevance assessment model used in the ad hoc and routing forums of TREC is difficult to apply to the complete MIETTA system. The evaluation of the individual components such as the TNO free text retrieval engine, the natural generation system and the IE tools SPPC and IUTA can be found in their corresponding literature mentioned in the previous sections. We consider that an end user centered evaluation should be suitable for such complex systems, including following criteria:

- transparency and ergonomics of the search user interface and the result presentation,
- quality of machine translation and natural language generation,
- interaction of the hybrid search options.

5.   CONCLUSION

We have presented a novel framework for the uniform and multilingual access to web documents and the structured data and have implemented a practical application that successfully realized this framework. The MIETTA system allows the user to carry out a cross-lingual search in different sources of information at different levels of content granularity. This framework is highly suitable as a domain-specific information system and internet-portal. It can be easily transferred to other domains and is extensible to other languages.

Future work will be directed towards extending the framework to IE from web documents and to fully automatic document classification. In the current MIETTA system, template extraction from web documents combined with MG has not been considered due to limited resources. Such a combination, however, would make the system even more effective as it could provide both summaries of web documents and multilingual access to such summaries.

In the most recent search engine research, question-answering systems are regarded as the future generation of information system. In comparison to the classical information retrieval systems, question-answering systems allow users to send questions as queries to receive answers instead of just a list of documents. In the roadmap of the future question answering systems [Burger et al., 2001], the multilingual and cross-lingual systems and heterogeneous data sources belong to the important issues. The MIETTA strategy, namely, the combination of IE and MG can be adopted for answer generation in a cross-lingual and multilingual environment. In addition, the uniform framework for dealing with heterogeneous data sources is a good experiment for the future question answering systems [Lin, 2002].

ACKNOWLEDGEMENTS

The framework described here is grounded on the cooperation in the MIETTA consortium. I am grateful to the MIETTA colleagues for the useful discussions and contributions.

REFERENCES

Appelt and Israel. 1997. Building Information Extraction Systems. *ANLP-97 Tutorial,* 1997.
C. P. Braschler, and P. Schäuble.1999. Cross-Language Information Retrieval (CLIR) Track Overview. In *Proceedings of the eighth Text REtrieval Conference (TREC-8),* held in Gaithersburg, Maryland, November 17-19, 1999.

J. Burger, C. Cardie, V. Chaudhri, R. Gaizauskas, S.Harabagiu, D. Israel, C. Jacquemin, C. Lin, S. Maiorano, G. Miller, D. Moldovan, B. Ogden, J. Prager, E. Riloff, A. Singhal, R. Shrihari, T. Strzalkowski, E. Voorhees and R. Weischedel. 2001. Structures to Roadmap Research in Question and Answering (QandA). In *NIST DUC Vision and Roadmap Document*, 2001.

Stephan Busemann. 1998. Language Technology for Transnational Web Services. In *Proceedings of European Telematics: Advancing the Information Society Telematics Applications Programme Annual Concertation Meeting*, Barcelona, 1998, 101-105.

Stephan Busemann and Helmut Horacek. 1998. A Flexible Shallow Approach to Text Generation. In Eduard Hovy (ed.): In *Proceedings of the Nineth International Natural Language Generation Workshop (INLG '98)*, Niagara-on-the-Lake, Canada, August 1998, 238-247.

Jaime Carbonell, Yiming Yang, Robert Frederking, Ralf D. Brown, Yibing Geng and Danny Lee. 1997. Translingual Information Retrieval: A comparative evaluation. In *Proceedings of the Fifteeth International Joint Conference on Artificial Intelligence*, August 1997.

Jiang Chen and Jian-Yun Nie. 2000. Parallel Web Text Mining for Cross-Language IR. In *Proceedings of 6th International Conference on Computer-Assisted Information Retrieval (RIAO 2000)*, Paris, 2000.

Cowie and Lehnert. 1996. Information Extraction. In *Communications of ACM*, 39(1):51-78, 1996.

D. Crystal. 1997. *English as Global Language*. Cambridge University Press. 1997.

Mark W. Davis and William C. Ogden. 1997. Implementing cross-language text retrieval systems for large-scale text collections and the world wide web. In *AAAI Symposium on Cross-Language Text and Speech Retrieval. American Association for Artificial Intelligence*, March 1997.

Scott Deerwest, Susan T. Dumals, George W. Furnas, Thomas K. Landauer, and Richard Harshman. 1990. Indexing by latent semantic analysis. *Journal of the American Society for Information Science*, 41:391-407, 1990.

S. Dumais, T. Landauer and M. Littman. 1996. Automatic Cross-Linguistic Information Retrieval using Latent Semantic Indexing. In *Proceedings of SIGIR-96*, Zurich, August 1996.

G. Erbach, G. Neumann and H. Uszkoreit. 1997. MULINEX - Multilingual Indexing, Editing and Navigation Extensions for the World Wide Web. In David Hull and Doug Oard (eds.) *Cross-Language Text and Speech Retrieval — Papers from the 1997 AAAI Spring Symposium*, AAAI Press, Menlo Park, 1997.

Djoerd Hiemstra and Wessel Kraaij. 1998. Twenty-One in ad-hoc and CLIR. In *Proceedings of the Seventh Text Retrieval Conference (TREC-7)*, NIST special publication, 500-240.

Gregory Grefenstette. 1998. The problems of cross-language information retrieval. In *G. Grefenstette (ed.), Cross-language Information Retrieval. Chapter 1*. Kluwer Academic Publishers, Boston, 1998.

Gregory Grefenstette. 2001. Multilinguality on the Web. http://www.infonortics.com/searchengines/sh01/slides-01/grefen.pdf. 2001.

G. Grefenstette and Julien Nioche. 2000. Estimation of English and non-English Language Use on the WWW. In *Proceedings of RIAO'2000*. Paris, April. 2000.

R. Grishman and B. Sundheim. 1996. Message Understanding Conference - 6: A Brief History. In *Proceedings of the 16th International Conference on Computational Linguistics (COLING)*, pages 466-471, Kopenhagen, Denmark, Europe, 1996.

Jimmy Lin. 2002. The Web as a Resource for Question Answering: Perspective and Challenges. In *Proceedings of the third International Conference on Language Resources and Evaluation (LREC 2002)*. Las Palmas, Canary Islands, Spain. May, 2002.

Michael L. Littman, Susan T. Dumais, and Thomas Laudauer. 1998. Automatic cross-language information retrieval using latent semantic indexing. In G. Grefensttte (ed.), *Cross-language Information Retrieval*, chapter 5. Kluwer Academic Publishers, Boston, 1998.

G. Nunberg. 1996. The Whole World Wired. Commentary broadcast on 'Fresh Air', National Public Radio, Sept. 1996.

Douglas W. Oard. 1999a. Global Access to Multilingual Information. Presented at *IRAL99*, Taipei, 1999.

Douglas W. Oard. 1999b. Cross-Language Text Retrieval Research in USA. In *3rd ERCIM DELOS Workshop*, Zurich, Switzerland, 1999.

J. Piskorski and G. Neumann. 2000. An Intelligent Text Extraction and Navigation System. In *Proceedings of 6th International Conference on Computer-Assisted Information Retrieval* (RIAO-2000), Paris, 2000.

G. Salton 1971. *Automatic Processing of Foreign Language Documents*. Preentice-Hall, Englewood Cliffs, NJ, 1971.

Gerard Salton and M. McGill. 1983. *An Introduction to Modern Information Retrieval*. McGraw-Hill, New York, 1983.

Peter Schäuble and Páraic Sheridan. 1997. Cross-Language Information Retrieval (CLIR) Track Overview. In *Proceedings of TREC-6*, 1997.

V. Trau. 1999. Characterisations of Web Server Contents. FH Wiesbaden, University of Applied Sciences, Web Seminar, January, 1999.

Tschanz and S. Klein. 1996. Web-enabled Cooperation in Tourism. In *Proceedings of EMOT Work shop*, Modena, Italian 1996.

Gerhard Weikum. 2002. The Web in Ten Years: Challenges and Opportunities for Database Research. Invited Keynote, In *Proceedings of 10th Italian Database Conference (SEBD: Sistemi Evoluti per Basi di Dati)*, Portoferraio, Isola d'Elba, Italy, 2002.

J. L Xu. 2000a. Multilingual Search on the World Wide Web. In *Proceedings of the Hawaii International Conference on System Sciences HICSS-33*, Maui, Hawaii, January, 2000.

Feiyu Xu, Klaus Netter and Holger Stenzhorn. 2000b. MIETTA-A Framework for Uniform and Multilingual Access to Structured Database and Web Information. In *Proceedings of Information Retrieval for Asian Language (IRAL 2000)*, Hong Kong. 2000.

Feiyu Xu and Hans-Ulrich Krieger. 2003. Extraction of Domain-Specific Events and Relations via a Combination of Shallow and Deep NLP. DFKI research report. 2003.

Chapter 10

GENERIC HIERARCHICAL CLASSIFICATION USING THE SINGLE-LINK CLUSTERING

Willy Picard and Wojciech Cellary

Department of Information Technology
The Poznań University of Economics
Mansfelda 4, 60-854 Poznań, Poland
{picard, cellary}@kti.ae.poznan.pl

Abstract   Up to date, research on automatic classification focused mainly on the efficiency of algorithms in regard to a given aspect of a dataset. The issue of classification of a given dataset in regard to various aspects is generally not addressed. In this chapter, a multi-facet hierarchical classification technique based on the single-link clustering is proposed. First, the single-link clustering is formally presented. Then, the concepts underlying the generic hierarchical classification technique are given. Next, analysis domains modeling a given facet of a dataset are described. A new language devoted to generate analysis domains is presented. Further, classification of analysis domains is discussed. Finally, examples of applications of the generic hierarchical classification are given.

Keywords: hierarchical classification, multi-facet analysis, ultra-metrics, single-link clustering, analysis domain language.

1.   Introduction

With the growth of the amount of information available on the Internet, data classification is a necessity. Classification of information should be hierarchical in order to allow fast focusing on information classes of higher interest. Information classification problem is a subject of intensive research. Two classification methods that are the mostly used in practice are: Kohonen Self-Organizing Maps Algorithm and the Hierarchical Bayesian Clustering. The Kohonen Self-Organizing Maps Algorithm [6, 7] is based on a unsupervised neural network mapping high dimensional input data onto a two-dimensional output space while preserving relations between the data items. The Hierarchical Bayesian Clustering [5] is based on Bayesian probability theory. It maximizes the probability that a cluster is included in another cluster. Both these methods are focused on the most efficient way of the dataset classification according to a given criterion. However, in practice, a dataset needs to be classified in many ways called below a "generic hierarchical classification". For example, scientific papers can be classified according to their domains, keywords, lengths, editors, relations with other papers, etc.

The Kohonen Self-Organizing Maps Algorithm is not suitable to the generic hierarchical classification, because the granularity of the data classification is determined by the predefined, fixed size of the output space.

The Hierarchical Bayesian Clustering is also not well suitable to generic hierarchical classification, because each new classification criterion would need the definition of a new probabilistic function for cluster aggregation. These probabilistic functions are difficult to built and even more difficult to intuitively understand for a human.

The approach to the generic hierarchical classification proposed in this chapter is based on the single-link clustering, which has strong mathematical basis presented in Section 10.2. The single-link clustering is based on the use of ultrametrics. It has been proven that the notions of ultrametric and hierarchical classification are equivalent. Thus, an ultrametric defines a hierarchical classification. Furthermore, an ultrametric may be derived from any metric. So, any metric defines a hierarchical classification.

The classes resulting of a classification based on a metric d are sets of elements that are similar according to the criterion defined by the distance d. The more similar two elements are, the less the distance between them is. The definition of a new classification criterion would imply the definition of the similarity between elements. Thus, a new classification criterion would imply the definition of a new metric. As the notion of metric is intuitive, new classification criteria may be easily defined.

In this chapter, first, the mathematical basis of the single-link clustering is presented. Then, the multi-facet analysis concept is introduced. Next, the data retrieval mechanism is described and formalized, as well as the classification technique used. Finally, some examples illustrate the power of the multi-facet classification technique.

2.   Single-link Clustering

The goal of any classification is to group items according to their proximity. The concept of promixity can be considered as the similarity between items. The more two items are similar, the closest their are.

2.1   Partition

Similarity between items is expressed by a mathematical concept of an *equivalence relation*.

DEFINITION 10.1 *An **equivalence relation** $\mathcal{R}$ on a set A is a relation that is reflexive ($\forall a \in A$, $a\mathcal{R}a$), symmetric ($\forall a, b \in A$, $a\mathcal{R}b \Leftrightarrow b\mathcal{R}a$), and transitive ($\forall a, b, c \in A$, $a\mathcal{R}b$ and $b\mathcal{R}c \Rightarrow a\mathcal{R}c$).*

Examples of equivalence relations are: "have the same car" or "live in the same country". An example of an equivalence relation on natural numbers is the "=" relation. The keyword of equivalence relations is the word "same".
Equivalence relations partition the universe into subsets (called *classes*):

DEFINITION 10.2 *A partition P of a set A is a collection of subsets $\{A_1, \ldots A_k\}$ such that any two of them are disjoint (for any $i \neq j$, $A_i \cap A_j = \emptyset$) and such that their union is A ($\bigcup_{i \in [1, \ldots n]} A_i = A$).*

Every element of A is a member of exactly one subset of the partition P. Assume that relation $\mathcal{R}$ is an equivalence relation on the set A. Let $[a]$ denote the set $\{b \in A \mid a\mathcal{R}b\}$, where $a \in A$.

LEMMA 10.3 *For $a \in A$, the sets $[a]$ constitute a partition of A.*

Proof. Let assume that $a, b \in A$ exist, where $[a] \neq [b]$ and $[a] \cap [b] \neq \emptyset$. Let c be any element of $[b] - [a]$. Let d be any element of $[a] \cap [b]$. First, $a\mathcal{R}d$, because $d \in [a]$. Second, $d\mathcal{R}b$, because $d \in [b]$, and $b\mathcal{R}c$, because $c \in [b]$ and $\mathcal{R}$ is symmetric. By transitivity, $d\mathcal{R}c$. Finally, by transitivity, $a\mathcal{R}c$, which means that $c \in [a]$. The last result is in contradiction with the fact that $c \in [b] - [a]$. Thus, for every $a, b \in A$, either $[a] = [b]$ or $[a] \cap [b] = \emptyset$, which means that, for $a \in A$, the sets $[a]$ constitute a partition of A. $\square$

LEMMA 10.4 *Any partition $\{A_1, \ldots, A_k\}$ of A defines an equivalence relation by letting $a\mathcal{R}b$ iff a and b are members of the same A_i.*

Proof. <u>Reflexivity.</u> $\forall a \in A, \exists i \in [1, \ldots, k]$ such that $a \in A_i$. Clearly, a and a are members of the same A_i, which means that $a\mathcal{R}a$.

<u>Symmetry.</u> If $a\mathcal{R}b$, $\exists i \in [1, \ldots, k]$ such that $a \in A_i$ and $b \in A_i$. Also b and a are members of A_i, and therefore $b\mathcal{R}a$.

<u>Transitivity.</u> Assume that $a\mathcal{R}b$ and $b\mathcal{R}c$. Thus, there exist $i, j \in [1, \ldots, k]$ such that a and b are members of the same A_i and b and c are members of the same A_j. However, by definition of a partition, b cannot be a member of two

different A_i and A_j. So $A_i = A_j$ and a and c are members of the same A_i, proving $a\mathcal{R}c$.   □

By the proof of the two above lemmata, partitions and equivalence relations are exchangeable notions.

2.2   Indexed Hierarchy

Let assume that A is a finite set. Let $\mathcal{P}(A)$ denote the set of all subsets of A.

DEFINITION 10.5 *A hierarchy $\mathcal{H}$ on A is a subset of $\mathcal{P}(A)$ such that:*

$$A \in \mathcal{H}, \tag{10.1}$$
$$\forall a \in A, \quad \{a\} \in \mathcal{H}, \tag{10.2}$$
$$\forall (h_1, h_2) \in H^2, \quad \begin{cases} h_1 \cap h_2 = \emptyset, \\ \text{or} \quad h_1 \subset h_2, \\ \text{or} \quad h_2 \subset h_1. \end{cases} \tag{10.3}$$

DEFINITION 10.6 *An indexed hierarchy on A is a couple $(\mathcal{H}, f)$, where $\mathcal{H}$ is a hierarchy and f is an application from $\mathcal{H}$ to $\mathbb{R}^+$ such that:*

$$\forall a \in A, \quad f(\{a\}) \quad = 0, \tag{10.4}$$
$$\forall (h_1, h_2) \in H^2, \, h_1 \subset h_2, \quad h_1 \neq h_2, \quad \Rightarrow f(h_1) < f(h_2). \tag{10.5}$$

2.3   Ultrametrics

DEFINITION 10.7 *An ultrametric on a set A is an application δ from $A \times A$ to $\mathbb{R}^+$ such that:*

$$\forall (a, b) \in A^2, \quad \delta(a, b) = 0 \Leftrightarrow a = b, \tag{10.6}$$
$$\forall (a, b) \in A^2, \quad \delta(a, b) = \delta(b, a), \tag{10.7}$$
$$\forall (a, b, c) \in A^3, \quad \delta(a, b) \leq \sup[\delta(a, c), \delta(b, c)] \tag{10.8}$$

LEMMA 10.8 *Consider δ an ultrametric on a set A. The relation $\mathcal{R}_{\delta_0}$ defined by*

$$\forall \delta_0 \in \mathbb{R}^+, a\mathcal{R}_{\delta_0}b \Leftrightarrow \delta(a, b) \leq \delta_0 \tag{10.9}$$

is an equivalence relation.

Proof.   <u>Reflexivity.</u> $\forall a \in A, \delta(a, a) = 0$. Therefore $\delta(a, a) \leq \delta_0$, which means that $a\mathcal{R}a$.

<u>Symmetry.</u> If $a\mathcal{R}_{\delta_0}b$, then $\delta(a, b) \leq \delta_0$. By symmetry of ultrametrics, $\delta(a, b) = \delta(b, a)$. Therefore $\delta(b, a) \leq \delta_0$, which means that $b\mathcal{R}_{\delta_0}a$.

Transitivity. Assume that $a\mathcal{R}_{\delta_0}b$ and $b\mathcal{R}_{\delta_0}c$. Thus, $\delta(a,b) \leq \delta_0$ and $\delta(b,c) \leq \delta_0$. Because of equation 10.8, $\delta(a,c) \leq \sup[\delta(a,b), \delta(b,c)] \leq \sup[\delta_0, \delta_0] \leq \delta_0$, proving $a\mathcal{R}_{\delta_0}c$.   □

As shown in Section 10.2.1, equivalence relations and partitions are exchangeable notions. Therefore, let $\mathcal{P}(\delta_0)$ denote the partition that consists of classes resulting from the equivalent relation $\mathcal{R}_{\delta_0}$.

LEMMA 10.9 *Let A be a finite set. If $\mathcal{H} = \bigcup_{\delta_0 \in \mathbb{R}^+} \mathcal{P}(\delta_0)$, then $\mathcal{H}$ is a hierarchy.*

Proof. Let us show that $A \in \mathcal{H}$. As A is finite, there exists a maximum distance between two its elements. The partition associated with the maximum distance is the set A.

It is obvious that $\forall a \in A, \{a\} \in \mathcal{H}$, because $\{a\} = \mathcal{P}(0)$.

Finally, for the condition 10.3, consider some arbitrary h_1 and $h_2 \in \mathcal{H}$. Then, $\exists(\delta_0, \delta_0') \in \mathbb{R}^+$ such that $h_1 \in \mathcal{P}(\delta_0), h_2 \in \mathcal{P}(\delta_0')$. If $h_1 \cap h_2 = \emptyset$, the condition is observed. Otherwise, consider $a \in h_1 \cap h_2$. h_1 can be written as $h_1 = \{b \in A \mid \delta(a,b) \leq \delta_0\}$. Respectively, $h_2 = \{b \in A \mid \delta(a,b) \leq \delta_0'\}$. If $\delta_0 \leq \delta_0'$, then $h_1 \subset h_2$. Otherwise, $h_2 \subset h_1$, which concludes the proof.   □

LEMMA 10.10 *Let f be an application from $\mathcal{H}$ to $\mathbb{R}^+$ such that*

$$\forall h \in \mathcal{H}, f(h) = \min\{\delta_0 \mid h \in \mathcal{P}(\delta_0)\}.$$

Then, the couple $(\mathcal{H}, f)$ is an indexed hierarchy.

Proof. $\forall a \in A, \{a\} \in \mathcal{P}(0) \Rightarrow f(\{x\}) = 0$. Moreover, consider some arbitrary h_1 and $h_2 \in \mathcal{H}$, such that $h_1 \subset h_2$ and $h_1 \neq h_2$. Consider a being a member of h_1. Therefore:

$$\{\delta_0 \mid h_1 \in \mathcal{P}(\delta_0)\} \subset \{\delta_0 \mid h_2 \in \mathcal{P}(\delta_0)\},$$

and then

$$\min\{\delta_0 \mid h_1 \in \mathcal{P}(\delta_0)\} \leq \min\{\delta_0 \mid h_2 \in \mathcal{P}(\delta_0)\}.$$

So, $f(h_1) \leq f(h_2)$. Moreover, $h_1 \neq h_2$ and $h_1 \subset h_2$ implies that there exists an element b which is a member of h_2 but not a member of h_1. Consider $a \in h_1 \cap h_2$. Then,

$$f(h_1) < \delta(a,b) \leq f(h_2),$$

which means that $f(h_1) < f(h_2)$.   □

LEMMA 10.11 *Consider an indexed hierarchy* $(\mathcal{H}, f)$. *An application* δ *from* $A \times A$ *to* $\mathbb{R}^+$ *is an ultrametric if*

$$\forall (a, b) \in A^2, \delta(a, b) = \min_{h \in \mathcal{H}} \left\{ f(h) \,|\, (a, b) \in h^2 \right\}.$$

Proof. <u>Reflexivity.</u> By definition, $\delta(a, a) = 0$, because $f(\{a\}) = 0$. If $\delta(a, b) = 0$, then

$$\exists h \in \mathcal{H} \text{ such that } a \in h, b \in h, f(h) = 0.$$

If $h \neq (\{a\})$ (i.e. $a \neq b$), $f(h) > f(\{a\}) = 0$, which is impossible. Then $a = b$.

<u>Symmetry.</u> The demonstration is obvious.

<u>Condition 10.8.</u> Consider h_1 such that $\delta(a, b) = f(h_1)$, h_2 such that $\delta(a, c) = f(h_2)$, h_3 such that $\delta(b, c) = f(h_3)$. As $c \in h_2 \cap h_3$, then $h_2 \cap h_3 \neq \emptyset$. Because $\mathcal{H}$ is a hierarchy, let assume that $h_2 \subset h_3$ (if $h_3 \subset h2$, the proof is similar). Then,

$$f(h_2) \leq f(h_3). \tag{10.10}$$

Therefore, a, which is a member of h_2, is also a member of h_3 (b does so). As

$$f(h_1) = \min_{h \in \mathcal{H}} \{f(h) \,|\, (a, b) \in h^2\},$$

$h_1 \subset h_3$. Then,

$$f(h_1) \leq f(h_3). \tag{10.11}$$

Because of inequalities 10.10 and 10.11,

$$f(h_1) \leq \sup [f(h_2), f(h_3)],$$

which proves Condition 10.8.   □

From Lemmata 10.10 and 10.11, the notions of an ultrametric and an indexed hierarchy are exchangeable, as illustrated in Figure 10.1. When δ_0 changes, different classes are created and the hierarchical aspect of the classification is visible in the embedment of classes.

2.4   Path Metrics

DEFINITION 10.12 *A path p between two elements a and b in a set A is a list of elements $p = (a_1, a_2, \dots a_n)$ such that:*

$$\forall i, \quad a_i \in E,$$
$$a_1 = a,$$
$$a_n = b.$$

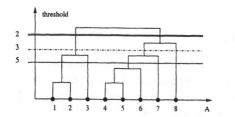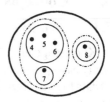

Figure 10.1. Equivalence between indexed hierarchy (on the left side) and ultrametric (on the right side, the classes for various values of δ_0)

DEFINITION 10.13 *Let d be a metric on A. A step $s_d(p)$ of the path p for the metric d is:*

$$s_d(p) = \sup_{i=1}^{n-1} d(a_i, a_{i+1}).$$

DEFINITION 10.14 *The path metric δ_d for metric d on a set A is an application from $A \times A$ to $\mathbb{R}^+$ such that:*

$$\delta_d(a, b) = \inf_{p \in \mathbb{P}(a,b)} s_d(p),$$

where $\mathbb{P}(a, b)$ is the set of all the paths from a to b in A.

LEMMA 10.15 *Each path metric is an ultrametric.*

Proof. Conditions 10.6 and 10.7 are obvious. Let prove condition 10.8.

$$
\begin{aligned}
\delta_d(a, b) &= \inf_{p \in \mathbb{P}(a,b)} s_d(p) \\
&\leq \inf_{p \in \mathbb{P}_c(a,b)} s_d(p),
\end{aligned}
$$

where $\mathbb{P}_c(a, b)$ is the set of all the paths from a to b in A containing c. By definition of $s_d(p)$,

$$
\begin{aligned}
\delta_d(a, b) &\leq \inf_{p_1 \in \mathbb{P}(a,c)} \inf_{p_2 \in \mathbb{P}(c,b)} \sup \left[s_d(p_1), s_d(p_2) \right] \\
\delta_d(a, b) &\leq \sup \left[\inf_{p_1 \in \mathbb{P}(a,c)} s_d(p_1), \inf_{p_2 \in \mathbb{P}(c,b)} s_d(p_2) \right] \\
\delta_d(a, b) &\leq \sup \left[\delta_d(a, c), \delta_d(c, b) \right],
\end{aligned}
$$

which proves Condition 10.8. □

A path metric may be derived from every metric. As every path metric is an ultrametric, and every ultrametric is equivalent to an indexed hierarchy,

Every metric defines an indexed hierarchy.

3.   Concepts

3.1   Analysis of a Set of Data

Knowledge extraction is mainly basing on various analyses of a dataset. In many cases, users cannot conduct these analyses manually, because the amount of data to be analyzed is too high. Therefore, software tools need to be developed to provide users with synthetic views of a given dataset.

An analysis support system has to provide users with a possibility of various analyses of a dataset to well understand different aspects of the given dataset. For instance, a user may want to analyze the involvement of different scientists in the scientific community, or to analyze the correlation between authors and a given research topics.

To analyze a dataset , both the abstract objects to be analyzed and the analysis criteria must be defined.

3.2   Mapping Functions

Objects to be analyzed are generated by a mapping function f from space S to a set denoted D_f. S is the dataset space. Different mapping functions are used to analyze different aspects of the dataset.

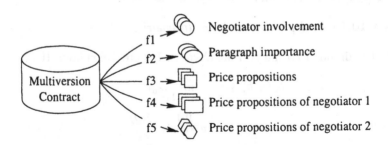

Figure 10.2.   Mapping functions

To illustrate the use of various mapping functions to analyze different aspects of a dataset, consider a negotiation process in which various negotiators are trying to reach an agreement on a contract, each offer being considered as a new contract version. The various aspects of the dataset generated during the negotiation process can be analyzed with the help of various mapping functions as presented in Figure 10.2. Mapping function f_1 generates a set of objects modeling negotiator involvement. Mapping function f_2 generates a set of objects modeling paragraph importance. Mapping functions f_3, f_4, and f_5 generate sets of objects modeling price propositions for various subsets of the analyzed dataset.

3.3   Hierarchical Classification

In a highly concurrent environment, the result of an analysis should be a hierarchical classification [8]. Given a set of objects, a classification splits it into subsets of similar objects, denoted classes. Hierarchical classification provides users with a set of embedded classes. Users can then choose a granularity level (the number of classes) of the classification. For instance, the same set of authors will be split into few classes if a general involvement characteristics is required, or into many classes if detailed characteristics of authors involvement is required.

As the proposed solution is based on metrics, and ultrametrics, the criteria used to analyze set D_f are defined in a human understandable way, so that users may choose and define the criteria they want.

4.   Analysis Domains

4.1   Domain Objects

Domain objects are used to model various facets of the dataset to be classified. Domain objects may for instance represent the editors of scientific papers, the relationships between news and press agencies, etc. As a consequence, domain objects must be flexible enough to represent various data types.

Each domain object is an element of an *analysis domain*. An analysis domain is a set of domain objects modeling a facet of a dataset. Formally, let D_f denote the analysis domain modeling facet of a dataset, denoted f.

A domain object DO_i is uniquely identified in a given set of domain objects by its identifier do_i. Formally,

$$\forall (DO_i, DO_j) \in D_f^2, \; do_i = do_j \Leftrightarrow DO_i = DO_j$$

$$\forall (DO_i, DO_j) \in D_f \times D_{f'}, \; do_i = do_j \text{ and } DO_i \neq DO_j \Rightarrow D_f \neq D_{f'}$$

A domain object DO_i consists of:

- a unique identifier, denoted do_i,

- a set of attributes, and

- a type.

An attribute is a pair $(name, value)$. Each attribute models a property of the domain object. To illustrate the use of attributes, let us assume that a book is modeled by a domain object denoted DO_{book}. The attributes of DO_{book} are pairs $('author',' JohnSmith')$, $('editor',' Kluwer')$, and $('title',' the\, ACME\, prototype.')$.

An attribute name is a character string. A character string consists of one or many characters defined in the Unicode standard [9]. In case of Internet data classification, no limitations are assumed on the used languages. As a consequence, attribute names should not be limited to one or a few sets of languages and their characters. The use of Unicode allows for an international audience.

An attribute value is a domain object, because domain objects are able to model complex data types. A domain object may, for instance, model an editor, with attributes *name* and *address*. The value of the *editor* attribute in the former example may be such a domain object.

Also identifiers are domain objects in order to associate semantics with the identifiers. For instance, the identifier do_{book} may be a domain object modeling a "book identity". Identifier do_{book} may have the following attributes: *ISBN* (International Standard Book Number), and *checkDigit* (last digit of an ISBN used to check ISBN validity). The domain object DO_{book} is then identified by a domain object defining the ISBN identifier and its check digit.

Object domain types are Unicode character strings. Object domain types are used for two purposes. First, an object domain type associates some semantics with an object domain. In the former example, the type of DO_{book} may be *book* to indicate the meaning of the data DO_{book} models. Second, domain object types allows domain object structure to be defined. The structure of domain objects representing books may be defined as follow:

- identifier: type *extendedISBN*,

- attributes:

  - author: type *Person*,
  - editor: type *Editor*,
  - title: type *String*.

Types of identifier and attribute values are corresponding to domain object types.

The following six primitive domain objects may be considered as the atomic data elements for domain object building:

- String,
- Integer,
- Long,
- Float.
- Double,
- Boolean.

Primitive domain objects do not refer to any other domain object type. Primitive objects have only one attribute denoted *value*. The value of this attribute depends on the domain object type. Primitive domain object values are presented in Table 10.1.

Table 10.1.   Primitive domain objects

Type	Description	Size/Format
String	Character string	from 0 to $2^{31} - 1$ Unicode characters
Integer	Integer	32-bit two's complement
Long	Long integer	64-bit two's complement
Float	Single-precision floating point	32-bit IEEE 754 (defined in [3])
Double	Double-precision floating point	64-bit IEEE 754 (defined in [3])
Boolean	A boolean value (true or false)	true or false

4.2   Analysis Domain Definition

Domain objects are generated according to an *Analysis Domain Function (ADF)*. An ADF is a function whose image is an analysis domain. Formally,

$$f \text{ is an ADF} \iff \begin{cases} f \text{ is a function on analysis domains } D_{orig_i} \\ Im(f) = \{DO\}, \text{ where } DO \text{ are domain objects} \end{cases}$$

When two or more analysis domains exist for an ADF, the function is said to be *multi-variable*. A special analysis domain, denoted $\emptyset$, is defined by $card(\emptyset) = 0$. The existence of the analysis domain $\emptyset$ allows to distinguish *transformer* functions from *generator* functions.

DEFINITION 10.16 *An ADF f is a* generator *function iff only one origin domain of f exists that is $\emptyset$.*

A generator function creates an analysis domain without the need of preexisting data in the form of an analysis domain. A generator function may for instance generate the number π, or retrieve data from a database.

DEFINITION 10.17 *An ADF f is a* transformer *function iff at least one origin domain of f is different from $\emptyset$.*

A transformer function transforms an existing analysis domain into another analysis domain. A transformer function may for instance transform an analysis domain modeling books into another analysis domain representing the number of books for each author.

ADF functions may be embedded according to the *composition law*. The composition law allows "pipelines" of functions to be defined, in which an analysis domain being the results of an ADF is an origin domain of another ADF.

DEFINITION 10.18 *The ADF composition law, denoted* ∘, *defines an ADF* f_o *from ADF(s)* f_i *as follow:*

- *for single-variable functions,* $f_o = f_1 \circ f_2 = f_1(f_2)$;

- *for multi-variable functions,* $f_o = f_1 \circ (f_2, \ldots, f_n) = f_1(f_2, \ldots, f_n)$,

where f_1 *is a transformator function, while* f_2 *and* f_3 *are either generator or transformator functions.*

4.3   Analysis Domain Language

The *Analysis Domain Language (ADL)* is used to define ADFs. ADL is a dialect of XML — the eXtensible Markup Language. The eXtensible Markup Language [2] describes a class of data objects, called *XML documents,* and partially describes the behavior of computer programs that process them. XML is based on SGML – the Standard Generalized Markup Language [4]. XML documents are conforming to SGML documents by construction. There are multiple reasons for using XML for ADL:

- it is an emerging standard developed by the WWW consortium;

- it is a general-purpose and extensible language;

- it allows defining language grammar that can be automatically validated by a parser;

- it is designed and optimized for parsing structured documents;

- the parsing software for XML is available;

- it can be easily integrated with other XML-based web standards;

- it allows defining human-readable data in a standardized way.

ADL is basing on four elements: *Metaobjects, ObjectSets, Tags,* and *Functions.* Metaobject correspond to domain objects. ObjectSets correspond to analysis domains. Tags are basic elements of processing. Functions correspond to ADFs.

4.3.1   Modules.   ADL is structured in *modules*. A module groups metaobject definitions, definitions of functions generating these metaobjects and potentially implementation of needed features – as tags. A module may for instance define metaobjects modeling books and related-informations, functions for retrieval of book informations from a database and some new tags needed to access a database.

XML Namespaces [1] is used to avoid name collisions. Metaobject, function and tag names are universal, their scope extends beyond the module that contain them. Each module is responsible for associating itself with a URI. A module may use metaobjects, functions and tags defined in another module. A namespace referring the URI of the used module must be defined and associated with a prefix. An XML namespace must be associated to every used module.

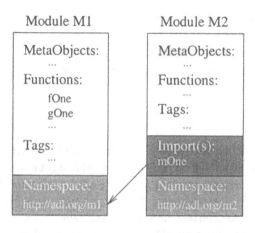

Figure 10.3.   Modules in ADL.

An example of the use of XML Namespaces for modularization of ADL is presented in Figure 10.3. Metaobjects, functions and tags defined in module M_1 may be used in module M_2 as qualified names. M_2 may, for instance, associate the prefix *mOne* to module M_1. Function *fOne* defined in M_1 may be then used in M_2 as *mOne:fOne*.

A module is defined in an XML document. A module definition document contains:

- the name of the module,

- a URI defining the associated namespace,

- potentially a list of tag definition references,

- potentially a list of function definition references, and

- potentially a list of metaobject definition references.

An example of module definition document is given below:

```
<module name="testModule"
        uri="http://nessy.pl/adl/testing">
  <tags>
    <tag-decl name="if"
                 definition="if.tdl"/>
    ...
  </tags>
  <functions>
    <function-decl name="BooksFromDB"
                      definition="retrieveBooks.fdl"/>
    ...
  </functions>
  <objects>
    <object-decl name="Book"
                    definition="Book.odl"/>
    ...
  </objects>
</module>
```

In the module definition document given above, a module named `test-Module` is defined. The URI `http://nessy.pl/adl/testing` is associated with this module. First, a tag named `if` is defined. Its definition can be found in the `if.tdl` tag definition document. Second, a function named `BooksFromDB` is defined. Its definition can be found in the `retrieveBooks.fdl` function definition document. Finally, a metaObject named Book is defined. Its definition can be found in the `Book.odl` metaobject definition document.

ADL provides a module — denoted the *core* module — which groups basic functionalities of ADL. The *core* module provides primitive metaObjects and fundamental tags for ADL. The namespace for the *core* module — the URI it is associated with — is *http://nessy.pl/adl/core*.

4.3.2   Expressions.   In ADL, expressions are defined as ${ *some Expression* }. An expression can contain:

- variable references,

- operators, and

- literals.

Variable reference

Variable references are done by names. If a variable *myVariable* has been defined, the expression ${*myVariable*} returns the variable *myVariable*. To test if *myVariable* is set, the expression ${*isEmptyObject.myVariable* } may be used.

Operators

The following operators are defined:

- relational operators: ==, !=, <, >, <=, >=
- arithmetical operators: *, +, -, /, div, mod
- logical operators: ||, &&, !
- operator `empty` that checks if a metaobject is unset or if an objectSet contains some metaobject;
- operator ”.” that retrieves metaobject attribute. For example, ${*myMetaObject.myAttribute*} retrieves the attribute *myAttribute* from metaobject *myMetaObject*;
- operator "[]" that retrieves metaobject from objectSet according to their IDs. For example, ${*myObjectSet[myMetaObjectID]*} retrieves the metaobject identified by *myMetaObjectID* from the objectSet *myObjectSet*.

Literals

The following literals are defined:

- logical: `true` or `false`,
- integers,
- floats,
- character strings surrounded by single or double quotes. The backslash character "\" is used to escape single and double quote characters, i.e. "”" is obtained by "\”". The backslash character must be entered as "\\".
- Unset value: `null`.

4.3.3   MetaObjects.   MetaObjects are defined in an XML document. A metaObject definition document contains:

- the name of the metaObject type,
- the name of the type of the metaObject identifier, a list of the attributes and their type if the metaObject is not a primitive,
- the type of the value if the metaObject is a primitive.

An example of metaObject definition document is given below:

```
<object-def type="Book">
  <id type="extendedISBN"/>
  <attributes>
    <attribute name="author" type="Person"/>
    <attribute name="title" type="String"/>
    <attribute name="editor" type="Editor"/>
  </attributes>
</object-def>
```

In the metaObject definition document presented above, a metaObject named Book is defined. It is identified by a metaObject whose type is `extendedISBN`. Three Book attributes are defined: `author` (of type Person), `title` (of type String) and `editor` (of type Editor). As attributes are defined, the metaObject Book is not a primitive metaObject.

An example of a primitive metaObject definition document is given below:

```
<object-def type="String">
  <value type="java.lang.String">
</object-def>
```

In the metaObject definition document presented above, the `String` primitive metaObject is associated with the `java.lang.String` class. No ID is defined as the `java.lang.String` is responsible for unique self-identification.

4.3.4   ObjectSets.   An objectSet is a set of metaObjects. All metaObjects of a given objectSet have the same type. An objectSet may be empty, i.e. no metaObject is a member of the objectSet. The emptiness of an objectSet may be check with the `isEmptySet` operator. If objectSet *OS* is empty, *isEmptySet_OS* is true. The emptiness of an objectSet may also be checked with the size operator. The size operator returns the size of an objectSet. The size of an objectSet is the number of metaObjects it contains. If the objectSet *OS* is empty, *OS.size* equals to 0.

The *core* module provides tags for basic operations on objectSets. Four operations are defined: objectSet creation (`declare` tag), metaObject addition to an objectSet (add tag), metaObject deletion from an objectSet (`remove` tag), and deletion of all metaObjects from an objectSet (`clear` tag). The `for-each` tag is an iterator on objectSets.

All ADF origin domains are objectSets. The image (in the mathematical sense) of all ADF is an objectSet. Figure 10.4 illustrates the relationship between ADF (functions) and objectSets.

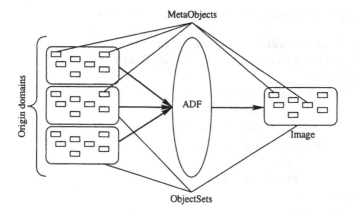

Figure 10.4. ObjectSets and ADF

4.3.5   Tags.   Tags associate *processing entities* with XML tags. A processing entity is an independent software or a part of a software, such as a database access layer or a statistical library. The XML tags associated with processing entities can be used in function definitions. Tags are the only mechanism to extend ADL. When new features are needed, a new XML tag may be associated with a processing entity that implements the needed feature.

Two kinds of tags may are defined:

- empty tags, and

- non-empty tags.

An empty tag corresponds to an XML empty tag. An empty tag does not have any content. In a function declaration, an empty tag is called by the insertion of the associated empty XML tag.

A non-empty tag corresponds to a non-empty XML tag. A non-empty tag has content, with one or many children tags. In a function declaration, a non-empty tag is called by the associated non-empty XML tag.

Processing entities may be written in various programming languages. For the Java[TM] language, which has been chosen for the implementation of the ADL compiler, two interfaces have been defined: one for empty tags, and the other for non-empty tags.

Tags are defined in an XML document. A tag definition document contains:

- the name of a tag,

- the name of programming language a tag is implemented in,

- optionally – tag parameters specific to the chosen programming language.

An example of tag definition document is given below:

```
<tag-def name="SQLQuery" lang="java">
  <javaClass name="pl.nessy.db.SQLQuery">
    <params>
      <param name="connection"
             type="String"
             required="true"/>
      <param name="query"
             type="String"
             required="true"/>
    </params>
  </javaClass>
</tag-def>
```

In the tag definition document presented above, a tag named SQLQuery is defined. It is implemented in the Java[TM] programming language. All children (connection and query) elements are specific to tag implementation in Java[TM].

4.3.6   Functions.   Functions are the core of ADL. An ADF is expressed in ADL as a function. Each function models a potential facet of a given dataset. A function processes zero, one or many objectSets. The result of the processing of a function is an objectSet. Generator ADFs, as defined in Section 10.4.3.7, are functions that do not process any objectSet. Transformers ADFs are functions that process at least one objectSet.

Functions are defined in an XML document. A function definition document contains:

- the name of a function,

- optionally – the names of modules the function uses,

- optionally – the objectSets to be processed and the type of metaObjects they contain,

- the name of the resulting objectSet and the type of metaObjects it contains,

- the processing actions to be performed.

The processing actions may be calls to tags and functions. Calls to tags are done by inserting the associated XML tags. To call functions, a special tag defined in the *core* module is applied.

An example of function definition document is given below:

```
1.  <function-def name="BooksFromDB"
2.     xmlns:core="http://nessy.pl/adl/core"
3.     xmlns:col ="http://nessy.pl/adl/collections">
4.
5.     <param  name="isbnList"  type="ISBN"/>
6.     <param  name="bookDB"     type="BookFromDB"/>
7.     <result name="books"      type="Book"/>
8.
9.     <processing>
10.       <declare name="tempBooks" type="Book"
11.               isASet="true"/>
12.       <core:for-each var="bookFromDB" items="bookDB">
13.         <core:declare name="localBook" type="Book"/>
14.         <core:set
15.           obj="localBookList"
16.           attribute="title"
17.           value="${bookFromDB.title}"/>
18.
19.         <col:ifContains
20.           col="isbnList"
21.           item="${bookDB.isbn}">
22.           <core:set
23.             obj="localBook"
24.             attribute="id"
25.             value="${bookDB.isbn}"/>
26.         </col:ifContains>
27.
28.         <add to-set="tempBooks" name="localBook"/>
29.       </core:for-each>
30.
31.     </core:execute name="col:deleteDoublons"
32.                    into="books">
33.       <core:param value="tempBooks"/>
34.     </core:execute>
35.   </processing>
36. </function-def>
```

In the function definition document presented above, a function named BooksFromDB is defined. It uses the core module (line 2) and a possible col module responsible for extended collection manipulation (3.). The function processes two objectSets isbnList and bookDB containing metaObjects of type ISBN and BookFromDB (lines 5 and 6), respectively. The resulting objectSet books contains metaObjects of type Book (line 7).

4.3.7   The *core* Module.   The *core* module defines a set of primitive metaObjects and tags. Primitive objects are defined in Section 10.4.1. As presented in Table 10.2, tags in the *core* module are classified in five categories:

- variable declaration,

- metaObject attribute setting,

- control flow statements,

- function call, and

- objectSet manipulation operations.

Table 10.2.   Tags defined in the *core* module

Tag category	Tag(s) name
Variable declaration	declare
MetaObject attribute setting	set
Control flow statement	choose, if
Function call	execute
ObjectSet manipulation	add, for-each, remove, clear

5.   Classification of Domain Objects

5.1   Parametric Analysis

The goal of classification is to provide a synthetic view of an aspect of a given dataset. The choice of a facet corresponds to the choice of an ADF. The result of the execution of an ADF is an analysis domain, i.e. a set of domain objects. The ADF defines the facet of the dataset to be analyzed, generating domain objects modeling a given facet.

As domain objects may model complex views of a dataset, and the interests of a given user may be different from other users' interests, many analyses may be performed on the same domain objects. For this reason, the concept of parametric analysis is proposed.

DEFINITION 10.19 *An analysis is* parametric *if various criteria may be used to perform various analyses of a given analysis domain.*

A given analysis domain consists of a set of domain objects. All domain objects of a given analysis domain are of the same type. As a consequence, the type of an analysis domain may be defined as follows:

DEFINITION 10.20 *The type of an analysis domain* AD *is the type of domain objects of the analysis domain* AD.

The domain object type – and thus the analysis domain type – defines the attributes of all domain objects of this type. So, given an analysis domain, the attributes of domain objects of the analysis domain are known.

Analysis criteria need the presence of some attributes. Attribute values are data to be analyzed. Attribute names are semantics associated with data to be analyzed. Therefore, every analysis criterion is associated with a given domain object type. As a consequence, the type of an analysis criterion may be defined as follows:

DEFINITION 10.21 *The type of an analysis criterion* AC *is the type of domain objects the* AC *is associated with.*

A given analysis domain may be associated only with the analysis criteria corresponding with the analysis domain type. A relationship many-to-many between analysis domains and analysis criteria exists. This relationship is a compatibility relationship.

DEFINITION 10.22 *An analysis domain* AD *and an analysis criterion* AC *are* compatible *iff the type of* AD *and the type of* AC *are the same*

The concept of parametric analysis is illustrated in Figure 10.5. Two different analysis domains may be analyzed according to various criteria. Each criterion

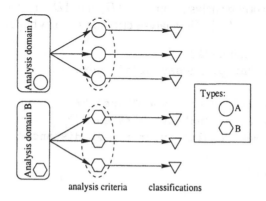

Figure 10.5. Parameterizable analysis

produces a classification. Each criterion is associated with an analysis domain type. In Figure 10.5, it is assumed that the domain analysis domain types of A and B are different. As a consequence, no criterion may be used for both analysis domain. The analysis domain A is *compatible* with the analysis criteria represented by a circle. The analysis domain B is *compatible* with the analysis criteria represented by a hexagon. Analysis of A and B are parametric: various criteria may be used to perform various analyses of both A and B.

5.2   Analysis Criteria Definition

An analysis criterion is a metric on a given analysis domain. Formally:

DEFINITION 10.23 *A function AC is an* analysis criterion *iff*

$$\begin{cases} AC \text{ is a function from } AD^2 \text{ to } \mathbb{R}^+ \\ \forall (x,y) \in AD^2, \quad\quad x = y \;\Leftrightarrow AC(x,y) = 0 \\ \forall (x,y) \in AD^2, \quad\quad AC(x,y) \;= AC(y,x) \\ \forall (x,y,z) \in AD^3, \quad AC(x,y) \;\leq AC(x,z) + AC(y,z) \end{cases}$$

Analysis criteria are a subset of transformer functions (*Cf.* Section 10.4.2), so they are ADFs. They can, therefore, be defined in ADL.

An analysis criterion is an ADF with two analysis domain, each of them containing only one domain object. The resulting domain contains only one domain object modeling the concept of distance between two domain objects.

Formally, let AC denote an analysis criterion on an analysis domain AD. The type of AC, as well as AD, is denoted *typeAC*. Let do_1 and do_2 denote two domain objects of AD. Let $r \in \mathbb{R}^{+*}$ denote the distance between do_1 and do_2 according to AC. Let AD_r denote the resulting analysis domain.

For AC, two origin analysis domains AD_1 and AD_2 are defined by $AD_1 = \{do_1\}$ and $AD_2 = \{do_2\}$. The analysis criterion AC may be defined as follows:

```
<function-def name="AC"
  xmlns:core="http://nessy.pl/adl/core">

  <param  name="first"  type="typeAC"/>
  <param  name="second" type="typeAC"/>
  <result name="result" type="typeAC_distance"/>

  <processing>
  ...
  </processing>
</function>
```

AD_r contains only one domain object do_r. The type of do_r — which is also the type of AD_r — is *typeAC_distance*. Domain objects of this type may be defined as follows:

```
<object-def type="typeAC_distance">
  <id type="core:Integer"/>
  <attributes>
    <attribute name="first"    type="typeAC"/>
    <attribute name="second"   type="typeAC"/>
    <attribute name="distance" type="Float"/>
  </attributes>
</object-def>
```

Processing actions to be performed to calculate the distance between do_1 and do_2 are defined by calls to functions or tags, like for every ADF. The user defining new analysis criterion has to check whether the set of processing actions she/he uses to define the processing of the analysis criterion defines a metric. The ADF compiler does not perform any checking of the conditions given in Definition 10.23.

5.3   Classifications

Given an analysis domain and an analysis criterion that are compatible, a classification can be processed. A classification is the result of the analysis process. The structure of the classification is based on the inter-class distance. Classifications allow analysis domains to be partitioned at various level of granularity by the threshold operation.

5.3.1   Classification Structure.   A classification is defined in terms of *classes* and *inter-classes distances*. A class may contain either other classes and an inter-class distance, or one or more metaObjects (with an inter-class distance always equal to 0). More formally, let C denote a classification on analysis domain DA. C is a set of classes denoted c_i. Classes are formally defined as follows:

$$\forall c_i \in C, \begin{cases} c_i = (\{c_j\}, d_i), \text{ where } \forall j, c_j \in C, d_i \in \mathbb{R}^{+*} \\ \text{or} \\ c_i = \{MO_j\}, \text{ where } \forall j, MO_j \in DA \end{cases}$$

$$\forall (c_i, c_j) \in C^2, c_i \subset c_j \text{ or } c_i \supset c_j \text{ or } c_i \bigcap c_j = \emptyset$$

Two kinds of classes exist. Some classes – denoted *atomic classes* – contains only metaObjects. Others – denoted *complex classes* – contains only classes and an inter-class distance.

The classification is an indexed hierarchy under the condition that an additional constraint is set on interclass distances:

$$\forall(c_i, c_j) \in C^2 \text{ such as } c_i \neq c_j, \; c_i \subset c_j \Rightarrow d_i < d_j,$$

where d_i (respectively d_j) is the inter-class distance associated with c_i (respectively c_j) and the inter-class distance of atomic classes equals 0.

Let a distance D on C be defined as follows:

- $c_i \subset c_j \Rightarrow D(c_i, c_j) = d_j$,

- if $c_i \cap c_j = \emptyset$, let $c_k \in C$ be such that $c_i \subset c_k$, $c_j \subset c_k$, and
  $\forall c_l \in C, c_l \subset c_k \Rightarrow \neg(c_i \subset c_l \text{ and } c_j \subset c_l)$. Then $D(c_i, c_j) = d_k$.

LEMMA 10.24 *In an indexed hierarchical classification, the inter-class distance d_i associated with class c_i observes $D(c_j, c_{j'}) \leq d_i$, where $c_j \subset c_i$ and $c_{j'} \subset c_i$.*

Proof. If $c_j \subset c_{j'}$, $D(c_j, c_{j'}) = d_{j'}$. As $c_j \subset c_i$, $d_j \leq d_j$. Therefore $D(c_j, c_{j'}) \leq d_i$.

If $c_{j'} \subset c_j$, a similar reasoning may be used.

If $c_j \cap c_{j'} = \emptyset$, there exists $c_k \in C$ such that $c_j \subset c_k$, $c_{j'} \subset c_k$, and $\forall c_l \in C, c_l \subset c_k \Rightarrow \neg(c_j \subset c_l \text{ and } c_{j'} \subset c_l)$. By definition, $D(c_j, c_{j'}) = d_k$. Or, as $c_i \in C$, $c_j \subset c_i$, and $c_{j'} \subset c_i$, by definition of c_k, $c_k \subset c_i$. Then $d_k \leq d_i$. As a conclusion, $D(c_j, c_{j'}) = d_k \leq d_i$. $\square$

5.3.2   Classification Generation.
Classification generation is an operation that, given an analysis domain and a compatible analysis criterion, generates a classification. Classification generation is based on ultrametric automatic hierarchical classification algorithm (cf. Section 10.2.3).

An analysis criterion is not an ultrametric. Analysis criteria only have to be metrics. However, a path metric – which is an ultrametric – can be derived from each metric (cf. Section 10.2.4). The path metric derivation is an operation whose computational complexity in terms of processing is very high. When the number of domain objects of an analysis domain is n, a function processing all possible paths between two domain objects can be computed in $O(n!)$ time.

Proof. Consider an analysis domain AD such that $\text{card}(AD) = n + 2$. Let do_1 and do_2 denote two domain objects in AD. Let P_{do_1,do_2} denote the set of paths from do_1 to do_2. Then,

$$\text{card}(P_{do_1,do_2}) = n! \sum_{p=0}^{n-1} \frac{1}{(n-p)!}$$

As $\lim_{n \to \infty} \sum_{p=0}^{n-1} = e - 1$,

$$\lim_{n \to \infty} \text{card}(P_{do_1,do_2}) = \lim_{n \to \infty} n! \sum_{p=0}^{n-1} \frac{1}{(n-p)!} \simeq n!(e-1)$$

Therefore, a function processing all possible paths between two domain objects can be computed in $O(n!)$ time.   □

We conclude that the path metric derivation operation cannot be performed directly because of the high complexity of the algorithm.

Another solution to derive ultrametric from metric is based on characteristics of ultrametrics:

LEMMA 10.25 *In an ultrametric space, all triangles are isosceles.*

Proof. Let δ denote an ultrametric on a space A. Let assume that three elements of A exist, a, b, and c, such that the triangle (a, b, c) is not isosceles. Assume that $\delta(a, b) < \delta(b, c) < \delta(a, c)$ — other cases are equivalent to this one by permutation of a, b, and c. Therefore, the condition $\delta(a, c) \leq \sup[\delta(a, b), \delta(b, c)]$ is not observed. As a conclusion, the hypothesis that a non isosceles triangle may exist is false.   □

Using this characteristics of ultrametrics, we define the "isoscelization" operation. The "isoscelization" operation transforms every triangle in an isosceles triangle in which the three sides s_1, s_2, and s_3 observes the following: $\forall (i, j, k) \in [1, 2, 3]^3$, $s_i \leq \sup[s_j, s_k]$.

DEFINITION 10.26 *The "isoscelization" operation transforms*

a triangle (a, b, c) such that $\begin{cases} \delta(a, b) = s_1 \\ \delta(a, c) = s_2 \\ \delta(b, c) = s_3 \\ s_1 \leq s_2 \leq s_3 \end{cases}$

into a triangle (a, b, c), where $\begin{cases} \delta(a, b) = s_1' = s_1 \\ \delta(a, c) = s_2' = s_2 \\ \delta(b, c) = s_3' = s_2 \end{cases}$.

The "isoscelization" operation is illustrated in Figure 10.6. The original triangle is the one on the left side. The transformed triangle is the one on the right side. The original triangle is a scalene triangle. After modification, the longest side – s_3 in the figure – is altered so that its length equals to the length of side s_2. Side s_2 is the side whose length is between s_1 – the smallest side – and s_3 – the longest side.

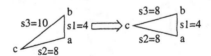

Figure 10.6. The "isoscelization" operation.

If the "isoscelization" operation is performed on all the triangles existing in a space A measurable with distance d, all the triangles will be isosceles. A new distance δ may be then defined on A as follows: the distance between two elements of A — denoted a_1 and a_2 — is the length of the segment $a_1 a_2$ (in the space in which all triangles are isosceles).

It is worth to emphasize that the new distance δ obtained as explained above is an ultrametric. The proof is obvious as the constraints defining an ultrametrics, defined in Section 10.2.3, are observed. Constraints 10.6 and 10.7 come directly from properties of the metric d, and Constraint 10.8 is ensured by the "isoscelization" operation.

The complexity of the ultrametric processing based on the "isoscelization" operation is smaller than the processing based on path metrics. The complexity of the proposed algorithm is $O(n^3)$.

LEMMA 10.27 *Given a space A such that $card(A) = n$, the number of triangles existing in A equals $\frac{n(n-1)(n-2)}{6}$.*

Proof. A triangle consists of three points: a, b, and c. There are n possibilities for the choice of a. There are then $n-1$ possibilities for the choice of b. Finally, there are $n - 2$ possibilities for the choice of c. So, there are $n(n - 1)(n - 2)$ triplets in A. Each triangle is counted six times with permutations: (a, b, c) is the same triangle as (a, c, b), etc. Therefore, the number of triangles in A equals $\frac{n(n-1)(n-2)}{6}$.   □

The following algorithm may be used to perform the "isoscelization" of space A:

```
1. segments = orderedListOfAllSegments();
2. isoSegments = new List();
3. nonIsoSegments = orderedListOfAllSegments;
```

```
4.  while (nonIsoSegments.size() !=0 ) {
5.     [a,b]=nonIsoSegments.firstElement();
6.     for-each ( c in A, c <> a and c <> b ) {
7.        isoscelization(a,b,c);
8.     }
9.     isoSegments.add([a,b]);
10.    nonIsoSegments.remove([a,b]);
11.    nonIsoSegments.sort();
12. }
```

The complexity of the presented algorithm is $O(n^3)$.

Proof. The number of segments in a space whose cardinal is n equals $\frac{n(n-1)}{2}$. For each segment, the loop defined between lines 6 and 8 is executed $n - 2$ times. Therefore, the algorithm complexity is $\frac{n(n-1)}{2} \times (n - 2) \simeq O(n^3)$.   □

5.3.3   Threshold Operation.

Lemma 10.24 allows to define a *threshold* operation on classifications. The threshold operation provides various partitions of the analyzed analysis domain according to a threshold.

Two additional concepts are required to define the threshold operation: the concept of *class contents* and the concept of *t-max class*.

DEFINITION 10.28 *The contents of a given class c_i of a classification C is a set of domain objects, denoted* $Contents(c_i)$.

- *For atomic classes, the class contents is the class itself, i.e.* $Contents(c_i) = c_i = \{MO_j, \text{where } \forall j, MO_j \in DA\}$.

- *For complex classes, the class contents is the union of contents of all embedded classes, i.e.* $Contents(c_i) = \bigcup_j Contents(c_j)$ *with the notations used in Section 10.5.3.1.*

The class contents operation is illustrated in Figure 10.7. The full classification C is presented in a). Domain objects are represented by circles. Five domain objects exist in C, denoted a, b, c, d, and e. Classes are represented by ellipses. Eight classes exist, denoted c_i, where $i \in [1, \ldots, 8]$. The "is-embedded-in" relationship is represented by lines between classes. Classes c_2 and c_3 are, for instance, embedded in c_1. For atomic classes (c_i, where $i \in [4, \ldots, 8]$), $Contents(c_i)$ is the set of domain objects contained in c_i. $Contents(c_4)$ is therefore $\{a\}$. When a class is a complex class, the class contents is a set of object domains which is calculated recursively with the $Contents()$ function. Therefore, $Contents(c_2) = Contents(c_4) \cup Contents(c_5) \cup Contents(c_6) =$

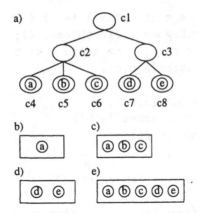

Figure 10.7. The *class contents* operation. a) the full classification C; b) $Contents(c_4)$; c) $Contents(c_2)$; d) $Contents(c_3)$; e) $Contents(c_1)$

$\{a, b, c\}$.
$Contents(c_3) = Contents(c_7) \cup Contents(c_8) = \{d, e\}$. Finally,
$Contents(c_1) = Contents(c_2) \cup Contents(c_3) = \{a, b, c, d, e\}$.

DEFINITION 10.29 *Given $t \in \mathbb{R}^{+*}$, a class c_i is a t-max class iff*

$$d_i \leq t \text{ and } \neg(\exists c_j \text{ such that } c_i \subset c_j \text{ and } d_j \leq t)$$

In the classification presented in Figure 10.8, classes are represented by ellipses, distances associated with classes are given inside ellipses, "is-embedded-in" relationship is represented by lines between ellipses. In this classification example, c_2 is a 3-max class: the distance d_2 associated with c_2 observes $d_2 = 3 \leq t = 3$, and there is no class c_j such that $c_2 \subset c_j$ and $d_j \leq 3$ (the only class that contains c_2 is c_1, but $d_1 = 7$). Class c_3 is also a 3-max class: the distance d_3 associated with c_3 observes $d_3 = 2 \leq t = 3$, and there is no class c_j such that $c_3 \subset c_j$ and $d_j \leq 3$ (the only class that contains c_3 is c_1, but $d_1 = 7$).

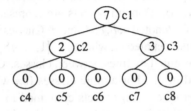

Figure 10.8. Classification example

DEFINITION 10.30 *Given a threshold t, the threshold operation T_t creates a partition P_t of a classification C. P_t is the set of contents of all t-max classes of C. Formally,*

$$P_t = \{Contents(c_i), \text{ where } c_i \text{ is a } t - max \text{ class}\}$$

Various threshold operation results are illustrated in Figure 10.9. When $t = 0$, the partition obtained by the threshold operation is a set of atomic classes. With the classification given in Figure 10.9 a), $P_0 = P_1$, because all 0-max classes are all 1-max classes. Similarly, $P_5 = P_7$, because all 5-max classes are 7-max classes.

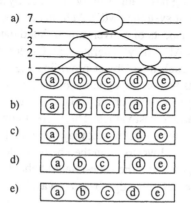

Figure 10.9. The threshold operation. a) Classification; b) P_1; c) P_2; d) P_3; e) P_7

The threshold provides the granularity of the obtained partition. The higher the threshold is, the lower the number of classes in the obtained partition is. In the context of knowledge extraction, this characteristics of the threshold operation is a key feature as it allows:

- various analysis levels; when the threshold is low, the generated partition consists of many classes, representing a fine-grained analysis. When the threshold is high, the generated partition consists of a few classes, representing a high-level analysis, giving an overview of the analyzed facet;

- fast focusing on details; starting from a high-level analysis, a user can select a few classes in the partition which are of special interest. These classes can further be analyzed in details by the application of a threshold operation with a lower threshold. The repetition of this technique allows to focus quickly on interesting details.

6.   Applications

The universality of the ADL language – which is the basis of the proposed multi-facetanalysis mechanism – allows for knowledge extraction in various areas and according to various criteria. Four knowledge extraction criteria may be distinguished: time-related, structural, contents-based, and combined.

Time-related knowledge extraction may be used to study the evolution of datasets and retrieve knowledge related to this evolution. Examples of time-related knowledge extraction are the study of a stock market evolution, or the analysis of a standardization process. Time-related knowledge extraction requires means of accessing past data, usually provided by a time-aware database or a content management system (CMS). ADL accessing these data source are used to model various aspects of a given time-related dataset. In the case of a stock market study, an ADL may generate metaObjects modeling the overall evolution of auctions, each metaObject providing the highest and the lowest values of the auction, as well as the dynamic of the auction. Auctions may then be classified according to various criteria, such as their dynamics or the mean value of their highest and lowest values. Therefore, knowledge concerning the dynamics of auctions in the stock market may be extracted from the generated hierarchical classification. Investors can then better understand the structure of the stock market, and, knowing the time-related behavior of various auctions, invest in a better – at least knowledge-based – way.

Structural knowledge extraction is based on the structural characteristics of data. In the case of the Web, structural knowledge extraction may base on the hypertext characteristics of data. Examples of structural knowledge extraction are the analysis of data source relevance on a given topic, or study of the organization of a web site. Structural knowledge extraction requires means of structure retrieval. ADL tags, specialized in structure retrieval, may be developed and reused. A tag retrieving a Web page and the hyperlinks it contains may be used by many ADFs. In the case of a study of data source relevance, an ADF may generate metaObjects modeling the the page structure, each metaObject providing the number of links in a given page, the list of addresses of these links, and the number of pages having at least one link to this page. Web pages may then be classified according to various criteria, such as their "reference" status (the highest number of links to a given page exists, the highest its "reference" status). Web pages may also be classified according to the number of links to other pages, providing a classification of web pages to identify resources catalogs. Therefore, people interested in a given topic may have a faster access to important informations – "reference" pages – or may identify the pages containing meta-informations about the given topic. The structural knowledge extraction allows for identification of main elements in a given dataset.

Contents-based knowledge extraction may be used to study the organization of datasets in regard to its contents. Examples of contents-related knowledge extraction are the study of a set of documents to find main topics, or the classification of documents in regard to their relevance to a given topic. Content-based knowledge extraction requires means of filtering document contents, so that words with a low information quantity – such as "the", "a", or "is" – are not taken into account in the contents of documents. Tags filtering contents may be used by many ADFs which may model various aspects of a given set of documents. An ADF may for example generate metaObjects modeling the relevance of a document to the "physics" topics, each metaObject providing the number of occurrences of words "physics", "astrophysics", and "gravitation" in a given document and the identifier of the document. Documents may then be classified according to various criteria, such as their relevance to the gravitation topic or their relevance to the astrophysics topic. Another ADF may generate metaObjects modeling words and the number of their occurrence of words in the whole set of documents. Words may then be classified according to their frequency in the set of documents, allowing for topics extraction. Contents-based knowledge extraction allows for topics retrieval and identification of relevant documents to a given topic.

Combined knowledge extraction allows for dataset analysis in regard to mixed criteria: time-related, structural, and contents-based. An example of combined knowledge extraction is the study of centers of interest in the Java^{TM} community in the last five years. A database can be used to stored web pages from Java-related web sites. An ADF may extract keywords from the database, another ADF may retrieve web pages associated with these keywords, and a structural analysis may be performed to retrieve relationships between keywords. Then, a last ADF may retrieve time-related data associated with the keywords. Finally, various classifications may be performed on the resulting metaObjects according to various criteria: center of interests can be classified according to the number of occurrence of a given word in the stored Web pages with a scaling factor implying a highest interest in "new" keywords; another classification can stress on the structural knowledge retrieval with an influence of the number of occurrence of a given word, etc. Combined knowledge extraction provides complex analyses in which many factors are taken into account.

7.   Conclusions

The generic hierarchical classification using the single-link clustering technique provides a solution to the problem of multi-facet analysis of a given dataset. The proposed technique may be the basis for knowledge extraction taking into account various aspects of a given dataset.

Two ideas that are the basis of the generic hierarchical classification technique are: first, the interests of various users concerning a given dataset can be different, second, expression of the subject and the criteria of the analyses must be easily understood be humans and extensible. As a consequence, the language ADL, used for definition of both the subjects of the analysis and the criteria, provides uniform means of expressing the various facets of a dataset to be analyzed.

Various application fields are possible for the generic hierarchical classification using the single-link clustering: time-related, structural, contents-based, and combined knowledge extraction. The combined knowledge extraction takes into account data evolution, structure of a dataset, and contents, allowing to extract information concerning structured, time-changing data.

The generic hierarchical classification technique opens new directions of research. An example is the use of software agents in electronic negotiations. Using the proposed analysis mechanism, advanced behavior models can be build for negotiating agents. Psychological and social models may base on data retrieved from the analysis of various facets of the negotiation process. An agent may for example have a "collaborative" behavior, i.e. may look for negotiators having similar proposals to build a group of negotiators in order to increase its weigh in the negotiation process.

References

[1] Bray T, Hollander D, and Layman A (1999), Namespaces in XML, W3C Recommendation, http://www.w3.org/TR/1999/REC-xml-names-19990114/

[2] Bray T, Paoli J, Sperberg-McQeen CM, and Maler E (2000), Extensible Markup Language (XML) 1.0 (Second Edition), W3C Recommendation, http://www.w3.org/TR/2000/REC-xml-20001006/

[3] IEEE (1987), IEEE Standard for Binary Floating-Point Arithmetic. ANSI/IEEE Std. 754-1985. *ACM SIGPLAN Notices 22*, 2.

[4] International Organization for Standardization (1986), Information Processing – Text and Office Systems – Standard Generalized Markup Language (SGML). Tech. Rep. 8879:1986(E), ISO, Geneva, Swissland.

[5] Iwayama M and Tokunaga T (1995), Hierarchical Bayesian Clustering for Automatic Text Classification. In *Proceedings of IJCAI-95, 14th International Joint Conference on Artificial Intelligence*, pp. 1322–1327.

[6] Kohonen T (2001), *Self-Organizing Maps*, 3rd ed. Information Sciences. Springer-Verlag, New York.

[7] Kohonen T (1990), The Self-Organizing Map. In *Proceedings of the IEEE*, vol. 78, pp. 1454–1480.

[8] Picard W (2001), Collaborative Document Edition in a Highly Concurrent Environment. In *First International Workshop on Web-Based Collaboration, at the 12th International Workshop on Database and Expert Systems Applications, DEXA 2001*, pp. 514–518.

[9] Unicode Consortium (2000), *The Unicode Standard, Version 3.0*. Addison-Wesley.

Chapter 11

CLUSTERING OF DOCUMENTS ON THE BASIS OF TEXT FUZZY SIMILARITY [*]

Piotr S. Szczepaniak [1, 2], Adam Niewiadomski [1],

[1]   *Institute of Computer Science, Technical University of Lodz*
      Sterlinga 16/18, 90-217 Lodz, Poland
[2]   *Systems Research Institute, Polish Academy of Sciences*
      Newelska 6, 01-447 Warsaw, Poland

Abstract: This chapter focuses on application of a fuzzy similarity measure of textual records to clustering of textual documents. The method, rooted in the theory of fuzzy sets, is based on concepts used in comparison of natural language words and sentences. In particular, the fuzzy relation is the kernel of the presented idea.

Keywords: document classification, clustering of textual documents, fuzzy set, fuzzy similarity measure, text comparison

1.   CLUSTERING OF DOCUMENTS – BASIC CONCEPTS

Defining a document cluster, one may generally adopt the view having roots in [1,2] and say that

a cluster is a group of documents that are more similar to one another than to the members of any other cluster.

In clustering the problems involved cover: representation of documents, choice of a similarity measure, and a grouping method. For any kind of clustering it is crucial to define the term 'similarity' so that it can be measured in some well-defined way. In metric spaces, the distance norm is

[*] This work has partly been supported by the NATO Scientific Committee via the Spanish Ministry for Science and Technology; grant holder – P.S.Szczepaniak; host institution – Politechnical University, Madrid, Spain, 2002/2003.

used for determination of the distance from a data vector to the prototype of a considered cluster or for evaluation of the distances between objects of a group. The definition of the distance for textual objects is a more complicated task; examples like Jaccard, Cosine and Dice Coefficients can frequently be found in literature, e.g. [3-5]. The similarity of two documents is usually determined on the basis of the number of topical terms that appear in both of the documents under consideration.

Clusters can be well-separated or overlapping, and their number as well as the reference documents (prototypes) may be known or may not exist before the clustering procedure is started.

Clustering enables more effective information retrieval already when part of a large collection of diverse documents is dealt with, but the real importance of the problem becomes evident when the largest library, namely the Web, is to be used [3].

Diverse algorithms (models) for ranking Web documents according to the likelihood of relevance assigned by a system to a given user query have been developed. Following the taxonomy proposed in [3] the models may be divided into two groups; namely classic and alternative ones. Classic models include vector-space ones as well as probabilistic and Boolean models. The number and variety of alternative models are remarkable; they cover: fuzzy set models, extended Boolean models, generalised vector space models, neural network models, etc. Since ranking and clustering are closely related, the same or slightly modified approaches are in use.

1.1   Hard Partition

The objective of the document partition is to create c clusters in the collection B of documents. Let us assume that the number c is known or desired. The hard partition as defined by Bezdek [1] can be applied here.

Let $p(B)$ denote the power of set B. The hard partition of B is a family of sub-collections $\{ B_i \mid 1 \le i \le c \} \subset p(B)$ which possesses the following properties:

$$\bigcup_{i=1}^{c} B_i = B$$

$$B_i \cap B_j = \varnothing, \qquad 1 \le i \ne j \le c,$$
$$\varnothing \subset B_i \subset B, \qquad 1 \le i \le c.$$

In other words, sub-collections B_i:
- collectively form collection **B**,
- are disjoint,
- are non empty and any single B_i is a full collection.

If the documents of the sub-collection fulfill some similarity requirement, we will speak about the cluster.

In the literature, the situation when each document of the collection belongs exactly to one cluster is frequently called a hierarchical clustering.

It is easy to notice that the decision about the membership of documents in a cluster is not always simple. As an illustration, consider a collection of eight documents related to two topics, i.e. dealing with two subjects to various extents estimated by a domain expert (Fig.1).

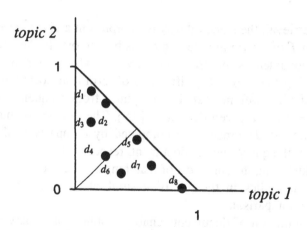

Figure 1-1. Evaluation of document content

The co-ordinate of document d_i on *topic1* axis says in how high percentage, according to the expert's opinion, the considered document deals with topic *no1*. Similarly, the co-ordinate on *topic2* axis gives analogous information concerning topic *no 2*.

Here, one can see two separated sub-collections $B_1 = \{ d_1\ d_2\ d_3 \}$ and $B_2 = \{ d_6\ d_7\ d_8 \}$ and two documents d_4, d_5 which lay in between and may be assigned to one of the groups or may even create a new sub-collection.

On the other hand, it can be said that to a certain extent each of the eight documents belongs to some extend to both clusters – their membership is fuzzy. This statement is particularly apt with respect to documents that lay on the border.

1.2   Fuzzy Clustering

Fuzzy clustering applied to different tasks of information retrieval took a remarkable place in publications last years. The topics that were frequently addressed include matching of queries with documents, representation of user profiles, and document-document matching.

As mentioned above, to perform clustering a suitable representation of documents, a similarity measure, and a grouping method should be selected and implemented.

In information retrieval, the standard way is to represent a given set B of documents and a set T of querying/indexing terms by vectors. In the vector space model, each document is represented by a vector whose elements are numbers characterising the *weight* (significance) of term t_j in document d_i. These so-called indexing weights can be computed from frequencies of occurrence of the terms in a given document [8,9]. The degrees of match between a query and the documents are computed by comparison of the vectors that represent the query and the document, respectively.

For document clustering, the same test of matching can be used; the only and simple modification lies in the use of a similarity measure for the document-document comparison.

Numerical representation of documents enables application of any hard or fuzzy clustering method. Respecting the topic of this section, the popular fuzzy c-means algorithms should be mentioned [10,11]. This is a large family of methods that work iteratively and form clusters by minimising an objective function. The clusters are called fuzzy because the membership of the considered documents in given clusters is graded.

The clustering idea presented in the following applies hard partitioning as defined in section 1.1 but uses a novel method for fuzzy evaluation of similarity between textual documents, cf. also [12,13].

2.   FUZZY TEXT SIMILARITY

2.1   Basic Definitions

Fuzzy set and fuzzy relation

The concept of a fuzzy set was introduced by Zadeh in 1965 [6]. To each element of a considered space, he added a positive real number from the [0,1] interval interpreted as a "membership level (or degree)". Formally, a fuzzy set A in a non-empty space X is a set of ordered pairs

$$A = \{<x, \mu A(x)>: x \in X \}, \tag{2.1}$$

where $\mu_A: X \rightarrow [0,1]$ – the membership function.

A fuzzy relation can be defined on the basis of (2.1), cf.[7].

Fuzzy relation R in the Cartesian product of two non-empty spaces X and Y is a set of pairs:

$$R = \{<(x, y), \mu_R(x, y)>: x \in X, \ y \in Y \}, \tag{2.2}$$

where $\mu_R: X \times Y \rightarrow [0,1]$ is the membership function. The positive real number $\mu_R(x, y)$ is usually interpreted as a degree of relationship between x and y.

If it has the following properties:
a) reflexivity, if and only if
$$\mu R(x, x) = 1 \quad \forall x \in X \tag{2.3}$$
b) symmetry, if and only if
$$\mu R(x, y) = \mu R(y, x) \quad \forall x, y \in X \tag{2.4}$$
a fuzzy relation is called a "neighbourhood relation" and can be interpreted as a model of non-transitive similarity.

2.2   Method

In a natural fashion, the introductory stage in the development of the method for the full text comparison should be a method for comparison of single words.

Here, a fuzzy relation

$$RW = \{(<w_1, w_2>, \mu_{RW}(w_1, w_2)): \; w_1, w_2 \in W\}$$

on W – the set of all words within the universe of discourse, for example a considered language or dictionary – is proposed as a useful instrument.

A possible form of the membership function $\mu_{RW}: W \times W \to [0,1]$ may be

$$\mu_{RW}(w_1, w_2) = \frac{2}{(N^2 + N)} \sum_{i=1}^{N(w_1)} \sum_{j=1}^{N(w_1)-i+1} h(i, j) \quad \forall w_1, w_2 \in W \qquad (2.5)$$

where:

$N(w_1)$, $N(w_2)$ – the number of letters in words w_1, w_2, respectively;

$N = \max\{N(w_1), N(w_2)\}$ – the maximal length of the considered words;

$h(i,j)$ – the value of the binary function,

        i.e. $h(i, j) = 1$ if a subsequence, containing i letters of word w_1 and beginning from the j-th position in w_1, appears at least once in word w_2; otherwise $h(i, j) = 0$;

$h(i, j) = 0$ also if $i > N(w_2)$ or $i > N(w_1)$.

Note that $0,5 \, (N^2 + N)$ is the number of possible subsequences to be considered.

Example:

Let us take the sample pair of words w_1 = *REFERENCE* and w_2 = *REFEREE*.

Here $N(w1) = 9$ *and* $N(w2) = 7$, $N = max\{ N(w1), N(w2)\} = 9$, $\mu_{RW}(w_1, w_2) = \mu_{RW}(w_2, w_1) = 22/45 = 0{,}489$.

Such a construction of the membership function μ_{RW} reflects the human intuition: "the more common subsequences two given words contain, the more similar they are". Note that the method determines the syntactical similarity only for a given pair of words. The value of the membership function contains no information on the sense or semantics of the arguments.

Basing on the measure (2.5) it is possible to introduce the similarity measure for documents. Here, the document is considered to be a set (not a sequence) of words. Let us define a fuzzy relation on the set of all documents B, with the membership function of the form

$$\mu_{RB}(d_1,d_2)=\frac{1}{N}\sum_{i=1}^{N(d_1)}\max_{j\in\{1,...,N(d_2)\}}\mu_{RW}(w_i,w_j)\qquad(2.6)$$

where:

d_1, d_2 – the documents to be compared;

$N(d_1)$, $N(d_2)$ – the number of words in document d_1 and d_2
  (the length of d_1 and d_2, respectively);

$N = \max\{N(d_1), N(d_2)\}$;

μ_{RW} – the similarity measure for words defined by (2.5).

It is very frequently needed to find a common point (the same syntax or close semantics) in two textual documents. Generally, there are two groups of methods for determining this dependence. The first allows computation of a real non-negative number which is interpreted as the *distance* between a given pair of documents; the smaller – closer to zero – that distance is, the closer to each other the documents are. In the second group of methods the result is a real number from the interval [0,1] which is interpreted as the value of the membership function needed in the definition of a fuzzy relation. This relation models the *similarity* between two given documents, and is defined on the set of all words – W. It is often a *neighbourhood relation*, which means that it is reflexive and symmetrical on W. The value 1.0 of that function means that the considered documents are identical; on the other hand the value close to zero suggests that the documents are different. The comparison offered by (2.6) is of the latter kind.

3. CLASSIFICATION OF DOCUMENTS

The problem at hand is as follows. Given a collection B of N textual documents, find a family of $c<N$ sub-collections $\{B_i \mid 1\le i \le c\}$ that group

documents being more similar to one another than to members of other clusters or at least more similar to their own cluster centre than to others.

Before the grouping process is started, basic decisions related to the representation of documents as well as to the definitions of similarity measure and cluster centre should be taken. To some extent, the choice of an existing grouping method or development of a new one reflects those preliminary decisions.

3.1   Preliminary Decisions

Representation of documents

The documents can be given in their original full text version. They may also be restricted to the most representative part (for example to abstract, summary, or both when considering scientific papers). In a very restrictive case, a sequence of keywords/indexing terms can be used. Of course, preprocessing involving elimination of stopwords and lexical analysis is a very advantageous procedure. For the similarity measure proposed in section 2, stemming of the remaining words (i.e. removing affixes) is not necessary.

Definition of similarity measure

The fuzzy similarity measure is applied. Here, the reference to section 2 is given.

Cluster centre

It is assumed that the centre of a cluster is a document of collection B or its representation. Considering the grouping method it is a document that is already partly transformed as being modified by preprocessing. For simplicity of presentation, in what follows the name 'document' is used without taking the above subtleties under consideration.

Cluster centre is a document that is the most similar to all the other documents in the sub-collection it represents.

Formally, assuming that the sub-collection of documents B_k $\{d_1, d_2, d_3, ..., d_k\}$, $k < N$, form a cluster due to the similarity of documents, the cluster center (reference document) is defined as the document d_i, $i \leq k$, whose index i maximizes the sum

$$\sum_{j=1}^{k} \mu_{RB} (d_i, d_j) \text{ for all } i = 1, 2, \ldots, k \tag{3.1}$$

with μ_{RB} computed according to (2.6). In the following, the centre of a cluster will be denoted as v_i.

It is worth remarking, however, that groups that may become clusters need to be predetermined.

Membership assignment

For each document in collection **B**, the degree of membership in a cluster is determined on the basis of the maximum of similarity of d_i to each cluster center

$$\mu_{i,j} = \max_{i \leq N, j \leq C} \{ \mu_{RB} (d_i, v_j) \} \tag{3.2}$$

where:

$\mu_{i,j}$ – is the grade of membership of the i-th document in the cluster v_j;
$\mu_{RB} (d_i, v_j)$ – is the fuzzy similarity of document d_i to the centre of cluster v_j;
v_j – denotes the centre of the j-th cluster.

Formula (3.2) means that the given document d_i belongs fuzzily to the cluster whose centre v_j is the most similar to d_i over all cluster centres v_1, v_2, ..., v_c.

Note that by this statement we preserve the fuzzy membership but on the other hand we actually perform a hard partitioning as defined in section 1.1.

The last task is the choice of existing or development of a new mechanism for grouping documents with the use of the defined similarity measure.

3.2   Grouping – a heuristic algorithm

There are many ways to perform clustering. Effectiveness and precision are the requirements that may be contradictory. Moreover one should be aware that more or less simple computational procedures that are applied offer solutions which may not coincide with human intuition or knowledge, in particular when dealing with textual information.

To approach some compromise one can try to reduce the number of document comparisons. This may be achieved by performing two stages of computations: initialisation of clusters and classification.

Initialisation

$1°$ Take a possibly representative sub-collection of documents B_{ip} – 'initial population'.

$2°$ Determine the similarity between all the documents of the sub-collection – formula (2.6).

$3°$ Choose c different documents – prototypes of cluster centres v_j . Their mutual similarity should lie under some threshold.

Of course, a large number of variations for initialisation may be created. For example, the use of keywords may be simpler and faster (but not necessarily better) choice.

Grouping

$1°$ Take a new document d_{new} from $B \setminus B_{ip}$.

$2°$ Compute the similarity of d_{new} to all actual centres v_j .

$3°$ Add document d_{new} to the cluster of the highest similarity of its centre – (3.2), and change this centre if necessary – (3.1).

$4°$ Are all the documents examined ?
   If *yes*, then go to step $5°$.
   If *not*, then go to step $1°$.

$5°$ Prepare all the c clusters to access, and *stop*.

Remark: Due to computations done in step $3°$ the similarity of all clusters as well as the similarity of all documents to all cluster centres are known. This information may be useful if one decides to give access to less relevant documents

- independently of their cluster membership;
- only through those clusters whose centres are somewhat similar to the most relevant one.

4.   SUMMARY

The presented method identifies groups of documents which are similar to a given number of reference documents – cluster centres. The reference documents may be known a priori, or determined during the initialisation stage from the so-called 'initial population' of examined documents. The method is able to deal with full text documents, with the most informative document fragments, or more traditionally - with keywords/index terms. Obviously, the method is not a panacea for every task of clustering or ranking but it may be useful for rough sorting and grouping of well structured and specialised documents related to a well defined domain in which, by the domain restricted vocabulary, there exists freedom of the natural language.

In textual database searching or clustering, the methods used so far for text comparison have been based mainly on the classical identity relation, according to which two given texts are either identical or not (if we neglect some simple preprocessing operations). This work is a contribution to a group of results that show that the *fuzziness* in the sense of Zadeh [6] is sufficient to establish more sophisticated methods for text similarity analysis. The application of fuzzy relations enables formalization of the human language intuition concerning similarity of textual information. The presented measures for comparison of natural language texts increase the chance that textual documents will be grouped properly. The described solution is not sensitive to grammatical mistakes or other misshapen language constructions. Moreover, last but not least, the implementation of the fuzzy similarity method should not be the cause of any serious inconvenience.

REFERENCES

Bezdek J.C. (1981). Pattern Recognition with Fuzzy Objective Function. Plenum Press, New York.

Jain A.K., Dubes R.C. (1988). Algorithms for Clustering Data. Englewood Cliffs, Prentice Hall.

Baeza-Yates R., Ribeiro-Neto B. (1999). Modern Information Retrieval. Addison Wesley, New York.

Lebart L., Salem A., Berry L. (1998). Exploring Textual Data. Kluwer Academic Publisher.

Ho T.B., Kawasaki S., Nguyen N.B. (2003). Documents Clustering using Tolerance Rough Set Model and Its Application to Information Retrieval. In: Szczepaniak P.S., Segovia J., Kacprzyk J., Zadeh L. (Eds.) Intelligent Exploration of the Web. Physica-Verlag, A Springer-Verlag Company, Heidelberg, New York.

Zadeh L. (1965). Fuzzy Sets. Information and Control, **8**, pp. 338-353.

Pedrycz W., Gomide F. (1998): An Introduction to Fuzzy Sets; Analysis and Design. A Bradford Book, The MIT Press, Cambridge, Massachusetts and London, England.

Kraft D.H., Chen J. (2001). Integrating and Extending Fuzzy Clustering and Inferencing to Improve Text Retrieval Performance. In: Larsen H.L., et al. (Eds.). Flexible Query Answering Systems. Physica-Verlag, A Springer-Verlag Company, Heidelberg, New York.

Kraft D.H., Chen J., Martin-Bautista M.J., Amparo-Vila M. (2003). Textual Information Retrieval with User Profiles using Fuzzy Clustering and Inferencing. In: Szczepaniak P.S., Segovia J., Kacprzyk J., Zadeh L. (Eds.) Intelligent Exploration of the Web. Physica-Verlag, A Springer-Verlag Company, Heidelberg, New York.

Bezdek J.C. (1980). A Convergence Theorem for the Fuzzy ISODATA Clustering Algorithms. IEEE Trans. on Pattern Analysis and Machine Intelligence, **2**, pp.1-8.

Bezdek J.C., Hathaway R.J., Sabin M.J., Tucker W.T. (1987). Convergence Theory for Fuzzy c-Means: Counterexamples and Repairs. IEEE Trans. on Systems, Man, and Cybernetics, **17**, pp.873-877.

Niewiadomski A.: Appliance of fuzzy relations for text document comparing. Proceedings of the 5th Conference NNSC (Zakopane, Poland, June 6-10), pp. 347-352.

Szczepaniak P.S., Niewiadomski A. (2003). Internet Search Based on Text Intuitionistic Fuzzy Similarity. In: Szczepaniak P.S., Segovia J., Kacprzyk J., Zadeh L. (Eds.) Intelligent Exploration of the Web. Physica-Verlag, A Springer-Verlag Company, Heidelberg, New York.

Chapter 12

INTELLIGENT AGENTS FOR DOCUMENT CATEGORIZATION AND ADAPTIVE FILTERING USING A NEURAL NETWORK APPROACH AND FUZZY LOGIC

Frank Teuteberg
Business Informatics, European University Viadrina, Frankfurt (Oder), Germany

Abstract: This chapter presents a multi-agent system for document categorization and adaptive filtering. A neural network approach is proposed to automate the process of agent-based categorization and adaptive filtering of electronic information sources from the WWW. Results from training and testing those networks are presented and discussed. Fuzzy logic is used to handle impreciseness in agent communication and collaboration.

Key words: Fuzzy Logic, Information Filtering, Intelligent Agents, Multi-Agent Systems, Neural Networks, XML

1. INTRODUCTION

The World Wide Web (WWW) is semi-structured and dynamically changing. The number of WWW sites is huge and still growing fast. Therefore, it can be a time consuming task to find the appropriate information sources. Keyword-based search engines are often not of much help whenever qualitative criteria are important to describe the user's information needs. For this reason, it is desirable that information agents support the extraction, filtering and categorization of information in the WWW.

The problem our research is motivated by is to find e-commerce applications which are "interesting" from a business point of view. "Interesting" means, for example, that a WWW site provides support for business transactions. One way to find "interesting" e-commerce applications is using a keyword-based search engine (e.g. Alta Vista) or going through "yellow pages" in the WWW and analyzing the respective WWW sites "manually". This is obviously a time-consuming task. Automation of categorization and filtering of electronic information sources in the WWW is desirable. "Interesting" applications are defined by means of two classification schemes (Kurbel, Szulim and Teuteberg, 2000). These e-commerce applications are entered into a database of e-commerce applications (Internet Database, IDB for short), which has been developed at European University Viadrina in Frankfurt (Oder), Germany. The purpose of IDB is to document the state-of-the-art of business Internet use.

We also study the automatic categorization of WWW applications into pre-defined high-level categories of the Yahoo! taxonomy. Our categorization differs from the manually generated Yahoo! taxonomy in that it is automatic and thus capable of categorizing WWW applications faster than the manual categorization of WWW applications.

The remainder of the chapter is organized in the following manner. In the next section, we discuss neural networks for categorization tasks. In section 3, we give a brief overview of the multi-agent system for document categorization and adaptive filtering, which is implemented in Java, and thus can run on all Java-enabled platforms. In section 4, we discuss technology issues related to agent communication and agent collaboration. FIPA-ACL (FIPA Agent Communication Language) is used as the agent communication language. For representing and processing fuzzy negotiation vocabulary we use XML (Extensible Markup Language) as the data interchange language. In XML entities, attributes, and relationships between entities can be defined with tags like <sender>, <receiver>, etc. We also argue for the advantages of encoding agent messages in XML. In sections 5 and 6, we present and discuss results from training and testing neural networks for the categorization of e-commerce applications into the categories "interesting" and "not interesting". We also present results from the automated categorization of WWW applications into pre-defined high-level categories of the Yahoo! taxonomy. Finally, section 7 summarizes some conclusions.

2. NEURAL NETWORKS FOR DOCUMENT CATEGORIZATION AND ADAPTIVE FILTERING

Neural networks are attractive for categorization tasks because of their capability to learn from noisy data and to generalize (Bishop, 1995). A typical neural network consists of at least three layers: an input layer, one (ore more) hidden layer(s) and an output layer. Figure 12-1 illustrates the steps of using a neural network for the categorization of business applications in the WWW into the categories "not interesting" and "interesting". Before a neural network can by applied to a particular categorization task it has to be trained. For this purpose, a set of data is given as input to the network, and the weights of the neural connections are adjusted in a way that the output of the network approximates the desired output. To set the weights, the mean squared error (MSE) is computed. The MSE is the sum of the squared differences between the desired output and the actual output of the output neurons averaged over all training exemplars. A small value, close to zero, indicates that the network has learned well and is suited for the categorization problem.

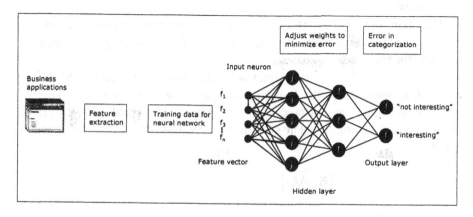

Figure 12-1. Neural network for categorization of business applications (Kurbel, Singh, Teuteberg, 1998)

3.   OVERVIEW OF THE MULTI-AGENT ARCHITECTURE

In this section, we briefly describe the architecture of our multi-agent system for document categorization and adaptive filtering and discuss relevant technology issues related to our system (Teuteberg, 2001). Our multi-agent system is composed of a large number of agents collectively trying to satisfy the user's request. We differentiate among the following types of agents (see figure 12-2) with distinct and clearly defined functions, for example:

– Stationary Agents: Stationary Agents act locally on the computer of the user;

- Mobile Agents: By migrating to heterogeneous information resources Mobile Agents can search the information resources locally;
- User Interface Agents: Each user must first register itself with one (or more) User Interface Agents. User Interface Agents support a variety of interchangeable user interfaces and result browsers;
- Service Agents: Service Agents provide their capabilities, e.g., information search services, information gathering services, etc., to other agents;
- Facilitator Agents: Facilitator Agents manage communications among the various agents and databases in the environment. For example, they manage a "Yellow Pages" directory for locating appropriate agents with appropriate services;
- Wrapper Agents: Wrapper Agents extract contents from information sources;
- Database Agents: Database Agents manage specific information resources. They translate messages into local access languages such as SQL for relational databases.

The "Agent" class is an abstract class that has to be extended to define application specific agents. Subordinate agents such as "Stationary Agent" or "Mobile Agent" are instances of the agent class "Agent". For handling multiple users the multi-agent system uses multiple instances of a specific agent class.

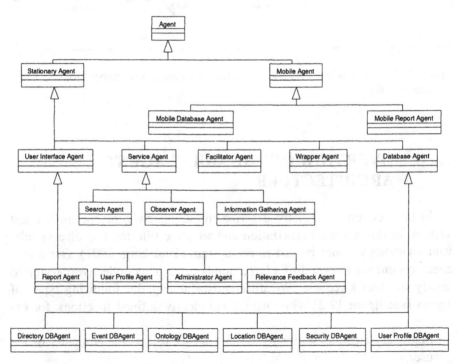

Figure 12-2. Class hierarchy of agents

For developing the different types of agents we use the AgentBuilder toolkit (Reticular Systems Inc., 1999). The AgentBuilder toolkit consists of several development tools and a run-time execution environment. The AgentBuilder toolkit and the run-time execution environment are implemented using the Java programming language.

The Reticular Agent Mental Model (Reticular Systems Inc., 1999) is the underlying mental model of our multi-agent architecture. This model consists of beliefs, commitments, capabilities, intentions and behavioural rules:

- *Beliefs* represent the current state of the agent's internal and external world and are updated as new information about the world is received;
- *Commitments* represent agreements, usually communicated to another agent, to achieve a particular state of the world at a particular time;
- *Capabilities* define the actions that the agent can perform;
- *Intentions* are the goals an agent wants to achieve at a particular time;
- *Behavioural rules* determine the actions an agent takes at every point throughout the agent's execution. Behavioural rules are represented as WHEN-IF-THEN statements.

Rules and capabilities are static, whereas the agent's beliefs, commitments, and intentions are dynamic and can change over the agent's life cycle.

Figure 12-3 describes the format for behavioural rules in our multi-agent-system.

NAME rule name
WHEN Message Condition(s)
IF Mental Condition(s)
THEN
Private Action(s)
Mental Change(s)
Message Action(s)

Figure 12-3. Format of behavioural rules

Figure 12-4 shows an agent's belief model. This belief model contains a belief about the current time, the agent's (Observer Agent's) start-up time, the address, the name of another known agent (Facilitator Agent) and a belief about the status of two stocks (SAP and Intershop Communications) the agent is observing.

```
Mental Model (Beliefs)
Time: <currentTime> Mon Jun 09 15:21:22 PDT 2000
Time: <startupTime> Mon  Jun 09 15:19:58 PDT  2000
Agent: <SELF> Observer Agent
Address: http://curie.euv-frankfurt-o.de:5000/1
Agent:  Facilitator Agent
Stock_Market_Record: <1> Name = SAP, Symbol = 716463, Quantity = 18, Price = 164,
Stop_Loss  = 150
Stock_Market_Record: <2> Name = Intershop Communications, Symbol = 622700,
Quantity = 18,  Price = 4, Stop_Loss = 3
```

Figure 12-4. An agent's mental model (beliefs)

The diagram of an agent's environment is shown in UML (Unified Modeling Language) notation (for details see (OMG, 1999) in figure 12-5.

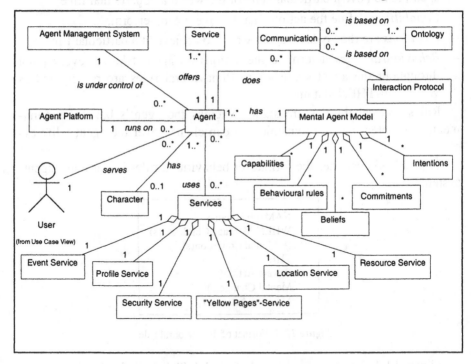

Figure 12-5. An agent's environment

The multiplicity specifications used in figure 12-5 indicate how many entities (elements) of one entity may be connected to other entities. Multiplicity in UML is analogous to cardinality in other modeling languages.

For example, an agent is offering at least one (1) or many (*) services (for example adaptive filtering). The agent communication is based on interaction protocols and ontologies, which determine the vocabulary for agent communication. Each agent uses different services for performing specific tasks. For example, a "Yellow-Pages"-Service for locating appropriate agents with appropriate services.

In our multi-agent-system an interpreter (see figure 12-6) continually monitors incoming messages and takes appropriate actions.

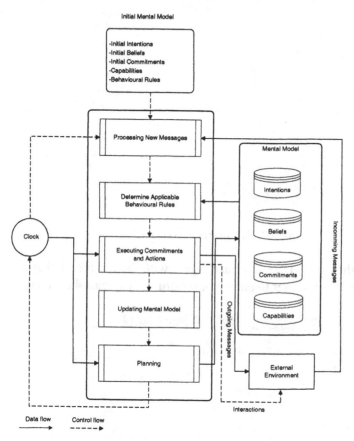

Figure 12-6. Agent execution process (Reticular Systems Inc., 1999)

At start-up, each agent is initialized with an initial mental model consisting of initial beliefs, initial commitments, initial intentions, capabilities, and behavioural rules. Over the agent's life cycle the agent interpreter updates the agent's initial mental model.

When a user connects to the agent server, a User Interface Agent is brought up on the user's screen as a Java window. Figure 12-7 shows the interface of a User Interface Agent. Via User Interface Agents the user can give feedback, compose messages, register itself, view messages, create agents, view results and visualize the state and performance of the multi-agent system.

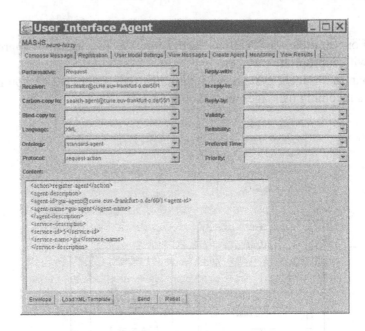

Figure 12-7. User Interface Agent GUI

Figure 12-8 shows the User Interface Agent with the Microsoft character *"Merlin"*, which asks the user to enter a password with at least 4 characters.

12-8. User Interface Agent GUI with character "Merlin"

The character "Merlin" will be invoked by a function *Password()*, when the user is entering a password with less than 4 characters (see figure 12-9).

```
function Password() {
AgentX.Characters.Load ("Merlin");
Merlin=AgentX.Characters.Character ("Merlin");
Merlin.Show();
Merlin.Play ("GestureLeft");
Merlin.Speak("Please enter a  password with at least 4 characters!");
Merlin.Hide();
}
```

12-9. Function Password()

4.   AGENT COMMUNICATION AND AGENT COLLABORATION

Information agents in a multi-agent system have to understand each other when they are supposed to perform meaningful collaboration action. Agents advertise their capabilities by sending appropriate messages describing the kind of services they offer.

4.1   Message structure

The agents in our multi-agent system communicate using the FIPA Agent Communication Language. FIPA (Foundation of Intelligent Physical Agents) is an international association of organizations developing standards for agent technologies (FIPA, 2003a; FIPA, 2003b; Wooldridge, 2000).

To enable collaboration among the information agents XML (Extensible Markup Language) is used for the description of advertised and requested services of the agents (Glushko, Tenenbaum, Meltzer, 1999).

In the past two years industrial initiatives have adopted XML for electronic commerce in order to facilitate communication between collaborating applications across business boundaries. Examples are cXML by Ariba (cXML.org, 2003), ebXML by the Global E-Business Initiative, a joint effort of the United Nations CEFACT and OASIS (ebXML.org, 2003), and the BizTalk Framework promoted by Microsoft (BizTalk Framework, 2003).

Agents can easily interpret XML-based messages because of XML's power to describe both metadata and data. Furthermore, XML provides a rich syntax for creating transactions that allow information agents to communicate with each other in a platform independent way.

XML is a subset of SGML (Standard Markup Language). SGML is an ISO standard which was established to support distributed computing. Documents in XML contain data in the form of tag/value pairs. XML documents are constructed based on Document Type Definitions (DTDs). DTDs

(Connolly, 1997) can be used as templates to define content models within XML documents, the valid order of elements and the data types of attributes.

In figure 12-10 we give an example of a DTD for the messages that are used for inter-agent communications in our multi-agent system. The DTD for messages specifies that a performative element contains performatives such as cancel, confirm etc., and that at least one performative is required (#REQUIRED).

The term performative was introduced in speech act theory by Austin (Austin, 1962). A performative determines which action the sender wishes to be taken in response to his message. We assume that message-id, sender, receiver etc. are all #PCDATA. "#PCDATA" (parsed character data) means that an element can have data (text) and can be parsed.

```
<!ELEMENT message (message-id, performative, sender, receiver, reply-with, reply-by,
in-reply-to, envelope, language, ontology, content, sequence-number, transmission-time,
encoding-mode, carbon-copy-to, blind-copy-to, validity, reliability-fuzzy-set,
prefered-time-fuzzy-set, priority-fuzzy-set)>
<!ELEMENT message-id                                              (#PCDATA)>
<!ELEMENT performative (cancel | confirm | failure | inform | inform-if | not-understood |
query | query-if | query-when | request | request-if | request-when | )        #REQUIRED>
<!ELEMENT sender                                          ( #PCDATA)#REQUIRED>
<!ELEMENT receiver                                         (#PCDATA)#REQUIRED>
<!ELEMENT reply-with                                             (#PCDATA)>
<!ELEMENT reply-by                                               (#PCDATA)>
<!ELEMENT in-reply-to                                            (#PCDATA)>
<!ELEMENT envelope                                               (#PCDATA)>
<!ELEMENT language                                       (#PCDATA)#REQUIRED>
<!ELEMENT ontology                                       (#PCDATA)#REQUIRED>
<!ELEMENT content                                        (#PCDATA)#REQUIRED>
<!ELEMENT sequence-number                                        (#PCDATA)>
<!ELEMENT transmission-time                                      (#PCDATA)>
<!ELEMENT encoding-mode                                          (#PCDATA)>
<!ELEMENT carbon-copy-to                                         (#PCDATA)>
<!ELEMENT blind-copy-to                                          (#PCDATA)>
<!ELEMENT validity                                               (#PCDATA)>
<!ELEMENT reliability-fuzzy-set                                  (#PCDATA)>
<!ELEMENT prefered-time-fuzzy-set                                (#PCDATA)>
<!ELEMENT priority-fuzzy-set                                     (#PCDATA)>
```

Figure 12-10. DTD for messages

A schematic example of a speech act represented in a FIPA-ACL frame is given in figure 12-11. The XML part is embedded in the content field. The meaning of the keywords used in the FIPA-ACL messages is as follows (FIPA, 2003a):

- sender: agent sending the message;
- receiver: agent receiving the message;
- language: language of the content field;
- interaction-protocol: interaction protocol the message is subject to;
- ontology: ontology which is used to give a meaning to the expressions in the content field;

– content: the actual message by the sender.

Each agent must first register itself with the Facilitator Agent. The Facilitator Agent mediates among User Interface Agents, Database Agents and Service Agents. Service Agents, for example, advertise their capabilities by sending a message as shown in figure 12-11 describing the kind of service they offer. If the agent is already registered the request is denied and an error message is sent. Otherwise, the facilitator agent sends an *inform* message to the agent that wants to register.

```
request
        :sender   search-agent@curie.euv-frankfurt-o.de:50/1
        :receiver facilitator-agent@curie.euv-frankfurt-o.de:8900/1
        :language            XML
        :interaction-protocol    agent-request
        :ontology            agent-management-ontology
        :content             <? xml version=„1.0">
        <action>register-agent</action>
          <agent-id>search-agent@curie.euv-frankfurt-o.de:50/1
          </agent-id>
          <agent-name> search-agent</agent-name>
          <agent-type>service-agent</agent-type>
          <address> curie.euv-frankfurt-o.de:50/1</address>
          <ownership>Frank Teuteberg</ownership>
          <life-cycle-state>active</life-cycle-state>
            <services>
            <service-description>
              <service-id>1</service-id>
                <service-type>information retrieval
                </service-type>
                <service-ontology>information retrieval ontology
                </service-ontology>
                <service-name>ir-1</service-name>
                <service-properties>
                  <mobility>no</mobility>
                </service-properties>
            <service-description>
            </services>
        )
```

Figure 12-11. Speech act *request*

The interaction protocol for advertising capabilities (services) is exemplarily shown in figure 12-12. One user, one User Interface Agent (Agent *B*), two Service Agents (Agents *A* and *C*), one Facilitator Agent and a "Yellow Pages"-Service are involved into the interaction (see figure 12-12), which is as follows: After initialization the agents *A* and *C* advertise their services by means of the performative "advertise" to the Facilitator, which inserts the corresponding service descriptions into the directory of the "Yellow Pages"-Service. Afterwards the user requests a specific service *x*, which the User Interface Agent *B* still not offers. Therefore, Agent *B* sends a query to the Facilitator Agent, whether the service *x* is currently available. Agent *C* (currently not busy) is offering the requested service *x*. Therefore, Agent C performs the service and delivers the obtained results to the User Interface Agent *B*, which then edits the results in a user-friendly way.

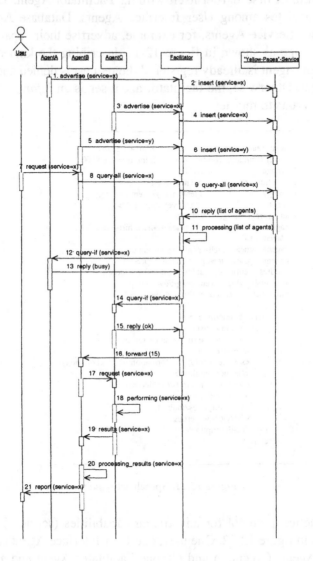

Figure 12-12. Interaction protocol for advertising agents' services

4.2 Fuzzy Logic for Agent Communication and Collaboration

In the past few years a number of multi-agent systems for document categorization and adaptive filtering have been developed, e.g. Amalthaea

(Moukas, Maes, 1998), InfoSleuth (Bayardo Jr. et al., 1998), RETSINA (Sycara, Pannu, 1998). The main difference between those systems and our multi-agent system is that most of those systems do not handle uncertainty in agent communication and collaboration. Therefore, we decided to integrate fuzzy logic for agent communication and collaboration in our multi-agent system. We extend FIPA-ACL with the message parameters validity, reliability-fuzzy-set, prefered-time-fuzzy-set and priority-fuzzy-set to allow the specification of validity, reliability and temporal behavioural constraints of messages.

Fuzzy logic is based on the fuzzy set theory, which was introduced by Zadeh (Zadeh 1965). Let x be an element of the universe Ω and $A \subseteq \Omega$. The non fuzzy (crisp) function $\mu_A: \Omega \rightarrow \{0, 1\}$ denotes the membership $x \in A$. The membership μ_A is 1 if $x \in A$ and 0 otherwise. Zadeh redefines the crisp function $\mu_A: \Omega \rightarrow \{0, 1\}$ to an interval by $\mu_A: \Omega \rightarrow [0,1]$ measuring the degree of membership. The closer the so-called fuzzy set $\mu_A(x)$ over Ω is to 1 the more x becomes a member of A (Tanaka, 1996).

A linguistic term such as "very reliable" of the linguistic variable reliability, for example, can be represented by means of the fuzzy set $\{(90, 0),$ $(95, 1), (100, 1)\}$, whereas the term „not reliable", for example, can be represented by means of the fuzzy set $\{(0, 1), (5, 1), (10, 0)\}$. Such fuzzy sets (Zadeh, 1965) can be used to calculate the degree of reliability of a specific message. Assuming that reliability of a message can be measured on an interval $[0,100]$.

In our multi-agent system planning and scheduling the execution of tasks and requests from other agents is based on fuzzy rules R_j to handle uncertainty in planning and scheduling:

R_j: If x_1 IS μ_{1j} AND ... AND x_n IS μ_{nj} THEN y IS v_j

Where $x_1 ... x_n$ are input variables, and y is an output variable. $\mu_{ij} \in [0,1]$ and $v_j \in [0,1]$ are fuzzy sets which are labeled with linguistic terms like "very high" or "low". The fuzzy sets are represented by membership functions like triangular or trapezoidal functions. A complete set of fuzzy rules is evaluated by max-min inference, resulting in an output fuzzy set v. The output fuzzy set v is then transformed into a crisp value by a defuzzification procedure. A typical fuzzy rule is given in table 12-1. For the implementation of fuzzy rules in a fuzzy planning module, we use DataEngine (http://www.dataengine.de). DataEngine is a tool for professional data analysis using fuzzy technologies, neural networks and statistical methods.

Table 12-1. Fuzzy rule

IF	Importance of performing a service	IS	„very high"
AND	Actual transfer rate	IS	„high"
AND	System performance	IS	„low"
AND	Availability of resources	IS	„high"
AND	Dependence on preceding actions	IS	„high"
AND	Buffer time	IS	„low"
THEN	Priority of performing a service	IS	„very high"
WITH	Certainty value 0.99		

Fuzzy rules can be qualified by a certainty value $\in [0,1]$. Allowing the certainty values (fuzzy rule weights) to be selected from $[0,1]$, they can be interpreted as a degree of support for a fuzzy rule. The pre-conditions in the fuzzy rule (see table 12-1) determine the maximum time a service agent has to begin performing a requested service. When a service agent is asked to perform a service, it consults with the fuzzy planning module first. The purpose of integrating fuzzy logic in our multi-agent system is to reduce imbalance in the system and to enhance the flexibility in scheduling and planning tasks.

5.   EXPERIMENTAL RESULTS – CATEGORIZATION OF E-COMMERCE APPLICATIONS

5.1   Coding of features

A crucial point in using neural networks for categorization tasks is to choose the right set of input features. The problem is to select those features, which represent a WWW application well.

Meaningful features of the WWW applications were extracted with the help of wrapper agents and coded as input patterns. In the vector space information retrieval paradigm (Salton, Buckley, 1988) each document has a vector V, where an element v_i is the weight of word or feature d for that document. In our work, we experimented with various ways of coding the weights v_i. We differentiate among several types of features, for example (Kurbel, Singh and Teuteberg, 1998):

– *Structural features:* Hyperlinks, frames, number of internal/external links, size of downloaded WWW applications in KB;

- *Elements of interactivity:* Elements which indicate a higher degree of interactivity (e.g. cgi/bin feature, certain Javascript elements (e.g. on-Select);
- *Technological features:* Standards, scripts and programming languages used;
- *Multimedia features:* Audio and video files embedded in WWW offer.

Binary coding indicates whether a feature is present ($v_i=1$) or absent ($v_i=0$) in a WWW application. Another type indicates the number of times a feature (e.g. a keyword) is present. The third type of coding exploits meta tags and the specific HTML syntax. A typical feature like "order form" is coded by 0 if it is absent, 0.25 if it is in the body tag, 0.5 if it is in the title tag, 0.75 if it occurs in the meta tag ("content" or "keyword"), and 1 if it is a hyperlink to another page within the same WWW offer (where perhaps an online order facility is provided).

Features (keywords) in meta tags, for example, are provided by authors of WWW sites if they want search robots to index their sites automatically. So keywords in meta tags might describe a WWW site well. Therefore, we assign a higher value (0.75) to keywords from meta tags than to keywords extracted from body or title tags.

A stop list, comprising high-frequency function words such as "a", "and", "the" is used to eliminate such words from consideration in the processing. The features left are then coded and represented in Excel spreadsheets. Figure 12-13 shows an excerpt from such a spreadsheet.

	A	B	C	D	E	F		HT	HU	HV	HW	HX	HY	HZ
1	http:	access	banking	internet	mail	password		size	.gif	.zip	button	frame	javascript	output
2	http://www.1stfed.com/	0.25	0.25	0.25	0.25	0		107034	1	0	1	0	0	0
3	http://www.abfs.com/ontrace.htm	0	0	0	0.25	0		8403	1	0	0	0	0	1
4	http://www.airborne-express.com	0	0	0.25	0.25	0		86236	1	0	1	0	0	1
5	http://www.aircanada.ca/cargo/english/n	0	0	0	0	0		10280	1	0	0	0	0	1
6	http://www.baxglobal.com/tracking/track	0	0	0	0	0		11744	1	0	0	0	0	1
7	http://www.bbi.co.uk/index.html	0	0	0.5	0	0		13494	1	0	0	0	0	0
8	http://www.bmo.com/	0	0.25	0	0.25	0		26026	1	0	1	1	0	0
9	http://www.canadatrust.com	0.5	0.5	0.25	0.25	0.25		670702	1	0	0	0	0	0
10	http://www.ccx.com/ccsi/home.html	0	0	1	0.25	0		9560	1	0	0	0	0	1
11	http://www.cdworld.com	0.25	0	0.5	0.25	0		94783	1	0	1	0	0	0
12	http://www.centralres.com/	0.25	0	0.25	0.25	0		57994	1	0	1	1	0	1
13	http://www.colonialbank.com/	0.25	0.25	0	0.25	0		130058	1	0	1	0	1	0
14	http://www.commerce.net/	0.25	0	0.25	0.25	0		258535	1	1	0	1	0	1
15	http://www.dealernet.com	0.75	0	0.25	0.5	0		81344	1	0	1	0	0	1
16	http://www.dhl.com/track/track.html	0	0	0	0	0		6196	1	0	0	0	0	0
17	http://www.eupc.com/eupc-e/index.htm	0	0	0.25	0.25	0		3068	1	0	1	1	0	1
18	http://www.export.nl	0.75	0	0.25	1	0		530022	1	0	1	0	0	1
19	http://www.fedex.com	0	0	0	0	0		21905	1	0	0	0	0	1
20	http://www.firstunion.com	0.25	0.75	0.25	0.25	0		216918	1	0	1	1	0	1
21	http://www.flavorohio.com	0	0	0	0.25	0		55260	1	0	0	0	0	0
22	http://www.ichat.com	0	0	0.25	0.25	0		62226	1	0	0	1	1	0
23	http://www.iebb.com/	0.25	0	0.5	0.25	0		15508	1	0	0	1	0	1
24	http://www.intermesse.com	0	0	0	0	0		6930	0	0	0	1	0	1
25	http://www.internet.net	0.25	0	0.75	0.25	0		167763	1	0	1	0	0	0

Figure 12-13. Excel spreadsheet with extracted features

Each row describes one WWW offer. The columns contain the extracted features. Wrapper Agents deliver the coded feature vectors to a neural network component in our multi-agent system. Then the networks were trained with those feature vectors.

5.2   Experimental Results

For training of the networks 227 e-commerce applications (122 MB, 12,756 HTML files) from IDB were downloaded with the help of Information Gathering Agents and classified manually into "interesting" and "not interesting". To limit the times for download, feature extraction and training, hyperlinks are followed down three levels.

Business-to-business applications were categorized under two points of view (Kurbel, Szulim and Teuteberg, 2000; Teuteberg, 2001b): a) direct communication between business partners, and b) communication with or via information exchanges. For the first group (direct communication), six main categories were defined:
1) Providing information;
2) Providing information plus contact offer;
3) Starting a transaction via Internet;
4) Starting and completing a transaction via Internet;
5) Business-process interfaces via Internet;
6) Inter-business cooperation via Internet.

WWW offers of categories 1) and 2) are declared "not interesting" whereas offers of categories 3) to 6) have the potential of being "interesting" for IDB.

In the second group (information exchanges), the following categories were used:
1) Simple catalog of firms and/or products;
2) Catalog with search option;
3) Product exchange;
4) Electronic market.

Here the categories 1) and 2) are regarded as the not interesting ones. Categories 3) and 4) contain those offers where the mediator operating the information exchange gives automated support for transactions between business partners. Those categories are considered "interesting".

For implementation of the neural networks, a commercial package called NeuroSolutions (www.nd.com) was used. This software enables users to create their own networks. It provides several options where choices have to be made, regarding, for example, the learning algorithm, the number of neurons, the number of hidden layers, and other network parameters. For the purpose of testing the trained networks, the 227 applications were randomly divided into four subsets according to the data shuffling method (Jeong, Williams, 1992).

The five best network configurations found before were then trained and evaluated with the four pairs of subsets. The best categorization results were reached with a hybrid PCA/MLP (PCA = Principal Component Analysis, MLP = Multilayer Perceptron) network (89.47 % correct). Significant improvements in the classification rate were achieved by introducing an indifference region (Kurbel, Szulim and Teuteberg, 2000). Instead of only two categories "interesting" and "not interesting", a third category "indifferent" was allowed. The percentage of e-commerce applications categorized incorrectly now dropped from 10.53 % to 5.26 %. A summary of the test results is given in table 12-2. The table shows the best result out of the four runs from data shuffling, for each network topology, and the *worst* result *[in brackets and italics]*. The network topologies and the parameters considered are characterized as follows:

1) Hybrid PCA/MLP network with 460 neurons in the PCA's output layer, 50 neurons in the first hidden layer of the MLP, 20 neurons in the second hidden layer of the MLP, and 1,000 training epochs;
2) Hybrid RBF/MLP network with 100 neurons in the hidden layer of the RBF (RBF = Radial Basis Function) network, 50 neurons in the first hidden layer of the MLP, 20 neurons in the second hidden layer of the MLP, and 1,000 training epochs;
3) MLP with three hidden layers, 50 neurons per hidden layer, and 100 training epochs;
4) Modular network with two hidden layers, 50 neurons per hidden layer, and 100 training epochs;
5) Generalized feed-forward network with two hidden layers, 50 neurons per hidden layer, and 100 training epochs.

It should be noted that the MSE varies with the training data and is not fully correlated with accuracy of categorization (see table 12-2).

Table 12-2. Categorization results

Network topology	MSE	Correctly Categorized	Indifferent	Incorrectly Categorized
1) PCA/MLP (460/50/20/1000)	0.002876934 *[0.006738572]*	89.47 % *[87.72 %]*	5.26 % *[7.02 %]*	5.26 % *[5.26 %]*
2) RBF/MLP (100/50/20/1000)	0.027539783 *[0.108368993]*	87.72 % *[80.70 %]*	5.26 % *[12.28 %]*	7.02 % *[7.02 %]*
3) MLP (3/50/100)	0.008454259 *[0.014019439]*	87.72 % *[82.46 %]*	3.51% *[5.26 %]*	8.77 % *[12.28 %]*
4) Modular network (2/50/100)	0.025483903 *[0.013499024]*	84.41 % *[80.70 %]*	7.02 % *[5.26 %]*	8.57 % *[14.04 %]*
5) Generalized feed-forward network (2/50/100)	0.217074692 *[0.389487624]*	70.18 % *[52.63 %]*	14.04 % *[15.79 %]*	15.76 % *[31.58 %]*

6.   EXPERIMENTAL RESULTS – YAHOO! CATEGORIZATION

For the automatic categorization of WWW applications into pre-defined high-level categories of the Yahoo! taxonomy (www.yahoo.com) the following network topologies and a Fuzzy-C-Means algorithm have been examined in this work (Teuteberg 2001a; Teuteberg 2001b):

1) Kohonen network with 520 features as input for a 2-dimensional self-organizing feature map with 3 x 5 neurons, and 400 training epochs;

2) Fuzzy Kohonen network with 520 features as input for a 2-dimensional self-organizing feature map with 3 x 5 neurons, and 400 training epochs;

3) Fuzzy-C-Means algorithm with exponent 1,9 (the exponent has influence on the degrees classified WWW applications belong to a specific category (e.g. Social Science).

For training of the networks and the Fuzzy-C-Means algorithm, we use a random sample of 2800 WWW applications with 200 in each of the 14 high-level Yahoo! categories Art & Humanities, Business & Economy, Computers & Internet, Education, Entertainment, Government, Health, News & Media, Recreation & Sports, Reference, Regional, Science, Social Science and Society & Culture. For the purpose of testing the trained networks and the Fuzzy-C-Means algorithm, the 2800 WWW applications were randomly divided into four subsets according to the data-shuffling method.

A summary of the categorization results is given in table 12-3. The table shows the best test result and the worst result *[in brackets and italics]*. The best categorization results so far were obtained with a Fuzzy Kohonen network (87.49 % correct).

Table 12-3. Yahoo! categorization results

	Correctly Categorized	Incorrectly Categorized
Kohonen network (520, 2, 3, 5, 400)	87.29 % *[84.86 %]*	12.71 % *[15.14 %]*
Fuzzy Kohonen network (520, 2, 3, 5, 400)	87.49 % *[85.57 %]*	12.51 % *[14.43 %]*
Fuzzy-C-Means (exponent: 1,9)	80.57 % *[78.43 %]*	19.43 % *[21.57 %]*

7. CONCLUSION

In this chapter, an approach for agent-based categorization and filtering WWW applications was presented. We focus on learning user preferences using a neural network approach. The results described in this chapter show that neural networks are capable of categorizing WWW applications with a reasonable rate of accuracy. All tested networks performed quite well. On the average 85 % of the WWW applications were categorized correctly.

We have integrated fuzzy logic in our multi-agent system to enhance the flexibility in scheduling and planning tasks. Thus, the multi-agent system can cope with a varying and suddenly changing system environment particularly with regard to actual transfer rates, system performance or availability of information sources and agents' services.

ACKNOWLEDGEMENTS

Section 5 is based upon research that was performed by Karl Kurbel, Kirti Singh, Daniel Szulim and the author at European University Viadrina Frankfurt (Oder), Germany.

REFERENCES

J. L. Austin. How to do things with words, Oxford University Press, Oxford, 1962.
R. J. Bayardo Jr., W. Bohrer, R. Brice, A. Cichocki, J. Fowler, A. Helal, V. Kashyap, T. Ksiezyk, G. Martin, M. Nodine, M. Rashid, M. Rusinkiewicz, R. Shea, C. Unnikrishnan, A. Unruh and D. Woelk. InfoSleuth: Agent-Based Semantic Integration of Information in Open and Dynamic Environments. in: M. N. Huhns and M. P. Singh (Eds.). Readings in Agents, Morgan Kaufmann Publishers, San Francisco, 1998, pp. 205-210.
C. M. Bishop. Neural Networks for Pattern Recognition, Oxford University Press, Oxford, 1995.
BizTalk Framework. http://www.Biztalk.org, 2003, February 12th, 2003.
cXML.org. http://www.cxml.org, 2003, February 12th, 2003.
D. Connolly (Ed.). XML: Principles, Tools, and Techniques. World Wide Web Journal, Volume 2, O'Reilly, Sebastopol, 1997.
ebXML.org. http://www.ebXML.org, 2003, February 12th, 2003.
FIPA. FIPA ACL Message Structure Specification. http://www.fipa.org, 2003a, February 12th, 2003.
FIPA. FIPA Interaction Protocol Library Specification. http://www.fipa.org, 2003b, February 12th, 2003.
R. J. Glushko, J. M. Tenenbaum and B. Meltzer. An XML Framework for Agent-based E-commerce; CACM 42 (3): 106-114, 1999.

J. Jeong and W. J. Williams. A Unified Fast Recursive Algorithm for Data Shuffling in Various Orders; IEEE Transactions on Signal Processing 40 (5): 1091-1095, 1992.

K. Kurbel, K. Singh and F. Teuteberg. Search and Classification of "Interesting" Business Applications in the World Wide Web Using a Neural Network Approach. in: K. Forcht. (Ed.). Proceedings of the 1998 IACIS Conference, Cancun, Mexico, 1998, pp. 75-81.

K. Kurbel, D. Szulim and F. Teuteberg. Kuenstliche Neuronale Netze zum Filtern von E-Commerce-Angeboten; Wirtschaftsinformatik, 42 (3): 222-232, 2000.

A. Moukas and P. Maes. Amalthaea: An Evolving Multi-Agent Information Filtering and Discovery System for the WWW; Journal of Autonomous Agents and Multi-Agent Systems, 1 (1): 59-88, 1998.

Object Management Group. OMG Unified Modeling Language Specification. Needham, 1999.

Reticular Systems Inc. AgentBuilder: An Integrated Toolkit for Constructing Intelligent Software Agents, Revision 1.3, February 18th, 1999.

G. Salton and C. Buckley. Term Weighting Approaches in Automatic Text Retrieval; Information Processing and Management, 24 (5): 413-523, 1988.

K. Sycara and A. S. Pannu. The RETSINA multiagent system: Towards integrating planning, execution and information gathering. in: K. Sycara and M. J. Wooldridge (Eds.). Proceedings of the 2nd International Conference on Autonomous Agents (Agents '98). New York, 1998, pp. 350-351.

F. Teuteberg. Agent-based Information Discovery in the World Wide Web Using a Neural Network Approach and Fuzzy Logic. in: The Society for the Study of Artificial Intelligence and the Simulation of Behaviour (Ed.). Proceedings of the AISB' 01 Symposium on Information Agents for Electronic Commerce. York (UK), 2001a, pp. 43-50.

F. Teuteberg: Agentenbasierte Informationserschliessung im World Wide Web unter Einsatz von Kuenstlichen Neuronalen Netzen und Fuzzy-Logik. Josef Eul, Lohmar, 2001b.

K. Tanaka. An Introduction to Fuzzy Logic for Practical Applications, Springer, New York , 1996.

M. J. Wooldridge. Semantic Issues in the Verification of Agent Communication Langauges; Journal of Autonomous Agents and Multi-Agent Systems, 3 (1): 9-31, 2000.

L. A Zadeh. Fuzzy Sets; Journal of Information and Control, 8: 338-353, 1965.

Chapter 13

THE VIRTUAL BOUTIQUE: MULTIMEDIA RETRIEVAL AND DATA MINING FOR E-COMMERCE AND E-BUSINESS IN THE FRAMEWORK OF A VIRTUAL ENVIRONMENT

Eric Paquet and Herna Viktor
NRC and University of Ottawa

Abstract: This chapter presents an approach for multimedia information retrieval employing an image-based algorithm. The Virtual Boutique is a novel, content-based system for multimedia information retrieval, based on virtual reality and visual information management. It supports realistic and fast rendering, extensive manipulation, reconfiguration and multimedia searching capabilities. The Virtual Boutique includes algorithms for searching through the inventory of an e-business, utilizing both images and three-dimensional objects. The chapter shows the application of The Virtual Boutique to an online boutique. In addition, it is illustrated how data mining can be used to determine patterns in consumer-interaction

Key words: content-based, data mining, e-business, e-commerce, e-store, multimedia, retrieval, three-dimensional, virtual environments, 3D

1. INTRODUCTION

New applications in e-business now require the development of systems combining the strengths of advanced information retrieval technique with multimedia. Such systems offer integrated tools for modelling, visualizing, accessing and retrieving the objects contained in large, online multimedia data repositories.

The use of multimedia information retrieval and its related technologies are relatively new in e-business. Currently, most e-commerce sites rely primarily on text and images, which are sometimes augmented with the use of broadcast video [1]. A number of research groups are current investigating the use of bi-dimensional and three-dimensional objects and visualization for e-commerce sites. However, these have not been successful from a commercial point of view. This is mainly due to the close relationship that exists between e-business and the advertising industry, which historically mainly relies on text and images. Here, images and videos can be created and manipulated very efficiently since the corresponding sensors and software both are mature technologies. By comparison, the use of three-dimensional modelling and visualisation are mainly perceived as a stronghold of specialists. That is, up to recently, these technologies were mainly used in scientific visualization, medical visualization and in computer-aided design (CAD) [2].

However, there are a number of factors, which increased the widespread utilization of this technology. Firstly, the use of special effects in the movie industry led to the creation of powerful systems capable of modelling, designing, implementing and virtualisation in three dimensions. Secondly, the use of three-dimensions in the games industry led to the creation of a group of personal computer users which find three-dimensional intuitive and natural. It is these users who prefer to shop on-line in a three-dimensional, intuitive boutique.

This chapter is organized as follows. In Section 2, we discuss appropriate standards for Web-based three-dimensional technology and shows how three-dimensional objects can be acquired through scanning. In Section 3, we discuss a morphological approach to describing bidimensional images. Section 4 portrays a system to automatically describe the shape of three-dimensional objects. This is followed, Section 5, by a description of the current implementation of the retrieval system. Section 6 describes The Virtual Boutique and shows how it is applied to an online boutique. In Section 7, we investigate the use of data mining to complement the current implementation of The Virtual Boutique. Section 8 concludes the chapter.

2.   MOVING TO THE WEB: DEFINING STANDARDS AND OBTAINING THREE-DIMENSIONAL OBJECTS

The creation of a multimedia standard that aims to provide a framework to ensure realistic rendering of three-dimensional objects is of critical importance in e-business. Users, especially those who are familiar with games and special effects in movies, expect high quality rendering. This section discusses the evolution of standards for three-dimensional information exchange over the Web and presents techniques to capture high quality three-dimensional objects.

When exchanging three-dimensional data via the Web, a common file format has to be defined. To this end, the VRML Consortium created the virtual reality modelling language (or VRML) together with the concept of a freely available VRML browser. In essence, VRML is a file format describing three-dimensional environment. In many aspects, VRML was ahead of its time and has been successfully used in numerous research prototypes [3]. However, this standard did and still suffers from a major drawback, namely the file size and inefficient ASCII format. That is, the lengthy download time remains unacceptable for most users and applications. The Consortium addressed this problem by subsequently developing a binary format, which was, due to numerous practical problems, never adopted. Recently, however, the Consortium, after being re-named as the Web3D Consortium, released a new format called X3D [3].

X3D is very similar to XML and contains the following functionality. Firstly, it defines the well-known, basic geometrical elements. Secondly, it supports the definition of new elements. Lastly, it allows the definition of a grammar that governs their mutual relationships. Consequently, X3D can be utilised for defining new three-dimensional formats.

Another attempt that has been made involves the creation of an international multimedia standard MPEG-4 [4]. This standard would be able to handle all kinds of media including three-dimensional objects. MPEG-4 provides a binary format called BIFF that integrates sound, image, video and three-dimensional objects. In this way, it is possible to synchronise objects and to make them interact with one another. From the three-dimensional point of view, the structure of MPEG-4 is very similar to the one of VRML. MPEG-4 can also support face and body animation, a characteristic very useful for avatars and virtual mannequins. This standard is now being using in industry. An interesting application is HotMedia™ from IBM™. It remains to be seen whether MPEG-4 will become the standard for Web-based three-dimensional objects.

The following observation is noteworthy. Care must be taken to ensure that, when providing the customer with a virtualised object, it appears to be realistic. Customer will not be tempted to buy an object if it appears "toy-like" or "plastic". This is mainly due to the fact that most three-dimensional objects are created using a model created by a computer. These models are usually quite limited in terms of the colour and texture of the objects, which are rendered. This problem can be easily overcome by scanning the real object in three-dimensions, as discussed next.

Different techniques are available for scanning, including the following three methods. When using a laser scanner [5], the object is scanned (with a laser) and the third dimension is obtained from the position of the reflected beam on a sensor by triangulation. When using a stereo vision system, a second sensor replaces the laser. The third dimension is obtained from the positions of corresponding points on the two sensors. Thirdly, the time of flight system measures the time taken by a laser pulse to make a round trip between the sensor and the object. Because of the high speed of light, modulation techniques are used to measure indirectly the duration of the motion.

Alternatively, the virtual objects are created by simply mapping real pictures or textures on the three-dimensional geometry. Photogrammetry [6] reconstructs three-dimensional objects and scenes from a set of pictures. The user specifies common points between two pictures and the system calculates the three-dimensional co-ordinates by using bundle adjustment. It is very convenient because the only hardware needed is a standard digital camera. Some systems are more adapted for large objects and scenes while some offer more precision: the right choice depends on the application.

This section discussed standard for using multimedia over the Web. This was followed by an overview of approaches to create realistic virtual representations. The next section overview an approach for describing bidimensional images using a morphological approach.

3.   DESCRIBING BIDIMENSIONAL IMAGES

The widespread use of images on the Internet, and in particular in e-business, comes as no surprise. A picture is easy to obtain and to transfer over the Web, especially since the use of digital cameras has become commonplace. Also, a picture conveys its message across language boundaries; making it very attractive in the global e-business marketplace.

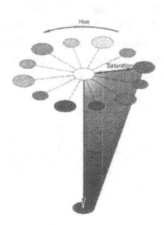

Figure 13-1. The hue-saturation-value or HSV colour representation.

This section portrays an algorithm used to describe or index bidimensional images for use in our multimedia retrieval system.

The algorithm presented here is inspired by [7-9] and is based on a morphological approach, thus considering the form and structure of images. In this approach, the chromatic distribution of each image is described with the hue-saturation-value representation (HSV). The HSV scheme, which refers to a cylindrical transformation of the red-green-blue (RGB) representation, is similar to the one adopted by painters for their palette. It thus reproduces many characteristics of the human visual system. The hue represents the tint e.g. red, green or blue. The saturation represents its intensity e.g. light red or deep red. The value is related to the amount of light in the scene. The HSV representation is shown in Figure 13-1.

Figure 13-2. The morphological approach: the hue and the saturation of the image are scanned randomly with a structuring element.

The bidimensional image descriptor is computed as follows. Firstly, points are randomly sampled on the image. For this purpose, a quasi-random sequence is used. For each sampled point, a structuring element is applied on the image. The shape of the structuring element depends on the particular application, but a rectangular element is perfectly adapted to most situations. Such a structuring element is shown in Figure 13-2.

Figure 13-3. Query for similar pieces in a broken vase database. All pictures were taken under the same background and lighting conditions. Only two results are illustrated here.

The structuring element is used to compute the local colour distribution. The distribution within the structuring element is represented by a bidimensional histogram. The first dimension represents the hue or the saturation quantified on a limited number of bins. Because of its variability, the value is not used in the image description. The second dimension represents the proportion of the colours relative to the others within the structuring element. For each position of the structuring element, the bidimensional histogram is computed and summing up the values obtained at the preceding iteration accumulates the quantities. From this process, a compact representation of the colour distribution is obtained.

Experience has shown this technique to be very efficient [10-11]. For example, Figure 13-3 shows the retrieval of vase pieces from a broken vase database containing about 400 pieces. All pictures were taken with a uniform contrasting background. Under that condition, our picture retrieval system can be applied to bidimensional shape retrieval if the objects under consideration can be characterized by their contour. In Figure 13-3, both contour and colour information are used in order to describe the object.

This section introduced a morphological approach to describe bidimensional images. Experience shows that this approach is successful to provide an information rich description of the images. The next section discusses a technique to describe the shape of a three-dimensional object.

4.   SHAPE DESCRIPTION FOR THREE-DIMENSIONAL OBJECTS

The National Research Council (NRC) of Canada has developed a system that automatically describes the shape of a large set of three-dimensional objects [10-11]. In this approach, the information about each object is written in a descriptor, which thus presents an abstract representation of the shape of the object. We include a brief description of the general idea [10-11].

The descriptor is computed as follow. Firstly, a scale, translation, rotation and reflection invariant reference frame is calculated from the principal axis of the tensor of inertia. The principal axes correspond to the Eigen vectors of the tensor of inertia. Assuming a triangular mesh representation for the object, the later is defined as

$$I = \left[I_{qr}\right] = \left[\frac{1}{n}\sum_{i=1}^{n}\left[S_i\left(q_i - q_{CM}\right)\left(r_i - r_{CM}\right)\right]\right] \tag{1}$$

Where S_i is the surface of a triangular face, CM is the centre of mass of the object and q and r are the co-ordinates x, y and z. The principal axes correspond to the Eigen vectors of the tensor of inertia and are obtained from the Eigen equation:

$$\left[I\mathbf{a}_i = \lambda_i \mathbf{a}_i\right]_{i=1,2,3} \tag{2}$$

It can be shown that the normalised principal axes are translation, scale and rotation invariant. By applying a suitable transformation to them, the reflection invariance can be obtained. More details about this transformation can be found in [10]. The axes of the reference frame are identified by their corresponding Eigen values.

The three-dimensional shape descriptor is based on the concept of a cord. A cord is defined as a vector that goes from the centre of mass of the model to the centre of mass of a given triangle. It is thus assumed that a triangular mesh represents the surface of the object. Note that the cord is not a unit vector since it has a length. As opposed to a normal, a cord can be considered as a regional characteristic. If the pyramid and the step pyramid are taken as an example, it can be seen that the cord orientation changes slowly on a given region, while the normal orientation can have important variations.

The distribution of the cords is represented by three histograms. The first histogram represents the angular distribution between the cords and the first Eigen vector. The second histogram represents the angular distribution between the cords and the second Eigen vector. The distribution of the radii is represented by a third histogram. This histogram is scale-dependent, but it can be made scale-independent by normalising the scale. The normalization operation can be performed based either on the maximum radius or on the average radius. Note that all descriptors must have an identical normalization in order to be comparable.

Each histogram is quantified over a certain number of bins. The histograms are normalised by the highest amplitude and each channel is quantified on one byte. A weight is associated to each cord. This weight corresponds to the area of the surface of the triangle to which the cord is attached. The weighting operation insures that the descriptors are, up to a certain point, tessellation invariant by taking into account the relative geometrical importance of each triangle. That means that the descriptors do not depend on a particular representation or tessellation of the object.

A descriptor based on the DAU4 wavelet transform is also proposed. The NxN matrix corresponding to that transform is:

$$W = \begin{bmatrix} c_0 & c_1 & c_2 & c_3 & & & & & \\ c_3 & -c_2 & c_1 & -c_0 & & & & & \\ & & c_0 & c_1 & c_2 & c_3 & & & \\ & & c_3 & -c_2 & c_1 & -c_0 & & & \\ & & & & \ddots & & & & \\ & & & & & & c_0 & c_1 & c_2 & c_3 \\ & & & & & & c_3 & -c_2 & c_1 & -c_0 \\ c_2 & c_3 & & & & & & & c_0 & c_1 \\ c_1 & -c_0 & & & & & & & c_3 & -c_2 \end{bmatrix} \tag{3}$$

The wavelet coefficients are obtained by applying the matrix W on the reference frame defined by the tensor of inertia. This choice is dictated by the fact that the wavelet transform is not translation and rotation invariant. In order to apply the transform to an object, the latter has to be binarized. The wavelet coefficients represent a tremendous amount of information. In order to reduce it, for each level of resolution of the transform a set of statistical moments is computed. For each moment, a histogram of the distribution of the moment is built. The channels correspond to the level of detail and the amplitude to the normalized moments. This histogram is the descriptor of the object.

The above-mentioned descriptor is very compact with a size of 120 bytes. Note that the size of the descriptor is totally independent on the size of the original three-dimensional file. That is, a file can represent an object, a part, a person or a scene.

Many other descriptors and indexation techniques have been proposed for three-dimensional models. These include silhouettes, Bayesian indexing, point signature and modal analysis. A discussion of these techniques falls beyond the scope of this chapter. Interested readers are referred to [12-17].

The following observation is noteworthy. Three-dimensional retrieval is mainly shape-based while bidimensional retrieval is context-based. In other words, the first one is metric-based while the later is appearance-based. However, both paradigms are powerful retrieval tools in an e-commerce environment. The next section discusses the implementation of the retrieval system for both images and three-dimensional objects.

5. IMPLEMENTATION OF INFORMATION RETRIEVAL SYSTEM

This section describes the implementation of the retrieval system, utilizing the image and shape descriptions as defined in Sections 3 and 4. The system is composed of three parts, namely the crawler, the analyser and the search engine.

The task of the crawler, which is also called spider or Web robot, is to periodically collect all the relevant bidimensional or three-dimensional files from a specified location. These files can be located on a disc, on a local network, an Intranet or over the Internet. The files located on the Internet are accessed through user specification of the domains and the URLs. While crawling over the Internet, the crawler uses the hyperlinks to gradually cover the portion of the Web that has been devoted to it and identifies the files of interest by their file extensions e.g. *.wrl for VRML files. That is, the crawler "spins a web" over the subset of the Internet it covers.

The second part of the system is the analyser, which uses as input the results as obtained from the crawler. The analyser examines the objects, as contained in the input files, and converts it to the description as discussed in Section 3.

The analyser proceeds as follows. First, it reads each file, as obtained by the crawler, and parses the dimensional information. All this information is subsequently mapped to an internal representation, i.e. the analyser acts as a translator.

- For three-dimensional objects, this information includes the vertices and colour, and other shape descriptions. If the object is not modelled as a triangular mesh, the surface is tessellated with a callback function. The tessellation is performed automatically for elementary surfaces, non-uniform rational beta splines – NURBS and polygonal meshes. Once the geometrical information is extracted, the descriptors are calculated and saved in a compressed representation. In addition, a thumbnail is also generated. This thumbnail is used as an abstract or compact representation for the three-dimensional object. It can be easily manipulated and carried over the network.

- For images, the dimensional information is used to create a descriptor in the form of a bidimensional histogram, as discussed in Section 3.

When all the descriptors have been computed, a specially designed and optimised object oriented database is created. For example, consider the CAESAR™ anthropometric database, as depicted in Figure 13-4. This database contains the descriptors of thousands of individuals scanned in three-dimensions, together with statistical and anthropometric data [18-19].

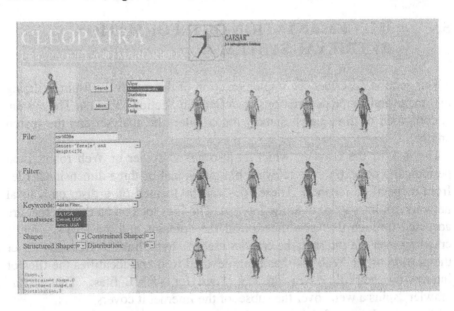

Figure 13-4. Query for a body in the CAESAR™ anthropometric database base on three-dimensional shape and weight.

The last part of the system is the search engine. The search engine provides the graphical interface to the user. It also implements the business logic between the interface and the OO database. Currently, the search engine is designed as a three tiers system. It consists of the client, the search engine logic and the database. In the research presented in here, the client is

The Virtual Boutique as described in Section 6. The second tier is a Java Servlet or an Enterprise Java Beans or EJB. This models the business logic and the interface between the business logic and the data. The third tier is the three-dimensional database.

Figure 13-4 shows the interface for a query to find similar bodies in the CAESAR™ anthropometric database with NRC's Cleopatra Search Engine. Here, the input to the query is a three-dimensional representation of an individual, referred to as an archetype, which appears on the left of the screen. That is, a query uses the query by example paradigm. The query returns images of individuals with similar shape, appearing on the right hand side of the screen. The outcome is subsequently filtered with statistical and anthropometric filters. For example, a filter may include a person's gender, income and/or age. The interface provides the filters and provides the user with options to select sub-databases. This interface provides us with an intuitive, natural tool for three-dimensional querying.

The strength of this approach is its extensibility and simplicity. Experience shows that the number of objects can easily reach more than 100.000 without compromising the system performances [11]. Also, the system can collect three-dimensional objects from a file system or from the Internet. It can be deployed on our dedicated object oriented database or on a commercial object-relational database such as Oracle8i™. The search engine is able to run as a stand-alone application or on an application server. In the later case, the search engine can be accessed from anywhere over the Internet.

This section described the three-part system used for acquiring and retrieving three-dimensional images. The next section introduces The Virtual Boutique, which incorporates both three-dimensional objects and images.

6.   THE VIRTUAL BOUTIQUE: VIRTUAL REALITY FOR E-BUSINESS

Recall that The Virtual Boutique implements the client of the search engine and is used by the online users to query the underlying database of an e-business site.

What is The Virtual Boutique? The Virtual Boutique is an online e-commerce store, which contains both images and three-dimensional objects, scanned into an environment consisting of a number of virtual rooms. This discussion will focus on the furniture department of the e-store, as depicted in Figure 13-5. The figure shows a global view of the furniture department, which includes a number of vases, tables, chairs and wall fixtures, amongst others. Here, we use images and three-dimensional objects to provide the consumer with a virtualised representation of the object.

The scenes, which are included in The Virtual Boutique, were created as follows. Initially, digital pictures of the scene (or boutique) were acquired. These pictures were taken using the same lighting conditions and the camera was using an object of known dimensions for calibration. Next, a three-dimensional representation of the scene was constructed using photogrammetry, as introduced in Section 2. A number of rules apply while taking the pictures, including the following. Firstly, there must be an overlapping between the pictures and each picture must be taken from a distinct viewpoint. It follows that, the further the distance between the viewpoints, the better the quality of the reconstruction. The density of the sampling depends on the complexity of the scene. While a few pictures are enough for a simple scene, many pictures may be required for a complicated scene. Figure 13-6 shows a room created using the above-mentioned process. This scene depicts a scene from the furniture store of an e-store. The room has been virtualised with photogrammetric techniques using only two digital pictures.

Figure 13-5. Global view of the furniture department of The Virtual Boutique

The design of The Virtual Boutique is based on the observation that, in essence, shopping is an unstructured, unorganised process. In a real store, the consumers move, discuss, touch and compare before purchasing. Many times, the consumer brings along a picture of an item he wishes to find, either physical or mentally. For example, a consumer shopping for a vase may bring along a clipping of a vase, which he previously saw in an interior design magazine. That is, he brings along an example and asks the vendor for a similar item. If the choice becomes too difficult, the consumer may put the various similar items next to one another to ease his choice. For example, the consumer shopping for a vase may place five different vases next to one another on the counter. This situation reflects that, for many people, choosing an item relative to others is easier than on an absolute basis.

The first paradigm involves interclass comparison, while the second paradigm enables intraclass comparison through relative visualisation. This is the most common paradigm in real shopping environment.

In The Virtual Boutique, the two above-mentioned paradigms of "comparison-based shopping" and "query by archetype" are implemented as follows. That is, a search within the Virtual Boutique is performed in two different ways. In the first approach, the descriptors for images or three-dimensional objects, as described earlier, are used to obtain similar items. In the second approach, the search is performed by using a lookup table of predefined classifications. Here, the outcome of the search is displayed by either replacing the reference object with the closest match or through a global reconfiguration of the boutique. Note that every object in the boutique can be manipulated, aiding the consumer to co-ordinate different objects, both from the appearance and spatial point of view.

Figure 13-6. The Virtual Boutique. The room has been virtualised with photogrammetric techniques. The objects have been generated with computer graphic techniques.

In the first case, a sequential shopping paradigm is used. The results are displayed in a sequential manner. The consumer selects an object and asks for similar or related objects. The boutique determines the closest match, using the method as described in Section 5. The system displays the result by replacing the original object in the scene. All subsequent results are displayed in the same manner. At the end of the process, the initial object is put back in place. This paradigm is very useful if the consumer tries to co-ordinates many objects together. For example, assume that a consumer wishes to buy a table and two chairs for his living room. Here, the main problem is to co-ordinate the three pieces of furniture in a meaningful way. By applying this paradigm to many objects, the consumer can evaluate different combinations and determine which one is the most appropriated for him.

In the second case, the consumer is allowed to reconfigure the whole scene using the outcome of a search, as depicted in Figure 13-7. Here, the consumer selects all the items of interest. It is subsequently displayed in the boutique. In this way, the consumer is creating a new composition of items, which may lead to him purchasing additional items (or even alternative) that originally planned. For example, consider the above-mentioned consumer who intended purchasing two chairs and a table. Through the reconfiguration of the scene, the consumer might decide to purchase a sofa, one chair, a table as well as a vase. Also, through virtualisation, this may lead to the consumer deciding to repaint his living room, leading to a purchase in the hardware department of our store. This scenario is also useful in environments where the shopper is a returning customer, who has previously purchased a combination of some items.

Figure 13-7. Reconfiguration of the Virtual Boutique. The left view shows the original boutique and the right view shows the same boutique where the sofas and the tables have been substituted by making a query to the three-dimensional shape search engine.

Note that the consumer can seamlessly switch between the two paradigms. Furthermore the boutique is divided in departments and the consumer can select a department according to his interests, i.e. furniture, hardware, electronic, etc. The user can select any item and cycle through them. Navigation within The Virtual Boutique is controlled through using the mouse and the keyboard [20]. The direction of the navigation and the inclination of the head are controlled by the mouse while the keyboard controls the displacements. The displacements include acceleration when the customer starts to move and deceleration when he becomes immobile. The collisions with the wall are elastic and reproduce the effect of a normal collision between a rigid wall and a human body. The lighting is designed in order to favour the visualisation and to create the required atmosphere.

A detailed discussion of the implementation issues of The Virtual Boutique falls beyond the scope of this chapter. Interested readers are referred to [21] for a discussion of the issues regarding compression, portability and performance related issues.

This section introduced The Virtual Boutique and showed its applicability for virtualising the rooms of the furniture department of an e-store. The next section discusses the use of the Virtual Boutique for data mining.

7.   VIRTUAL-REALITY AND DATA MINING: FUTURE RESEARCH DIRECTIONS

Data mining [22-26] is defined as the process of extracting non-trivial, previously unknown and potentially useful patterns from large data repositories. Data mining techniques includes classification and prediction, association rule mining and cluster analysis. In particular, the analysis of clickstreams, as contained in so-called e-webhouses, to determine consumer behaviour is currently an important topic in data mining [27].

This section presents our current ideas regarding the use of data mining to better understand the behaviour of consumers in The Virtual Boutique. The results of such an analysis can be used to target potential consumers, order the objects in the rooms, streamline the order of the rooms in The Virtual Boutique, determine trends in purchase behaviour, to create profiles of our consumers, amongst others [28-30].

The data obtained through the Virtual Boutique can be used to extract general business rules and information regarding consumer behaviour from the interaction of consumers with the boutique, as illustrated in the following examples. Clickstream analysis can be used to distinguish between customers who purchase items, versus those who do not. Data mining may determine that a typical consumer will return to the same object (e.g. a vase) six to eight times before purchasing it. On the other hand, a consumer who returns to a particular object more than ten times will typically abort the transaction. This type of consumer behaviour indicates that the second type of consumer does find the object attractive, but that one of the characteristics (e.g. the colour) is not ideal. Through pro-active marketing, a message should be displayed which for example suggest another similar item in a different colour.

Data mining can also be used to determine the walk-though behaviour of customers. If trends show that a particular room is unpopular, it should either be removed from the walk through or re-decorated. Similarly, the stock items in the boutique, which are only briefly visited and rarely purchased, should be removed from the inventory. Data mining can thus also be used to determine seasonal trends and shifts in fashion, for example in colour schemes and shapes.

In addition, from the navigation and the interaction of the consumer with the boutique it is possible to deduce if the disposition of the object is adequate and if the objects can be easily manipulated. It is also possible to determine the amount of time the consumer spends on each item and the combination and disposition of items favoured by the consumer. If a transaction does not lead to a sale, it is possible to analyse the whole process instant by instant in order to determine what went wrong.

CONCLUSIONS

Current advances in the games and movie industries have led to a new breed of consumers with a preference for e-business sites which includes images and three-dimensional objects, virtualisation and innovative information retrieval methods. The combination of intuitive information retrieval, realistic rendering of images and three-dimensional objects into a virtual environment is therefore a *sine qua non* condition for the further development of e-commerce and e-business. This chapter discussed The Virtual Boutique, which combines realistic rendering, multimedia integration, efficient and intuitive navigation and content-based searching capability into a single virtual environment.

The introductions of virtual reality-based environments for e-commerce enable the collection of a huge amount of data concerning consumers' habits. It is the opinion of the authors that the analysis, through data mining, of such so-called e- webhouses should lead to a better understanding of the behaviour patterns of e-business consumers.

ACKNOWLEDGEMENT

This chapter is based on prior work as reported in [20-21].

REFERENCES

1. V. C. Storey et al., "A Conceptual Investigation of the E-commerce Industry", Communications of the ACM 43, pp. 117-123 (2000).
2. E. Paquet and M. Rioux, "A Content-based Search Engine for CAD and VRML Databases", Dedicated Conference on Robotics, Motion and Machine Vision in the Automotive Industries, Proc. ISATA 31, 427-434, Dusseldorf, Germany (1998).
3. Web3D Consortium: http://www.web3d.com
4. MPEG-4: http://mpeg.telecomitalialab.com
5. J.-A. Beraldin et al, "3D Digital Imaging and Modeling", Proceedings Second International Conference on 3D Digital Imaging and Modeling, pp. 34-43, Ottawa, Canada (1999).
6. S .F. El-Hakim, "A Practical Approach to Creating Precise and Detailed 3D Models from Single and Multiple Views." International Archives of Photogrammetry and Remote Sensing, Volume 33, Part B5A, Commission V, pp. 122-129, Amsterdam, July 16-23 (2000).
7. P. van Beek et al., "Scalable Blob Histogram Descriptor", ISO/IEC JTC1/SC29/WG11 – MPEG-7 Proposal ID 430, Lancaster, England (1999).
8. T. Gevers and A. W. M. Smeulders, "Image Indexing using Composite Colour and Shape Invariant Features", ICCV, pp.576-581 (1998).
9. M. Flickner et al., "Query by Image and Video Content," IEEE Computer, pp.23-32 (1995).
10. E. Paquet and M. Rioux, "The MPEG-7 Standard and the Content-based Management of Three-dimensional Data: A Case Study", IEEE International Conference on Multimedia Computing and Systems, June 7-11, Florence, Italy, pp. 375-380 (1999).
11. E. Paquet et al., "Description of Shape Information for 2-D and 3-D Objects", Signal Processing Image Communication 16, pp. 103-122 (2000).
12. Y. Liu and F. Dellaert, "A Classification Based Similarity Metric for 3D Image Retrieval", CVPR, pp. 800-805 (1998).
13. Y. Gdalyahu and D. Weinshall, "Automatic Hierarchical Classification of Silhouettes 3D Objects", CVPR, pp. 787-793 (1998).
14. J. H. Yi and D. M. Chelberg, "Model-Based 3D Object Recognition Using Bayesian Indexing", Computer Vision and Image Understanding 69, pp. 87-105 (1998).
15. C. S. Chua and R Jarvis, "Point Signature: A New Representation for 3D Object Recognition", International Journal of Computer Vision 25, pp. 63-85 (1997).
16. F. Dell'Acqua and P. Gamba, "Simplified Modal Analysis and Search for Reliable Shape Retrieval," IEEE Trans. CSVT 8(5), pp. 656-666 (1998).
17. C. Dorai and A. K. Jain, "Shape Spectrum based View Grouping and Matching of 3-D Free-Form Objects," IEEE Trans. PAMI 19(10), pp. 1139-1146 (1997).
18. The CAESAR™ Project: http://www.sae.org/technicalcommittees/caesumm.htm
19. E. Paquet, K. M. Robinette and M. Rioux, "Management of Three-dimensional and Anthropometric Databases: Alexandria and Cleopatra", Journal of Electronic Imaging, 9, pp. 421-431 (2000).
20. E. Paquet, H. Viktor and S. Peters, "The Virtual Boutique: Virtual Reality and Information Management for E-business", Invited Speaker, International Conference on Advances in Infrastructure for Electronic Business, Science, and Education on the Internet - SSGRR, Telecom Italia, August 6-12, L'Aquila, Italy, CD (2001).

21. E. Paquet, H. Viktor and S. Peters, "The Virtual Boutique: a Synergic Approach to Virtualization, Content-based Management of 3D Information, 3D Data Mining and Virtual Reality for E-commerce", 3D Data Processing Visualization and Transmission - 3DPVT02, IEEE Proceedings, June 19-21, Padova, Italy, pp. 268-276 (2002).

22. J. Ham and M. Kamber, "Data mining concepts and techniques", Morgam Kaufmann, San Francisco, USA (2001).

23. G. G. Grinstein and M. O. Ward (2002). Introduction to data visualization. Information Visualization in Data Mining and Knowledge Discovery, U. Fayyad, G. G. Grinstein and A. Wiese (editors), Academic Press, London: UK, pp.21-26.

24. K. Thearling et al. (2002). Visualizing Data Mining Models, Information Visualization in Data Mining and Knowledge Discovery, U. Fayyad, G. G. Grinstein and A. Wiese (editors), Academic Press, London: UK, pp.205-222.

25. P. E. Hoffman and G. G. Grinstein (2002). A Survey of Visualization for High-Dimensional Data Mining, Information Visualization in Data Mining and Knowledge Discovery, U. Fayyad, G. G. Grinstein and A. Wiese (editors), Academic Press, London: UK, pp.47-82.

26. M. Foster and A. G. Gee, "The Data Visualization Environment, Information Visualization in Data Mining and Knowledge Discovery", U. Fayyad, G. G. Grinstein and A. Wiese (editors), Academic Press, London: UK, pp.83-94 (2002).

27. A. Biancardi and V. Moccia, "Integrating Applications into Interactive Virtual Environments", VISUAL'99, pp. 703-710 (1999).

28. E. F. Churchill et al., "Collaborative Virtual Environments", Berlin: Springer Verlag (2001).

29. Multiple authors, "Special Issue on Large Wall Displays", IEEE Computer Graphics and Applications, 20 (4), (2000).

30. Digital Light Processing: <http://www.dlp.com>

Chapter 14

A WEB-BASED APPROACH TO COMPETITIVE INTELLIGENCE

Peter Gerstl, Birgit Kuhn, Hans-Joachim Novak
IBM Germany

Abstract: Increasingly, companies are using the Internet to present themselves to customers and provide most up-to-date information and offerings. Hence it can be used to gain competitive information on a regular and timely basis. However, right now this process is mainly based on manual searches and is thus very costly and time consuming. This chapter discusses technical approaches supporting this process.

Key words: competitive intelligence, knowledge mining, automatic summarization, classification, Web crawler, categorization, language identification, clustering, text mining

1.   MOTIVATION

Increasingly, companies are using the Internet in various business related ways, e.g. to present themselves to customers, to provide up-to-date business information and offerings and to gather customer data by evaluating discussions held in discussion groups and mailing lists.

It is thus a natural consequence to also use the Internet as a valuable source for marketing and competitive analysis purposes on a regular and timely basis. The Internet is one of the biggest sources of competitive information: Companies can easily find competitor's Web sites, analyze competitor's product portfolios and keep updated on their sales strategy. With the same approach they can investigate popular Web sites that provide technical and market information in their area of business such as news feeds or industry portals.

It is equally important to analyze who is referring to a company by looking at the links pointing to particular web pages. Added business value comes from analyzing web links in a semantic manner and determining whether they refer to certain products, statements or campaigns.

This vast amount of information is available to every individual and company today and is already being heavily used and evaluated. This leads to a growing pressure to quickly and timely extract and interpret the content of parts of the Internet that are relevant in order to not fall behind the competition, and performing what is called "Competitive Intelligence".

Competitive Intelligence by means of knowledge mining usually involves the following three processes.

1. Document Gathering/Extraction

The natural first step in dealing with data on the Internet is to collect as much relevant data as possible. This is mainly done by various crawling techniques, as defined in section 2.3.

2. Information Interpretation

Once the document gathering step has been performed, the challenge is how to get this data to work and turn it into something meaningful, to turn it into *information*. Thus, the segregation of meaningful data and noise has to be done, and the meaningful data has to be interpreted. Up to now this is mainly done by manual inspection.

However, a variety of techniques are available to ease and speed up the interpretation process. For example, data mining techniques help to obtain consistent interpretations of data and help to predict trends by comparing company data over time. Categorization algorithms assist in grouping documents automatically according to content. And summarization is an invaluable tool in condensing data to the most relevant pieces, thus turning it into dense information.

3. Information Presentation

Once the data has been collected and turned into valuable information, an important step is to present this information in a way that allows users to take most advantage of it. For example, within one company different groups may be interested to work with competitive intelligence information, but focus on different aspects of the information. Thus, being able to present different views and ways of navigation to for example the sales force, the marketing group or a strategy council can be of vital company interest.

This paper describes a high level architecture in the form of a process model that implements such a system. The following sections introduce the process model, then talk about important considerations when using such a system, and finally provide a discussion and outlook regarding the topics covered.

2.   PROCESS MODEL AND HIGH LEVEL ARCHITECTURE

2.1   Overview of Knowledge Mining

Knowledge mining allows analyzing unstructured textual data. This is a key technology that helps companies provide users with easy access to relevant information at a low cost by automating many aspects of information extraction and analysis.

The first challenge in knowledge mining is to readily access information in unstructured text that is electronically available. The complete interpretation of knowledge stated in unrestricted natural language is still out of reach when using current technology. However, tools that apply pattern recognition techniques and heuristics are capable of extracting valuable information from arbitrary free-text. Extracted information ranges from identifying so-called important words, like names, institutions, or places mentioned in a document to whole summaries of a document.

Knowledge mining is especially important when dealing with huge collections of documents since analyzing them manually is usually not an option. The "mining" metaphor is used for both the knowledge discovery process, that is, identifying and extracting codified information from single documents and storing this information as metadata, as well as the analysis process of the distribution of these features across document collections detecting interesting phenomena, patterns, or trends.

A key element of knowledge mining is information that represents aspects of a document or document collection that helps to understand, for example, the document's content or use. This information is referred to as *metadata*.

Examples of meta data that characterizes the content of a single document are:

1.   The document title
2.   An abstract or summary
3.   Names, terms, or expressions occurring in the document
4.   The document language
5.   Categories a document belongs to

When dealing with documents in a highly structured domain, obtaining these types of meta data may simply amount to looking it up at the appropriate location in a database or form. When dealing with unstructured document collections or document collections with non-standard structure (e.g. Web pages from different sites and authors), knowledge mining may be the only way to obtain this kind of information. Knowledge mining provides capabilities to automatically create metadata, even if it is not explicitly available.

Advanced mining and retrieval algorithms are able to access relevant information in huge document collections, either by using the metadata to guide the retrieval process or by running statistical models against the metadata to find interesting relations between documents that may not be obvious when looking at the individual documents of the collection.

Meta data that has been extracted using knowledge mining algorithms is kept in the meta data store for further processing. This approach allows document- or collection-related information to be stored separate from the actual document content. Obviously, for documents that are available for read only access, such as foreign documents on the Web, keeping the content and metadata within the same repository is not an option at all. An important aspect when using this approach is to ensure that meta data is properly synchronized with the documents/collections it characterizes. This ensures that the addition or deletion of a document triggers the appropriate update on the meta data store.

Knowledge mining typically provides the following mechanisms for the automatic creation of metadata, namely:

1. **Categorization** assigns one or more categories to a document based on a user-defined taxonomy. This makes it possible to organize documents according to a well-defined classification scheme in order to easily locate and retrieve them within a certain area of interest (category). Industry portals usually organize their data according to a classification for the business area at issue.

2. **Summarization** extracts the most important sentences of a document. This helps the user decide whether to read the entire document. The user can specify the length of the intended summary. By doing so he directly influences the balance between the complexity of the extracted metadata and the amount of information in the document.

3. **Language identification** determines the language of a document. This is typically used to restrict documents by language and thus allow higher level analysis algorithms or manual readers to work with them on a language specific level.

4. **Information extraction** recognizes significant vocabulary items, like names, terms, and expressions, in text documents automatically. The typical use of this function is to identify product or company names that may help to uncover interesting relations between sites and pages.

5. **Clustering** divides a set of documents into similar groups or clusters. Clusters are automatically derived from the document collection. Clustering is an important tool, especially when dealing with huge document collections that need to be partitioned into smaller sets that can be dealt with more easily.

To exploit the knowledge mining functionality, documents must be organized such that they can be browsed and navigated. This is often realized by using a graphical user interface that allows the creation and maintenance of taxonomies. With such a tool the user can create a taxonomy, assign documents to each category of the taxonomy, and finally train the taxonomy based on these documents. Depending on the quality of the documents that have been selected for training, a number of iterations may be necessary to end up with a taxonomy that can be used to automate the classification process.

2.2   A Process Model for Competitive Intelligence

Figure 1 shows the process model of the proposed competitive analysis system. The knowledge acquisition process flows from left to right, with a feedback loop. Document gathering connects to the different information sources and collects data which may be of interest according to the criteria currently selected in the configuration, e.g. a potential Web sites of interest.

The filtering step reduces the amount of available information by focusing on criteria that have been proved to be useful for removing irrelevant data and organizing relevant data. While filtering may already involve some analysis, the main step involving mining is the step named 'analysis and store'. This step applies the mining functions specified in the configuration and stores the results in the meta data store for further analysis.

While the results of the filtering and analysis steps basically operate on the basis of single documents by creating metadata about these documents, the step that detects interesting information operates on sets of documents by detecting similarities and differences.

Finally the results of the previous steps are presented to the user and allows him to easily identify new and unconventional information. The user can provide feedback that helps to adjust the gathering, filtering, or analysis parameters.

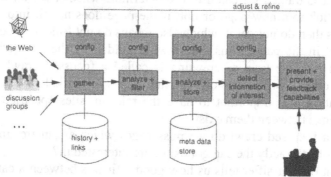

Figure 1 The Proposed architecture for a competitive intelligence system

2.3   Document Gathering

There are different ways to use a crawler for gathering information from the web.

The easiest method is to configure the crawler using a list of sites. If, for example, we know that each site in the list carries information about our competitors, we can use the capability of the crawler to read include and exclude lists and to only follow links down to a specified depth. This results in the crawler accessing the specified sites, and following all links down to the specified level. However, the crawler will not follow links which take it out of the set of domains specified in the configuration. Following all links without restriction would basically mean to crawl the whole Internet.

Using this method, how can we detect new information about our competitors?

Once the first crawl of the specified web space is done, we need to monitor the space for changes unless we want to risk that our gathered information becomes stale very soon. So the crawler checks the sites for updates to the pages it has crawled before. Moreover, when new pages come into existence which are linked to the existing ones the crawler will gather them provided the new pages are not beyond the specified crawling depth.

Though this approach is relatively straightforward, a prerequisite is that we know the names and Web sites of our competitors in the first place. We have to monitor the web constantly for new sites and add them to the list of sites to be visited by the crawler, otherwise we would risk to loose important information.

Fortunately, this does not have to be done manually. There are two methods to automatically detect sites about competitive information that can be easily realized. The first one uses the tools which are part of a knowledge mining system. We use our classifier to guide the crawler. We start off with a list of sites we know about, crawl them and classify them according to a taxonomy about competitive information we are interested in. Once the categorizer is trained we can use it to determine whether the crawler should follow a link to a new page or not; if the page does not fit into any of the categories then do not get it, which also means do not follow any of the links embedded in the page. Thus the crawl is guided by the categories we are interested in. This type of crawling is called a focussed crawl. Since the focused crawl will start off at the pages specified in the crawler configuration it is important to have the relevant sites specified where no explicit links between them exist.

Using a focussed crawl do we miss pages which are interesting *because* they do not fit exactly the categories we are interested in?

Given that our classifier tells us how good a fit was between a category and the crawled page we can choose a threshold such that doubtful cases are presented to the administrator of the system who then has make a decision.

The advantage of the focussed crawl is that it allows us to find pages about our competition which we were not aware of (and thus could not provide the crawler with in the first place).

The second method to automatically detecting sites about competitive information uses publicly available Web search engines. Using keyword searches we can gather lots of pages which are potentially interesting and then in later steps filter them according to more precise criteria. Furthermore search engine vendors or content providers tend to make Web services available that provide elaborate mechanisms to specify the data of interest.

In general, the gathering phase should not be too restrictive but rather gather far more information and filter later, in order to not miss any key information.

In the process of crawling we build up a database of the links which originate from each page we gather. Besides being necessary for our crawl this information is extremely valuable as it allows us to gain further insight: do any of our competitors point to each other or to us? Are any of the sites they point to also our customers? To which categories do the pages belong to which they point?

2.4 Data Filtering

The main purpose of this step is to reduce the amount of available information. This is typically done by specifying filtering criteria in the configuration for this step. In the following, typical filtering mechanisms are listed:

2.4.1 Filtering by Amount of "Readable" Content

Readable content refers to pieces of information that can be analyzed by the processes that follow in the chain of figure 1. Setting a threshold on the amount of readable content ensures that only those documents survive the filtering process which can be further analyzed. For example, if no means for processing information in images is available this step can filter out all pages that only contain images. Some mining functions such as summarization also require a minimum amount of text in terms of words, sentences, or paragraphs, to provide useful results.

2.4.2 Filtering by Language

Filtering by language uses automatic language detection (see 2.1) to identify the predominant language of a page. By specifying the languages of interest, the filtering step makes sure that only documents for which the automatic language detection comes back with a sufficiently high confidence value are passed on to the subsequent processing steps. If, for example, all further processing assumes that the document language is German, the filter component can ensure that only German documents are stored in the database.

This may be especially useful for removing redundancy by selecting the appropriate set of documents from multilingual Web sites.

2.4.3   Filtering by Key Words or Phrases

Filtering by key words or phrases uses feature extraction to specify a selection criterion with which all documents of interest need to conform. This takes advantage of the fact that the feature extractor maps different surface forms to a single canonical form. Specifying this canonical form as either *in* or *out* criterion makes sure that documents that contain variants of this form are treated properly.

Example: *in* criterion "vacuum cleaner"   -   *out* criterion "XY Company"

In general, the *in* and *out* criteria can be viewed as a simplified version of a general Boolean query, where the *in* criterion is a positive, and the *out* criterion a negative (= negated) element of a conjunction. A conflict resolution strategy, for example based on weights, should be established to define the behaviour for cases where both *in* and *out* criteria apply.
Using *out* criteria only makes sense in combination with other filtering approaches or if in criteria apply as well. If this is the only filtering technique used, any document not matching the *in* criterion will not pass the filter and no *out* criteria need to be specified.

2.4.4   Filtering based on Content Classification

Using topic classification (categorization) for filtering makes it possible to filter and organize documents according to predefined taxonomies of content-types. Similar to the *in* and *out* criteria in the previous section, categories in such a taxonomy can be classified as either *in* or *out* categories meaning that only documents that are assigned to an *in* category are passed on to the following components.

Note, that different taxonomies (sorting systems) can be used that correspond to different views on the data. An example for a product-related system is:

Taxonomy	Categories
Offering type	product description, support, services, consulting
Product type	vacuum cleaner, toaster, egg boiler
Type of terminology	expert, ordinary user, learner

2.4.5   Other Filtering Mechanisms

In addition to the filtering mechanisms described above, other approaches are possible, such as filtering by mime type, filtering by document type, etc. It really depends on the application scenario which of the above filtering mechanisms should be applied for best results.

2.5   Analyzing and Storing Data

The process of analyzing and storing information refers to (i) the identification of the structure of a document, (ii) processing the content parts based on content-type-specific mechanisms and (iii) storing the results of this processing (normalized document content and meta-data) in the meta data store.

Some of the processing may already have been done in the filtering step (because the type of filtering requires the availability of this kind of information). In this case this step simply amounts to storing the corresponding meta-data.

An important aspect of this step is the normalization (standardization) of content and meta-data and its mapping onto the well-defined structure of the database. This provides the basis for the next step in the chain that further organizes and groups documents.

The meta data created during the 'analyze and store' step usually contains:

1. data about the document source (URL, creation date, ...)
2. data about document structure and layout: amount of content, type and encoding of content, highlighted (= important) areas
3. data about textual content (language, topic classification, textual features)
4. data about other types of content (images, ...)
5. data about the link structure

Since Web pages may frequently be subject to changes or updates it may also be useful to store some information in a history such as the original documents and their link structure. Analyzing how Web content and its organization evolves over time can lead to interesting observations about portfolio or strategy changes that can help to detect future moves and repositioning of offerings ahead of time.

Depending on the actual system architecture, there may be a single analysis step that analyses the gathered documents, uses this information for filtering and stores the results in the meta data store so the two steps described in 2.4 and 2.5 collapse into one.

2.6   Detecting Information of Interest

This step uses the information made available by the previous steps to identify potential areas of interest. There major techniques in this area are:

2.6.1   Use of Interest Profiles

With a user interest profile, the user of the system can specify the information of interest. The primary mechanism to do this is by specifying important terms (key words) and/or categories the user is interested in by means of a query. Based on the meta data available, the system can select the documents that fit the user's profile (processing the query). The main advantage of this approach is that it helps to reduce the amount of data the user may need to browse manually and that the result sets which are presented already fit the users view which may be very different depending on the functional area he/she is responsible for, such as product planning, marketing, support, business processes, strategy etc.

2.6.2   Exploring the Dynamic Nature of the Observed Information

This is due to the fact that nearly all information, and particularly the information of interest in a competitive intelligence environment, changes over time. Thus, it is of crucial importance to detect how information on a topic evolves over time. Examples are:

1.   new offers from a competitor
2.   trends and tendencies in user's observations about a product

While it is interesting to observe changes between different versions of a Web page to find out about news or things that have been removed, it can be of equal interest to observe the evolution of a link structure over time, especially in relation to the categories of interest. If, for example, documents of the category 'last minute offers' are moved closer to the home page of a travel agency this may be an early indicator of a modified offering strategy or even a repositioning of this company. The system, however, can only indicate that some restructuring of the Web space has taken place and notify the user that this may be of interest for him. To find out whether the information is of any value remains the noble task of the human competitive intelligence analyzer.

2.6.3   Detecting Similar/Related Information

Information extraction and search results may provide information that can help to uncover implicit relations between documents such as introductions of campaigns or offerings of different competitors that have some important aspects in common. This can be an interesting approach for strategic and product planning and it may be used for trend analysis.

2.7   The Feedback Loop

Each of the three processes that help to focus on the relevant information (gather, filter, detect) has configuration parameters that specify how the corresponding step is accomplished. Thus the competitive analysis process provides a feedback mechanism that can adjust these parameters to make sure no important information is lost and the focus is set to the most promising areas.

Part of the feedback loop is based on the results of the analysis and thus works independent from user intervention, while the other part allows the user to tune the parameters of the individual steps according to insights from the data presented.

Adjusting the parameters of the gathering step usually means changing the focus of the crawler by adding or removing URLs or changing the crawling depth.

Adjusting the parameters of the filtering step typically means changing the list of languages of interest, changing the definition of categories by retraining one or more of the categorization schemes or adding new categories.

Adjusting the parameters of the detection step usually means tightening or releasing the criteria that detect changes, similarities, and differences.

3.   PROCESS DESCRIPTION

When setting up the system described above, the first step should be to carefully analyze the expected outcome of the system. This helps to choose those tools that are most beneficial to the expected outcome. This can be done based on a checklist like the following.

1. Focus on customers' view about own products or in information about competitor?
2. Main interest in current situation or market perspective?
3. Focus on detailed information or large coverage?
4. Information need well-understood or fuzzy?

While none of the criteria in the list may be seen as an either-or, the type of answer helps to indicate the approach to be taken. For example, the less the information need is understood, the more flexibility in specifying tuning parameters must be included in the system (e.g. Filtering criteria should not be too restrictive to exclude areas that may turn out to be important).

If the main goal is to find out whether customers like your product or not, a good starting point may be to crawl so-called consumer portals or newsgroups that are thematically related to the application area. The more convenient and well-established the product names, the easier it is to define filtering and analysis criteria to identify relevant pages. Usually, your company name and the product name or product type are a good start.

If the primary goal is to learn about the market situation of a product, a good starting point may be to identify your most important competitors and collect information about their products. Based on this information it may again be useful to crawl consumer portals and discussion groups to find out how your products are used and if the customers are satisfied.

Apart from these two examples there are a whole lot of other useful strategies and Web areas to start with, such as for example analysis reports and patent databases.

There are basically two different approaches to set up an initial system, independent of the area of use: either (i) start with a restrictive set of filtering and analysis criteria and expand them as more information becomes available or (ii) start with an almost non-exclusive set of criteria and narrow down the scope as it becomes more obvious where the focus should be set.

In its extreme form, the latter approach amounts to crawling a significant portion of the Web and creating a search index on which the analyst can set up queries. In general, the latter approach is a lot more labour-intensive since it puts the majority of burden onto the analyst while the first one always bears the risk to miss the relevant data.

The two approaches have an interesting parallel in the foundation of knowledge mining technology, where recall (focus on maximizing relevant information) usually is a direct counterpart of precision (focus on minimizing irrelevant information). Since any type of useful information that results from a competitive intelligence project is usually a success and economic factors are important to ensure the appropriate return of investment, it may be acceptable to miss some relevant information while keeping the amount of human intervention moderate.

An important advantage of the proposed architecture is that the configuration parameters can be stored and reused across variants of the information needed. If a similar investigation is to be done for a new product, only a subset of the configuration parameters needs to be re-specified, while a lot of valuable work can be preserved.

4.   DISCUSSION

This section discusses ethical aspects and technological limitations of competitive intelligence.

4.1   Ethic Aspects

Susan Warren (2002) claims competitive intelligence is really just the same as good old-fashioned spying, with the big plus that you never have to leave your desk. This of course raises all kinds of ethic, or even legal questions. Are companies allowed to spy on their competition? Are there any rules to protect companies from being spied on?

Truth is, the same rules apply as in old-fashioned, non-electronic spying on competition: as long as you access information which is publicly available and do not mislead anybody about your identity, there is nothing wrong with competitive intelligence (Susan Warren, 2002). After all, nobody would ever stop you from looking at your competition's packaging in supermarkets or trying to find out immediately when your competitor down the street drops his prices. As W. Michael Hoffman, executive director of the Center for Business Ethics at Bentley College in Waltam, Mass. puts it (Warren 2002), you cross the line if you anonymously coax proprietary information from an unsuspecting competitor. However, this does not imply that you have to tell you competitor every move you are taking - just like you would not announce, when going to into a supermarket, that you are in fact only there to spy and not to shop.

By crawling your competitor's web site you should always make sure to be "polite", that is to say that it should never be the case that the crawler is putting so many requests to the competition's server that the server's performance is impacted. This becomes particularly important if we look at a competitor's online store. We do not want to impact the business, but just aim to find out what the business is!

An example along the same lines is the observance of the file robots.txt that a lot of web servers provide. In this file the administrator states whether she wants the pages crawled or not. These instructions should always be observed by web crawlers, even though it is technically possible to ignore that information.

4.2   Technical Limitations

Possibilities for competitive intelligence with today's technology are great. However, it should not be forgotten that there are limitations.

For example, companies tend to more and more not use plain HTML text anymore on their websites, but encode text as bitmaps and flash. New products might be announced in a flashy bright banner, or whole sites can be captured as a single bitmap. In this case, standard web crawling and knowledge mining technologies would have to be expanded towards image recognition and afterwards recreation of the text. The results from applying knowledge mining techniques to images typically follow specific patterns. To explore these patterns further and define knowledge mining techniques to incorporate these patterns would be most helpful. However, this is more of a research topic at this stage than technology deployed in production environments.

Many companies have password protected parts of their web site. It is often exactly these protected sites, however, which contain the most valuable information for the competitive information gatherer. Thus, it is a necessity to create passwords for all relevant sites and then use these passwords to crawl this "hidden" information. This is not illegal, in fact this is currently done manually by many companies. However, this part may become technologically tricky as the crawler needs to pass on the password to the web site. Ideally, a mechanism for automatic updating of the password should also be in place. However, this is still very much a research topic.

Another problem that the automation of competitive intelligence faces is the fast pace at which the content of single pages or even the structure of the whole site changes. Also, the information which is of relevance might frequently change. This calls for a very flexible system, some of which is still a research topic. However, regular feedback loops for categorization, automatic detection of big changes in structure, and manual supervision are building blocks that help tackle this big challenge.

CONCLUSION

Knowledge mining techniques are ideally suited to gain competitive insight from web data. This paper showed that a computer system can provide competitive intelligence to its users by using what could now be called "standard techniques for knowledge mining". It helps detect new information which it submits to a human administrator for further scrutiny. The paper went on to describe different techniques used in the process of competitive intelligence and then described the typical process flow within such a system. The paper concluded with an ethical and technological discussion, placing competitive intelligence technology in a broader context.

REFERENCES

[Baeza-Yates & Ribeiro-Neto 1999] Baeza-Yates, R.; Ribeiro-Neto, B.: Modern Information Retrieval, Addison Wesley Publishing Co., 1999

[Endres-Niggemeyer 1998] Brigitte Endres-Niggemeyer (ed): Summarizing Information, Springer, Berlin, 1998

[Goldstein, Kantrowitz & Carbonell 1999] Goldstein J.; Kantrowitz, M.; Carbonell, J.: Summarizing Text Documents: Sentence Selection and Evaluation Metrics. In: Proceedings SIGIR '99, ACM, Berkeley, CA, 1999

[Joachims 1998] Joachims, T.: Text categorization with support vector machines: Learning with many relevant features. In: European Conference on Machine Learning (ECML), 1998

[Koller & Sahami 1997] Koller, D.; Sahami, M.: Hierarchically classifying documents using very few words. In: International Conference on Machine Learning (ICML), 1997

[Mani & Maybury 1999] Mani, I.; Maybury M.T. (eds.): Advances in automatic Text Summarization, MIT Press, Cambridge, MA, 1999

[Sparck Jones & Willet 1997] Sparck Jones, K.; Willet, P. (eds): Readings in Information Retrieval, Morgan Kaufmann Publishers, 1997

[Warren 2002] Warren, January 14: I-Spy - Getting the low-down on your competition is just a few clicks away, Special Report: E-Commerce, google.com/, 2002

[Witten, Moffat & Bell 1999] Witten, I.H.; Moffat, A.; Bell T. C.: Managing Gigabytes: compressing and indexing documents and images, Morgan Kaufmann Publishers Inc, 1999

[Yang 1999] Yang, Y.: An Evaluation of Statistical Approaches to Text Categorization Information Retrieval, May 1999

[Yang & Pedersen 1997] Yang Y.; Pedersen J.: A comparative study on feature selection in text categorization. In: International Conference on Machine Learning (ICML), 1997

Further references:

http://www.acm.org/sigir (Int. Conference on Research and Development in IR)

http://www.acm.org/sigkdd (Int. Conf. on Knowledge Discovery and Data Mining)

Chapter 15

LEARNING ONTOLOGIES FOR DOMAIN-SPECIFIC INFORMATION RETRIEVAL

Hele-Mai Haav

Institute of Cybernetics at Tallinn Technical University, Estonia

Abstract: Ontologies are used in information retrieval in order to improve traditional document search methods like keyword-based search or browsing hierarchies of subject categories on the Web. To make it possible to use ontologies for that purpose requires fast automatic or semi-automatic building of formal ontologies that can be processed by a computer. This paper describes a new approach to the automatic discovery of domain-specific ontologies in order to make it possible by intelligent agents to better "understand" the intended meaning of descriptions of objects to be retrieved from different web catalogues. The approach is based on automatic construction of domain-specific ontologies using Natural Language Processing (NLP) and Formal Concept Analysis (FCA). Besides the general framework of the approach, a principal architecture of a prototypical ontology design tool OntoDesign is presented. OntoDesign is a system for automatic construction of formal domain ontologies from given domain-specific texts by using FCA.

Key words: Ontology, Formal Concept Analysis, Concept Lattice, Learning of Concept Structures, Information Retrieval

1. INTRODUCTION

Research in ontology is becoming increasingly important in many fields of computer science, including database design, knowledge engineering, agent communication, semantic Web and information retrieval. One of the main motivations of ontology design is establishing a conceptually concise basis for communicating, sharing and reuse of knowledge over different applications.

Ontologies are used in information retrieval in order to improve traditional document retrieval methods like keyword-based search or browsing hierarchies of subject categories. First, domain-specific ontology is created by the domain-expert, and then documents are mapped to given ontology for retrieval [Helfin and Hendler 2000, OIL 2001]. Ontology-based search engines like OntoSeek [Guarino 1999], OntoBroker [Decker et al 1999], and SHOE [Helfin and Hendler 2002] use this approach.

Manual construction and description of domain-specific ontology is a complex and time-consuming process. It is extremely difficult for human experts to discover ontology from given data or text. As verification of the correctness of ontology has to be done by human experts with respect to their knowledge about domain, it can lead to inconsistency of the created ontology. One solution to the problem is to build ontology automatically or at least, use semi-automatic methods. Currently, there is a lack of approaches for automatic ontology building. A few proposals on ontology development by ontology extraction and learning can be found in [Woelk and Tomlinson 1994, Preece at al 1999, Decker et al 1999, Maedche and Staab 2000]. One possible candidate for construction of domain ontologies is Formal Concept Analysis (FCA) [Ganter and Wille 1999].

FCA is rather often proposed in the field of lattice-based information retrieval as formal basis for concept based document search [Eklund et al 2000, Haav and Nilsson 2001, Priss 2000, Kim and Compton 2001]. In these systems and approaches, FCA is used for establishing concept lattices as complex indexing structures for document retrieval. Each document is described by a set of keywords given by a domain expert. Concept lattice is constructed (computed) on the basis of relationships between keywords and documents. The resulting concept lattice is used for document retrieval and navigation of documents according to the lattice structure.

Lattice-based information retrieval systems construct a kind of "keyword ontology" of a domain. It is rather clear that this kind of ontology is very limited but yet useful for document retrieval purposes. As the algorithm of construction of concept lattice is complex, it is understandable that only given keywords are taken as descriptive attributes of documents instead of all words existing in the documents. An advantage of this kind of ontology-based search is that mappings from query to ontology and from ontology to documents matching the query are easily performed. On the other hand, conceptual structure obtained only from a set of given keywords is not complete domain ontology and cannot retrieve documents as intended by a user (a concept does not exist in the lattice) or can retrieve too many irrelevant documents (common sub-concept does not exist in the lattice).

The purpose of the approach presented in this paper is to learn domain-specific ontologies from given domain-specific texts in order to overcome the limitations of the "keyword ontology" based information retrieval techniques. As a formal method, FCA is used to discover conceptual relationships within a given domain.

The approach proposed in the paper constructs a formal concept lattice by algorithmic analysis of noun phrase patterns in domain-specific texts of an application domain. Noun phrases are extracted from the text using NLP tools. Resulting set of noun phrases together with references to text sources are stored into corresponding database table, which represents a context for the application domain in the form of binary relationship between objects and noun phrases used to describe given objects. FCA makes it possible to construct a formal concept lattice of the context. Formal concept lattice is considered as formal domain-specific ontology for a given application domain.

Resulting domain-specific ontology may be used for sharing knowledge of a domain, for information retrieval and navigation as well as for assisting a domain expert in ontology construction and verification. The main focus in this paper is on extraction of a conceptual structure (ontology) inherent in given domain-specific text sources for domain-specific information retrieval and navigation.

The rest of the paper is structured as follows. Section 2 introduces basic definitions concerning ontology and ontology expression. General framework of our approach of automatic construction of domain-specific ontologies is presented in section 3. Architecture of a prototype of an ontology design system OntoDesign is proposed and described in section 4. Section 5 is devoted to related works. Section 6 presents a conclusion and future work.

2. ONTOLOGY EXPRESSION

In this section a brief introduction to basic definitions of ontology and ontology description languages are presented in order to give a background for our ontology construction method proposed in the following sections.

2.1 Ontology Definition

Ontology is a conceptual representation of the entities, events, and their relationships that compose a specific domain. Two primary relationships are generalisation ("is-a" relationship) and composition ("part-of" relationship).

The definition of ontology is still a debated issue. One of the definitions proposed by T. Gruber and reported in [Uschold and Gruninger 1996] can be used here as follows:

"Ontologies are agreements about *shared* conceptualisations. Shared conceptualisations include conceptual frameworks for modelling domain knowledge; content-specific protocols for communication among inter-operating agents; and agreements about the representation of particular domain theories. In the knowledge-sharing context, ontologies are specified in the form of definitions of representational vocabulary. A very simple case would be a type hierarchy, specifying classes and their subsumption relationships."

N. Guariono and P. Giaretta [Guarino and Giaretta 1995] give another well-known definition: ontology is an explicit, partial account of conceptualisation. According to them, ontology is designed to express the intended meaning of a shared vocabulary. Conceptualisation is the formal structure of reality as perceived and organised by an agent independently of the language used (vocabulary) and the actual occurrence of the specific situation.

Depending on the subject of the conceptualisation, some authors [Van Heijst 1997] distinguish between *application ontologies, domain ontologies, generic ontologies* and *representation ontologies.*

According to them, top-level ontologies describe very general concepts like space, time, matter, object, event, action, etc., which are independent of a particular problem or domain. On the other hand, domain ontologies and task ontologies describe, respectively, the vocabulary related to a generic domain (like real estate, or automobiles) or a generic task or activity (like selling), by specializing the terms introduced in the top-level ontology.

As ontology is an agreement on the intended meaning, using ontology for information integration and sharing ensures the consistency of a system.

2.2   Ontology Description Languages

Ontologies should be expressed in a formal language so that given ontology expressions can be processed by computers. This is extremely important for automated web-services including search for information [Kim 2001, Maedche and Staab 2001].

Ontologies are usually described in one of the logic languages. The most widely used languages for ontology description are several variants of description logics and their extensions with rule bases. The language CLASSIC is most well known [Borgida et al 1997]. Classical frame-based languages are also widely used for ontology representation. One example may be Ontolingua [Gruber 1995]. Two interesting projects SHOE [Helfin and Hendler 2000] and ONTOBROKER [Decker, et al 1999] are based on an idea to annotate HTML pages with ontologies for concept-based retrieval purposes. In SHOE, description logic is used for ontology description.

ONTOBROKER relies on Frame Logic that supports a more powerful inference mechanism than description logic.

2.3 Lattice Structure as an Ontology Expression

We distinguish between formal and informal ontologies as in [Sowa 2000]. A formal ontology is specified by a collection of names for concepts and relation types organised in a partial ordering by the type-subtype relation.

2.3.1 An Example

As an example, we consider the real estate domain. Let us describe information retrieval in real estate web catalogues like EasyRent (www.easyrent.com). In these catalogues, real estate items are described by a set of common attributes as follows: area, street, city, floor, date of availability, etc. In addition, real estate objects are classified for search purposes according to attributes like price, number of bedrooms, number of bathrooms, type of house, apartment, and community features. Finally, a customer of the web service, the seller, gives a short comment about an item for sale. Comments are given as short and very specific natural language texts. An example of a typical text is as follows:

"This apartment is in a family house, parking slot, quiet street, small bedroom, big dining room, close to public transportation. Call to set up an appt."

The comments given in natural language share the understanding of valuable concepts of the real estate domain in a community of sellers and buyers of real estate items.

2.3.2 Lattice structure

Conceptual structures can be represented as lattices visualised by Hasse diagrams (see Fig 15-1) with concepts associated with nodes. Lattices can be used as means of representing formal ontologies. They are good candidates for ontology description because of some formal lattice properties.

A lattice is a partial order, where there always exist the supremum and infimum for any two elements as follows:

<u>Supremum</u>. For any two concepts c_1 and c_2 there exists a concept c_{sup} superior to c_1 and c_2 and being a specialization of any other concept c' superior to both c_1 and c_2.

Infimum. For any two concepts c_1 and c_2 there exists a concept c_{inf} inferior to c_1 and c_2 and being a generalization of any other concept c'' inferior to both c_1 and c_2.

For example, picking some concepts like house, apartment house, and rental house from the real estate domain above, we may construct a small conceptual structure described by the lattice as follows:

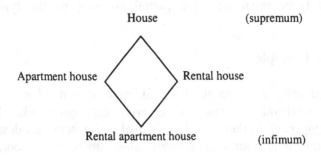

Figure 15-1. Is-a relationship of concepts from the real estate domain

The top element of the lattice represents the universal concept, which includes any other concept. Dually the bottom element represents the null concept, which is included in any concept. In the situation where the infimum of a pair of concepts is bottom ($\perp$), this expresses non-overlap (disjointness) of the concepts.

There are 2 operators, lattice join and lattice meet, in a distributive lattice. The operators obey the following axioms: idempotency, commutativity, associativity, absorption and distributivity, see [Davey and Priestley 1990].

The lattice operators according to lattice theory, see e.g. [Davey and Priestley 1990], induce a partial ordering relationship $\leq$ on the elements of a lattice. Generalisation of a concept is achieved by moving upwards and specialisation of a concept by moving downwards in the lattice diagram.

The lattice in Figure 15-1 represents conceptual inclusion relationships *apartment house* is-a *house*, *rental house* is-a *house*, etc, which are important for establishing ontologies. Is-a relationship is one of the most important ontological relationships.

The conceptual inclusion relationship has the following properties: reflexivity, antisymmetry, and transitivity. The concept *rental apartment house* in Figure 15-1 denotes multiple inclusion which implies multiple inheritance.

2.4   Formal Concept Analysis

Concept lattices can be discovered from a given context using Formal Concept Analysis (FCA) developed by Wille [Wille 1982]. Detailed definitions of FCA can be found in [Ganter and Wille 1999]. In FCA, a concept is understood as constituted by its extent (a subset of the objects) and its intent (a subset of available attributes). FCA relates lattices to a set of object-attribute relationships called a formal context. The Galois connection of a lattice applied to formal context represents an inverse relationship between object sets and attribute sets. Compared to specific concepts, more general concepts have fewer attributes in their intension but more objects in their extension.

FCA is applied in the system Toscana [Scheich et al 1993, Eklund et al 2000] for discovery relationships between attributes in relational database and for retrieval of objects in a database. The results of FCA are visualised using line diagrams. In section of related works, several interesting applications of FCA in relation to our approach are discussed.

Our approach is different compared to other applications of FCA. We use FCA for automatic construction of a formal ontology from domain-specific texts.

3.   LEARNING DOMAIN-SPECIFIC ONTOLOGIES USING NLP AND FCA

FCA is an algorithmic method for construction of concept lattices for a given context. By contrast to time-consuming manual building of domain ontologies the formal concept analysis establishes concept lattices automatically. FCA takes as basis two sets (called object set and attribute set) and a binary relationship between the two, and constructs a so-called formal concept lattice with a concept inclusion ordering.

Below, an application of FCA to automatic construction of formal domain-specific ontology is explained.

3.1   FCA of a Set of Domain-specific Texts

For our approach, objects for FCA can be any domain-specific texts that use domain-specific vocabulary and describe a domain-specific entity. A text describing a certain entity has a reference to this entity. Attributes of an object for FCA are noun-phrases present in the domain-specific text describing a given domain-specific entity. This means that attribute sets for FCA are not given but discovered by NLP.

Let a set of objects T correspond to domain-specific text sources (e.g. like comments on real estate items in web catalogue of our running example from section 2) described by a set of noun-phrases N chunked from these texts by NLP tool. Noun-phrases correspond to attribute sets for FCA. We assume that only one text (description) corresponds to each domain-specific entity. The largest set of noun-phrases N is the set of all noun-phrases present in the texts. We are interested in automatic construction of a formal concept lattice that we consider as formal domain-specific ontology. Let us consider a set of objects S from T; each object from S is then described by a subset of noun-phrases from N used in domain-specific texts. This is described as a binary relationship between text sources (objects) and noun-phrases denoted by R; i.e. a relationship between the sets S and N so that $R \subseteq S \times N$.

For example, recall our running example. In real estate web catalogues, real estate items for sale are described using very short texts with a very specific vocabulary. Descriptions of real estate objects are composed mainly from noun-phrases separated by commas. It is easy to chunk noun phrases from that type of descriptions of domain-specific entities. Nevertheless, property ads (i.e., domain-specific texts about domain-specific entities) are written having some intended model in mind. As different real estate web catalogues use slightly different descriptions of their items for sale, then sharing conceptualisation will help to better understand the meaning of property descriptions. If we assume that the ads are not read by human beings but rather by intelligent agents, then automatic construction of real estate domain ontology becomes an extremely important task.

For example, Table 15-1 represents real estate entities that are described by domain-specific texts called ads. For each ad there is a corresponding text source (e.g. ad A1 corresponds to texts about real-estate item one, etc.). Noun-phrases are extracted from sellers' textual comments of an object for sale. We do not show all the noun-phrases contained in the texts but rather we feel free to display only some noun-phrases chunked from ads of real estate domain. This is in order to obtain a small sample lattice in the example.

Table 15-1. A part of description of domain-specific texts (ads) and noun-phrases relationship

Object (Ad)	Noun-phrase
A1	{Family home, Parking slot, Public trans., Quiet street}
A2	{Family home, Parking slot}
A3	{Family home, Public trans., Quiet street}
A4	{Family home}
A5	{Family home, Public trans.}

Following [Ganter and Wille 1999] a formal concept is a pair of sets *(X, Y)*, where $X \subseteq S$ and $Y \subseteq W$ with respect to domain-specific text (ad) noun-phrase relationship R satisfying the following two conditions:

1. *X* is a set of texts (objects) containing all the noun-phrases in *Y*
2. *Y* is the set of noun-phrases common to all the texts (ads) in *X*

This pair of sets represents a formal concept with *extent X* and *intent Y*. Extent and intent of a formal concept determine each other and the formal concept. For example, one of the formal concepts of the context described in Table 1 is as follows:

{A1, A2, A3, A4, A4} × {Family home},

where the set *{ A1, A2, A3, A4, A4}* is the extent of a concept and the set *{Family home}* is its intent.

It is shown in [Ganter and Wille 1999] that the two conditions given above establish a so-called Galois connection between powersets of domain-specific texts (objects) (2^S) and noun-phrases (2^N). If we consider the set of all formal concepts *(X, Y)* derived from the relationship R (texts noun-phrase relationship) and define the partial order relation on this set so that

$$X \times Y \leq X' \times Y' \text{ iff } X' \subseteq X \text{ and } Y \subseteq Y',$$

then we will get the Galois lattice induced by the relationship R on S×N.

Each node in this lattice is a formal concept. The formal concept lattice corresponding to the relationships shown in Table 1 is displayed in Figure 2 as follows:

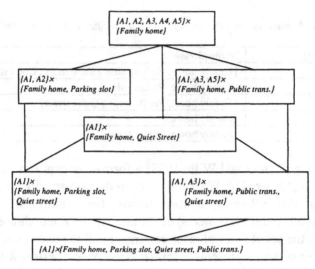

Figure 15-2. The formal concept lattice corresponding to domain-specific texts of real estate domain and noun-phrases relationship.

Sub and super-concept relationships between the formal concepts are represented by edges in the Hasse diagram in Figure 15-2.

If we have two formal concepts (X_1, Y_1) and (X_2, Y_2), then (X_1, Y_1) is called a sub-concept of (X_2, Y_2) provided that $X_1 \subseteq X_2$, which is equivalent to $Y_2 \subseteq Y_1$. Thus, X and Y are contravariant, smaller X sets correspond to large Y sets.

In this case (X_2, Y_2) conversely is a super-concept of (X_1, Y_1) written as

$$(X_1, Y_1) \le (X_2, Y_2),$$

where the relation $\le$ is called hierarchical order of concepts in [Ganter and Wille 1999a].

For example, {A1, A3, A5} × {*Family home, Public trans.*} is a super-concept of

   {*A1, A3*} × {*Family home, Public trans., Quiet street*}.

The sub and super-concept relationship also represents inheritance of properties by concepts.

It is easy to use such a lattice for retrieval of real estate items with certain set of properties. For example, if somebody is interested in a family home in a quiet street with a parking slot, then only one entity in our example will be retrieved, namely entity that is described in ad A1. But if somebody is just looking for a family home, then all the entities corresponding to ads A1, A2, A3, A4, A5 will constitute an answer to the query. In general, if more query terms are given, then fewer entities will be retrieved; i.e. a query is more precise.

Constructing a concept lattice from occurrence of domain-specific texts can also be seen as a way of learning conceptual relationships within a domain. For example, we may discover taxonomic relationships between concepts of a domain.

3.2 Formal Concept Lattice as a Formal Domain-specific Ontology

As shown above, the FCA constructs a formal domain-specific lattice, which can be also seen as a sub-lattice of some more general lattice of categories (top ontology). If lattices represent ontologies, then the merging domain ontologies to higher-level ontologies can be done automatically or semi-automatically.

We may reduce the concept lattice in Figure 15-2 so that it only shows attributes (noun-phrases in our case) of each formal concept. The lattice has then the following shape represented in Figure 15-3 below.

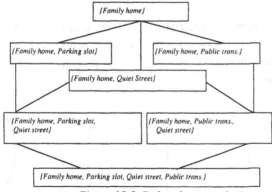

Figure 15-3. Reduced concept lattice.

This lattice displays only intension of concepts represented by noun-phrases and "is-a" relationships between concepts. It does not refer to objects forming an extent of a certain concept. We consider this lattice a useful conceptual structure learned from the given set of domain-specific texts describing domain-specific entities. In our approach, we consider this lattice as a formal domain-specific ontology. This ontology has all lattice properties, which are useful for ontology sharing, reasoning about concepts as well as navigating and retrieving of information.

Naturally, this example included too few objects to produce complete real estate domain ontology. Better learning result can be achieved by processing large number of domain-specific text sources. This enables to chunk more noun-phrases from domain-specific texts in order to refine the lattice.

The whole process of creating a domain-specific ontology was fully automatic. As we have made an assumption that noun-phrases used in domain-specific texts denote concepts used in the domain, then we may consider nodes with one attribute as concepts that have the same name as an attribute. For example, attribute *Family home* can be the name for the concept family home. This is the most general concept in the sample domain. More specific concepts with 2 attributes like *Family home and Parking slot* or *Family home and Quiet street* may need a different name to denote the concept. This cannot be done automatically; human intervention is needed in this case. Nevertheless, taxonomic relationships between concepts are present in the lattice.

4.   ONTOLOGY DESIGN TOOL OntoDesign

We have developed architecture of the prototypical ontology design tool OntoDesign, which is based on the methodology described in the previous section.

OntoDesign is a system for automatically constructing domain ontologies from a given set of textual descriptions of domain objects.

Figure 15-4 below presents components and principal structure of the OntoDesign prototype.

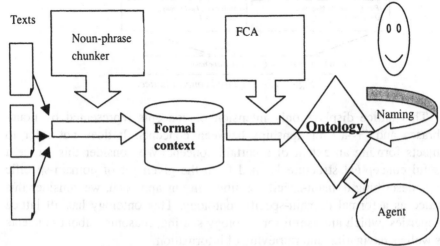

Figure 15-4. Architecture of the prototype of OntoDesign.

The system gets as input textual descriptions of domain entities written in some natural language. We support multilingual approach, because noun-phrase chunkers are available for many languages. We assume that those descriptions use domain specific vocabulary and are rather short. For example, suitable descriptions can be ads of real estate items in the real estate web catalogues, descriptions of products in product catalogues, technical descriptions of components. Rationale of these restrictions on the texts is that in this case noun phrases extracted from the text are really tightly related to the description of the domain and hopefully reflect the conceptualisation of the domain.

A resulting set of noun phrases together with references to the domain-specific text sources are stored into the database table, which represents a context for the application domain in the form of binary relationship between descriptions of entities and noun phrases.

FCA is performed on the database. As a result, the system should give a graphical output of the formal concept lattice that corresponds to the domain ontology. As formal lattice (even its reduced form) can be large, then a user is given tools for browsing the lattice.

Algorithm of construction of concept lattices is presented in [Ganter and Wille 1999]. One of the best algorithms for computing formal concepts is found in [Ganter 1984].

In practical applications, where the number of features per instance (number of noun-phrases for each domain-specific text in our case) is usually bounded, the worst-case complexity of the structure (lattice) is linearly bounded with respect to the number of instances [Godin 1991]. There exists also an incremental algorithm for updating the structure by adding (removing) instances or features to existing instances [Godin 1991].

The prototype system will be implemented in Java. The system is in early stage of development.

5. RELATED WORK

There exist only a few systematic methodologies for ontology building and development. One of them is OntoEdit [Sure et al 2002]. In many approaches, it is assumed that ontologies already exist, and no attention is paid to their construction. Usually it is assumed that ontologies are formalised manually by a domain expert. Nevertheless, there are attempts on ontology learning and ontology extraction [Woelk and Tomlinson 1994, Preece et al 1999, Decker, et al 1999, Maedche and Staab 2000]. For example, in KRAFT [Preece et al 1999], local ontology is extracted from shared ontology. In the system Infosleuth [Woelk and Tomlinson 1994] ontologies are constructed semi-automatically from textual databases. They use ontology-learning approach, where human experts provide a set of initial words denoting concepts from high-level ontology. The system processes documents, extracts phrases that include initial words, generates corresponding concept terms, and then classifies them into ontology. This is an iterative process, the result of which is verified by an expert in each step.

Our approach also constructs ontology by learning, but our method is not so dependent on an expert. Similarity is in using texts as descriptions of conceptualisation of domain and learning formal ontology from the given texts.

Interesting work is presented in [Maedche and Staab 2000] on discovering non-taxonomic relationships from texts using shallow text processing methods. Their technique is integrated into ontology learning tool TextToOnto.

FCA is used for bottom-up merging of ontologies in [Stumme and Maedche 2001]. In contrast to our approach, their mechanism is based on merging given ontologies using FCA techniques not on construction of ontologies.

6.   CONCLUSION

We have shown that FCA can be used for automatic construction of formal domain-specific ontologies from given set of domain-specific texts. Benefits of our approach include the following: automatic constructions of formal ontology of a domain, solid mathematical basis of ontology expression, easy instantiation of ontology, and easy retrieval of ontology instances. Nothing is entirely perfect. Limitations of the approach are related to naming of complex formal concepts and to mapping concepts to their descriptions, which should be done by a human expert by exploring the ontology lattice.

We have presented architecture of the ontology construction tool OntoDesign that is built on our approach presented in this paper.

We have not discussed extraction of non-taxonomic relationships between concepts even if FCA supports the generation of both, taxonomic and non-taxonomic relationships. This will constitute our future work. In addition, our future work will consider mapping lattice-based ontology to some logical language for reasoning purposes.

ACKNOWLEDGEMENTS

This research was partially funded by Estonian Research Foundation by the Grant no 4705. Special thanks go to K. Müürisep for comments on NLP tools.

References

[Davey and Priestley 1990] Davey, B. A. and Priestley, H. A., *Introduction to Lattices and Order*, Cambridge University Press, 1990

[Borgida et al 1989] Borgida, A. et al, Classic: A structural data model for objects. In ACM SIGMOD International Conference on Management of Data, Portland, USA, 1989

[Decker, et al 1999] Decker, S., Erdmann, M., Fensel, D., and Studer, R., Ontobroker: Ontology Based Access to Distributed and Semi-Structured Information. In R. Meersman et al. (eds.): Semantic Issues in Multimedia Systems. Proceedings of DS-8. Kluwer Academic Publisher, Boston, 1999, 351-369.

[Eklund et al 2000] Eklund, P., Groh, B., Stumme, G., and Wille, R., A Contextual-Logic Extension of TOSCANA, In Proc.of the 8th Int. Conference on Conceptual Structures, ICCS 2000, Springer Verlag, 453-467

[Ganter and Wille 1999] Ganter, B. and Wille, R., *Formal Concept Analysis, Mathematical Foundations*, Springer, 1999.

[Ganter 1984] Ganter, B., Two Basic Algorithms in Concept Analysis (Preprint 831), Darmstadt: Technische Hochschule, 1984

[Godin 1991] Godin, R., Missaoui, R., and Alaoui, H., Learning Algorithms Using a Galois Lattice Structure, *Proc. of the Third Int. Conference on Tools for Artificial Intelligence*, IEEE Computer Society Press, CA, 1991, 22-29

[Godin 1993] Godin, R., Missaoui, R., and April, A., Experimental comparison of navigation in a Galois lattice with conventional information retrieval methods, *Int. J. Man-Machine Studies*, 1993, (38): 747-767

[Gruber 1995] Gruber, T., Toward Principles for Design of Ontologies Used for Knowledge Sharing, International Journal of Human and Computer Studies, 43 (5/6): 907-928

[Guarino 1998] Guarino, N., Formal Ontology and Information Systems, In: N. Guarino (Ed), Formal Ontology in Information Systems, Proc. Of the 1st International Conference, Trento, Italy, June 1998, IOS Press, Amsterdam, 3-15

[Guarino et al 1999] Guarino, N., Masolo, C., Vetere, G., OntoSeek: Content-Based Access to the Web, IEEE Intelligent Systems, May/June 1999, 70-80

[Haav and Nilsson 2001] Haav, H-M. and Nilsson. J. F., Approaches to Concept Based Exploration of Information Resources, W. Abramowicz and J. Zurada (Eds), Knowledge Discovery for Business Information Systems, Kluwer Academic Publishers, 2001, 89-111

[Helfin and Hendler 2000] Helfin, J., and Hendler, J., Dynamic Ontologies on the Web, In: Proceedings of American Association for AI Conference (AAAI-2000), Menlo Park, California, AAAI Press 2000.

[Kim 2001] Kim, H., Predicting How Ontologies for Semantic Web Will Evolve, Communications of ACM, 2002, 45 (2): 48-55

[Kim and Compton 2001] Kim, M. and Compton, P., A Web-based Browsing Mechanism Based on Conceptual Structures, , In Proc.of the 9th Int. Conference on Conceptual Structures, ICCS 2001, CEUR Workshop proceedings

[Maedche and Staab 2000] Maedche, A. and Staab, S., Discovering Conceptual Relations from Text. ECAI 2000. Proceedingsof the 14th European Conference on Artificial Intelligence, IOS Press, Amsterdam, 2000

[Maedche and Staab 2001] Maedche, A. and Staab, S., Learning Ontologies for the SemanticWeb. IEEE Intelligent Systems, 16(2), March/April 2001. Special Issue on Semantic Web

[OIL 2001] Ontology Inference Layer, available at http://www.ontoknowledge.org/oil

[Preece at al 1999] Preece, A. D., Hui, K-J., Gray, W. A., Marti, P., et al, The Kraft arhitecture for knowledge fusion and transformation, In Proc. of 19th SGES Int. Conference, Springer, 1999

[Priss 2000] Priss, U., Lattice-based Information Retrieval", Knowledge Organization, 2000, 7 (3):132-142

[Scheich et al 1993] Scheich, P., Skorsky, M., Vogt, F., Wachter, C., Wille, R., Conceptual data systems. In: O. Opitz, B. Lausen, R. Klar (eds.): Information and classification. Springer, Berlin-Heidelberg, 72-84.

[Sowa 2000] Sowa, J.F., *Knowledge Representation, Logical, Philosophical, and Computational Foundations*, Brooks/Cole Thomson Learning, 2000.

[Stumme and Maedche 2001] Stumme, G. and Maedche, A., FCA-Merge: A Bottom-Up Approach for Merging Ontologies. In: IJCAI `01 - Proceedings of the 17th International Joint Conference on Artificial Intelligence, Seattle, USA, August, 1-6, 2001, San Francisco/CA: Morgen Kaufmann, 2001

[Sure 2002] Sure, Y., Erdmann, M., Angele, J., Staab, S., Studer, R., and Wenke, D., OntoEdit: Collaborative Ontology Development for the Semantic Web, In: The Semantic Web-ISWC 2002, Proceedings of the First International Semantic Web Conference, Sardinia, Italy, June 9-12, 2002, Springer, 2002, 221-235

[Uschold and Gruninger 1996] Uschold, M. and Gruninger, M., Ontologies: Principles, Methods and Applications. *The Knowledge Engineering Review*, 1996

[Van Heijst 1997] Van Heijst, G., Schreiber, A. T., and Wielinga, B. J., Using Explicit Ontologies in KBS Development. *International Journal of Human and Computer Studies*, 1997

[Woelk and Tomlinson 1994] Woelk, D. and Tomlinson, C., The Infosleuht project: Intelligent Search Management via Semantic Agents. In: Proceedings of the Second World Wide Web Conference '94:Mosaic and the Web, 1994

SUBJECT INDEX

302

Subject index 303

Q
Query language, 124, 171-173

R
RDF (Resource Description Framework), 1-11, 14, 15, 19-22, 139, 140, 153
RDF Schema, 2, 7, 8, 9
Recall, 10, 24, 33, 39, 41, 42, 106, 108, 154, 173, 278, 289
Redundancy, 116, 274
REES, 42
Resources, 3, 9, 119, 187, 296
Retrieval, 64, 66, 121, 128, 136, 165, 169, 186, 197, 215, 216, 217, 249, 265
Rhetorical structure analysis, 101, 109
Rhetorical structure theory, 109, 120

S
SGML, 196, 197
Search engine, 3, 24, 68, 70, 101-103, 115, 118,123-125, 127, 138-140, 155, 162, 164, 165, 167, 171, 172, 174, 182, 183, 185, 229, 230, 257-259, 262, 273, 283
Security, 18, 142
Self organizing maps, 185,186,197
Semantic frame, 101
Semantic Web, 1, 2, 9, 153, 297
Semantics, 1-5, 6, 7, 10, 21, 22, 48, 194, 206, 223, 224
Shallow text processing, 29, 30-32, 40, 42, 44-46, 48-52, 186, 187
Similarity, 29, 47, 113, 114, 115, 116, 118, 127, 129, 130, 159, 161, 164, 186, 187, 218, 220, 221, 222, 223, 224, 225, 226, 227
Software agents, 2, 3, 217
SProUT, 32, 49
SQL, 41, 143, 183, 202, 203, 232
Statements, 3

STP, see Shallow text processing
Summaries, 50, 101, 104, 119-121
Summarization, 43, 44, 46, 47, 50, 101-120, 267, 268, 273
Support vector machine, 110, 281

T
Taxonomy, 219, 230, 246, 270-272, 274
Temis, 43
Teragram, 43
Text mining, 46
TF (Term Frequency), 47, 112
Topic, 62, 112, 119, 120, 192, 215, 216

U
URI, 4, 6, 20, 22, 146, 147, 151, 197, 198, 199
URL, 20, 61, 103, 180, 275
User Interface, 65, 232, 235, 236, 239

V
Vector space model, 129, 130-133, 182, 221
VRML, 251, 257, 265

W
W3C, 2, 9, 22, 153

X
X3D, 251
XML, 2, 3, 5-8, 10, 11, 13, 14, 22, 69, 70, 72, 102, 138, 139, 143, 145, 152, 153, 196, 197, 200, 202, 229, 230, 237, 238, 247, 251
XMLNS, 5, 7, 22, 197
XMLSCHEMA, 8, 22
XSLT, 145

Z
Z39.50, 68